KARL RADEK

KARL RADEK
The Last Internationalist

Warren Lerner

Stanford University Press, Stanford, California 1970

Thanks are due for permission to use the following photographs:
to Verlag für Politik und Wirtschaft, Köln-Marienburg, for
Konrad Haenisch; to Radio Times Hulton Picture Library for
Zinoviev at Baku; to Paul Popper, Ltd. for Stalin in 1919; and
to Bertram D. Wolfe for Stalin and Kirov, Felix Dzierżyński,
and Lenin in 1922.

Stanford University Press, Stanford, California
©1970 by the Board of Trustees of the Leland Stanford Junior University
Printed in the United States of America
ISBN 0-8047-0722-7   LC 70-97915

To Vera Tansky, who many years ago told me why there were such men as Karl Radek

Preface

In April 1913, August Bebel, the leader of German socialism, received an impassioned message from the editor of the socialist newspaper in Bremen protesting the impending purge of one of the party's most talented young writers, Karl Radek. The editor claimed that Radek was the victim of a personal vendetta led by party conservatives and argued that German socialism could ill afford to lose a man of Radek's talents and intelligence. Bebel, who knew the circumstances that had led to Radek's plight, replied laconically: "If only all of Radek's qualities were as unimpeachable as his intelligence!" Thus he expressed what was to become an almost universal evaluation of Karl Radek, one of the most gifted and controversial socialists of his time.

For three decades, Radek functioned as a talented and aggressive apostle of international socialist revolution. An effective speaker and an imaginative tactician, he was widely acknowledged as a propagandist and journalist. A prolific writer in several languages, he combined knowledge, sarcasm, wit, and ingenuity in a way unmatched by any other writer of his genre. Yet his publications were not the contribution he prized most; he would not have wanted to be remembered as the H. L. Mencken of European socialism. Radek was an intensely political person, deeply involved in the cause of international revolution: to him, journalism was but one way to serve this cause.

Whatever else Radek failed to hold sacred, the realization of an international socialist revolution remained his constant goal. To a greater degree than almost any other important figure of the Marxist movement, Radek was *vaterlandslos*: the cosmopolitan whose political loyalties could never be defined in terms of nation or nationality. Lacking a national affiliation, he moved easily in and out of various socialist movements and eventually into the Communist International, where more than any other Bolshevik he was accepted as an internationalist to whom the world revolution was as important as the Russian Revolution. Unfortunately, in the last decade of his life, "the Stalin decade," the internationalism that had been his hallmark seemed buried under the weight of Stalin's "socialism in one country." The years after 1929 formed a sad epilogue to his dynamic career as a revolutionary internationalist.

Although no other biography of Karl Radek exists, a number of Western scholars, for example, E. H. Carr, Isaac Deutscher, Werner Angress, Otto Ernst Schüddekopf, and Richard Lowenthal, have dealt with him at length in various studies. Radek himself wrote something for publication almost every day of his adult life, and most of these writings have survived and are available to scholars. Virtually every person who came into contact with Radek recorded some impression of him—often an uncomplimentary one. Ruth Fischer and Angelica Balabanoff, for example, pictured Radek as irresponsible, shameless, and cynical—a detriment rather than an asset to the international socialist movement. Directly and indirectly, their accounts have colored many interpretations of Radek, even those of scholars reluctant to accept a negative evaluation of him.

Unfortunately, there is no substantial body of material available that reveals the private Radek—letters, diaries, or memoirs. His personal papers—assuming that there were any—have not survived, and Soviet and East European authorities have been slow to make available any archival materials they may have on him. For over thirty years he has been completely ignored by Soviet historians, a fate he shares with others of his generation, while Polish and East European historians deal with him only when they cannot avoid doing so. The biographer—and the reader—must be prepared to accept the limitations imposed by these problems.

Radek's career spanned an amazing variety of political and national milieux. To some extent, his history is the history of an era— of the time when the European socialist Left found itself caught in events that forced repeated choices between socialist ideals and national loyalties, between immediate and long-range revolutionary goals. This volume does not purport to be a study of the era; for a detailed coverage of the political movements involved, the reader will have to turn elsewhere. Nor does this work seek to present an exegesis of Radek's writings or to distill from them an "essential Radek." Instead of offering his readers eternal verities, Radek usually discussed specific objective conditions that demanded explanation or criticism. Unlike Lenin or Trotsky, he was not a system-builder. Radek's publications derived their importance from the context of his political activities; by and large, they cannot stand divorced from these activities. To invest his works with a universality that was not there would be a disservice to him and to history.

Radek made an extraordinary journey through the ranks of the European Left. His inspiration was the idea of a world revolution that would change society and thus eliminate the social ills of modern times. Though his actions were often crass or opportunistic enough to make one doubt his motives, the goal was always there. This volume is essentially a chronicle of his journey.

The book began as a doctoral dissertation, prepared at Columbia University under the guidance of Geroid T. Robinson, Oliver Radkey, and Henry Roberts, all of whom gave generously of their time and advice. The final version, considerably different both in scope and in content from the dissertation, was read and criticized, in whole or in part, by Richard Lowenthal, Alexander Erlich, Alexander Dallin, Clifford Foust, and John Curtiss. In my own stubbornness, I may have failed to profit adequately from their helpful suggestions, but I have not lacked good advice.

I would indeed be remiss if I failed to take note of the hospitality of numerous libraries in this country and abroad—a hospitality that was freely offered and most gratefully accepted. The necessary travel and overseas study were made possible by a grant from the ACLS–SSRC Foreign Area Fellowship Program.

My wife Francine read every word of the manuscript, challenged me with a frankness that others would not or could not employ, and improved the manuscript in every way. For whatever shortcomings and errors remain, I must, of course, assume sole responsibility.

W. L.

Contents

Eight pages of photographs follow p. 82

KARL RADEK

1. The Road to Marxism

In the late nineteenth century, the population of the Galician city of Lvov reflected the ethnic jumble of Eastern Europe. Settled by the medieval princes of Galicia, Lvov was acquired by Casimir the Great in the fourteenth century, and flourished as a Polish provincial capital for over four hundred years. Casimir offered sanctuary in Poland to the persecuted Jews of Western Europe, and many of them settled in Galicia, especially in the cities of Eastern Galicia. Lvov received an increasing influx of these Jewish immigrants, so much so that by the end of the nineteenth century, Jews made up over a third of the population. In 1772, as a result of the first partition of Poland, Lvov received a new name and national identity as the Austrian city of Lemberg. Now Austrian white-collar workers poured in to join the large Polish working class, while from the countryside Ukrainian peasants brought their wares to the city markets. The visitor could expect to hear a medley of German, Polish, Ukrainian, and Yiddish on the city streets.

For those of the Jewish community who considered themselves "emancipated" or "modernist," Lvov was the eastern outpost of Western civilization. Fifty miles to the east, across the Bug River, lay the sprawling empire of the Tsars. As a natural boundary the Bug River was not particularly formidable, but it separated the emancipated Galician Jew from a world he preferred to ignore. In Tsarist Russia and in some areas of Galicia itself, the majority of Jewish residents passed their entire lives in the ghettos and were largely oblivious to the political and social changes going on around them. The Russian Jew, accustomed to an openly anti-Semitic regime, associated almost exclusively with his coreligionists; there appeared to be no hope of his assimilation into the non-Jewish community. He accepted the hostility of the Gentiles and reciprocated it silently or summed up his feelings in one contemptuous word, "Goyim," which by its connotations expressed the narrow parochialism engendered by his isolation.

For the "modernist" Galician Jew—and not all Galician Jews could be described as modernist—such a solution was impossible: having recently escaped from the confines of the ghetto, he could not avoid involvement in the world around him. Nevertheless, he too found assimilation into Galician Gentile society virtually impossible. He did not care to identify with either the Ukrainian or the Polish Gentiles, for he dismissed the former as ignorant peasants —despite the presence of several noted Ukrainian professors on the faculty of the University of Lvov—and suspected the latter of clericalism, chauvinism, and chronic anti-Semitism. With the Austrians, however, the modernist Jew could feel some bond. German, which he considered the only proper means of communication between civilized men, was after all the language of Vienna as well as Berlin.[1] In the haphazardly run empire of the Habsburgs, there was often an opportunity for the "emancipated" Jew to find a minor post that would place him a notch above the Ukrainian peasant or ghetto-oriented Jew. The Austrian civil service was opened to all nationalities in 1867, and many Jews aspired to the security offered by a government post.

It was for this reason that Bernhard and Sophie Sobelsohn came to Lvov around 1880. Bernhard had been appointed to a minor position in the local post office. The couple settled among the "emancipated" Jews of the city and won quick acceptance in the Jewish community. Sophie gave birth to a daughter around 1882, and in 1885 bore a son.[2] The boy was named Karl, but his parents usually called him by the affectionate diminutive Lolek.

In 1890, the Sobelsohns' quiet, petty bourgeois existence was unexpectedly altered by Bernhard's sudden death. Sophie was equal to the task of raising the two children alone, but she had reservations about attempting to do it in Lvov. The city was simply not German enough; there were far too many East Europeans there, both Jewish and Gentile. At the urging of her Austrophile brothers, she moved the family to her old home in Tarnov, where she felt that her children would be safe from the Philistines across the Bug River. Although the city was much smaller than Lvov, the Jews of Tarnov were more "modern" and more German, and Sophie believed that a better education and cultural background would be available to her children there.[3]

To support her family, Sophie taught in a Tarnov kindergarten.[4] The children, particularly Karl, were often cared for at the homes of her brothers, who apparently assumed much of the responsibility for their education. Karl was an intelligent and bookish youngster, and his uncles had great hopes for him. Their chief goal was to keep him free of the ghetto mentality and to raise him as a cultured and assimilated Austrian citizen. They never gave him the opportunity to learn Yiddish; instead, they stressed the German language and German culture, particularly the culture of the German Enlightenment.[5] At an early age Karl was encouraged to read and reread Lessing's *Nathan the Wise*, a fictional tribute to Moses Mendelssohn, an eighteenth-century German philosopher who had advocated the cultural assimilation of German Jews. Karl's uncles believed that they themselves had achieved a rational adaptation to both German and Jewish culture, and they sought to impose the same adaptation on Karl. They saw their own modest positions in the Austrian civil service and the Austrian army as proof that a prudent Jew could build a rewarding middle-class existence in the Austria of Franz Josef. Karl's uncles held the Polish population of Tarnov in contempt, and taught the boy to regard Polish culture as alien and unworthy of study.[6]

But Karl was never comfortable in the artificial world created for him by his uncles. Though they attempted to surround him with playmates from that world, he remained an outsider. One of his classmates, writing a generation later, described the young Karl Sobelsohn thus:

He was short, skinny, and physically underdeveloped; from his earliest youth, he always had a pair of glasses perched upon his nose. Yet in spite of his general ugliness, he was very arrogant and self-confident. . . . Lolek was quite well known in Tarnov. His ugly nose, his gaping mouth, and the teeth sticking out [from below] his upper lip marked him clearly. He was forever carrying a book or a newspaper. He was constantly reading —at home, on the street, during recess in the school—always reading, day and night, even during classes. . . . As for the Jewish people and Jewish problems, he was not the least bit interested.[7]

His peculiar appearance and his arrogance made Karl unpopular with his classmates; again and again Sophie was forced to defend her son from the taunts of other children.[8] Karl's own response was to withdraw his interest entirely from the "emancipated" Jewish environment and to reject its heroes—Moses Mendelssohn, Heinrich Heine, and all the other Judeo-German idols.

Karl turned for inspiration to the cultural heritage he had been taught to abhor—Polish nationalism. He has recorded with evident nostalgia how at the age of thirteen he steeped himself in the works of "The Generation of 1831," a group of expatriate Polish Romantic writers who extolled Polish nationalism. He found the heroes of the Polish Romantics—men like General Jan Henryk Dąbrowski, who fought alongside Napoleon in the name of Polish liberation—much more exciting and worthy of notice than Nathan the Wise. He read with enthusiasm Adam Mickiewicz's great epic *Pan Tadeusz*, in which the Jewish musician Jankiel composes a paean to Polish liberation while the onlookers thunder: "Poland has not yet perished! March, Dąbrowski! March to Poland!" Jankiel, a Polish Jew, was more real than Moses Mendelssohn to the romantic youngster. Karl was so carried away by Mickiewicz's work that he briefly considered converting to Roman Catholicism if that would make it easier for him to involve himself in the cause of Polish nationalism.[9] Even Jankiel had not gone that far.

In line with his new zeal for Polish nationalism, Karl became a regular reader of *Naprzód* (*Forward*), a Cracow newspaper in whose pages Polish nationalism and socialist doctrine were mingled. *Naprzód* was readily available in Tarnov, which had no cosmopolitan press. Its socialist viewpoint was at best an incidental attraction to Karl; he read it primarily for its strident nationalism and for the glimpse it afforded him of the world beyond the walls of Tarnov.[10] Nevertheless, he could not avoid exposure to the paper's political message. He had read socialist tracts before, but without any great sympathy or understanding. Now he became intrigued by *Naprzód's* argument that the fight for national liberation and the fight against capitalist exploitation were one and the same. He read all the socialist literature he could find, both German and Polish, and the more he read, the more convinced he became that *Naprzód* was right: the fight for socialism and for Polish independence were one.[11]

He also became aware that *Naprzód's* view of the interests of Polish socialism and Polish nationalism as identical was not universally held. A few years before, in 1893, the Polish socialist movement had split over this fundamental issue. The Polish Socialist Party (PPS) insisted on national reunification and independence as one of its aims. Rejecting this goal as utopian and regressive, a splinter group led by Julian Marchlewski and Rosa Luxemburg formed a new party, the Social Democratic Party of the Kingdom of Poland (SDKP).[12] The PPS was largely active in Russian Poland, but Austrian Poland had a counterpart with the same ideological outlook—the Polish Social Democratic Party (PPSD), led by the Galician socialist Ignacy Daszyński. *Naprzód* clearly identified with the PPSD and so did Radek. He became active in a clandestine socialist study group and made what efforts he could among his acquaintances to enlist support both for socialism and for the Polish independence movement.[13]

At about the same time, Radek read *Syzyfowe Prace* (*The Labor of Sisyphus*), a contemporary novel by Stefan Żeromski. This book, first published in 1898, recounts the struggles of Polish students in a Russian gymnasium to preserve their national identity in the face of a policy of forcible Russification. Karl seems to have been fascinated by the book's secondary hero, Andrzej Radek, in whose role he often must have visualized himself. A boy of humble origin, Andrzej Radek was the spark of the students' radical organization; at student meetings he was always the first to start singing workers' songs or to speak eloquently on the connection between Polish nationalism and proletarian revolution. Karl was so impressed with this character that he began to refer to himself as "Radek," and in time dropped the name Sobelsohn entirely.[14]

The zealousness with which he played the role of Andrzej Radek ultimately led to Karl's expulsion from the Tarnov gymnasium in 1901 for political agitation.[15] This put an end to the family's efforts to shape Karl's future; the civil service position for which they had been grooming him was certainly now out of reach. Karl himself may well have been glad at the turn of events, for his expulsion provided him at last with a reason for leaving Tarnov. He tried to convince his family that he might be able to complete his education in Cracow.[16] His mother agreed to let him go, and in 1901 Karl set out for the greatest city of Austrian Poland.

The nineteenth-century Russian revolutionary Alexander Herzen wrote of himself that he entered Paris the way men of ancient times must have entered Rome or Jerusalem. It was with a similar outlook that Karl entered Cracow in 1901. There he somehow managed to conceal the circumstances of his dismissal from the school in Tarnov, and was permitted to enroll in a gymnasium. His new classmates seemed far more exciting and worldly than his friends in Tarnov, and certainly more politically knowledgeable. One of his new classmates, Marian Kukiel, undertook to introduce Karl to some of the local socialist groups.[17] Bolesław Drobner, then a leader of socialist youth groups in Cracow, still recalled sixty years later that his first impression of Radek was of an "extraordinarily gifted youth."[18]

It was in Cracow that Radek first began a systematic study of Marxism. In 1902, he wrote three short articles for the journal *Promien* (*Ray of Light*) as well as an article for *Naprzód* about the bakers' union in Tarnov.[19] Emil Haecker, the editor of *Naprzód*, was sufficiently impressed to offer Radek a job on the newspaper. Haecker recognized Radek's literary gifts and approved of his political goals. He assumed the role of Radek's political tutor and provided him with a steady flow of socialist literature, particularly that published by the PPSD.[20] In time, Haecker hoped to develop his protégé into an able and dedicated writer for the PPSD. He might have succeeded in this endeavor if Feliks Dzierżyński had not arrived in Cracow in 1903. Dzierżyński was somewhat of a legendary figure in Polish socialist circles. He had come from the most improbable of all backgrounds for a Polish socialist—from the Roman Catholic gentry—but early in life had rejected his inherited social status. Between repeated arrests by Tsarist police (and two spectacular escapes), Dzierżyński had organized several militant Lithuanian socialist factions into a single nonnationalist group, then persuaded the group to merge with the Marchlewski-Luxemburg group in Poland. This merger formed the nucleus of the Social Democratic Party of the Kingdom of Poland and Lithuania (SDKPiL). As the SDKP had done in 1893, the new party officially rejected the fight for Polish independence as impractical and diversionary.[21] Rosa Luxemburg was the ideological leader of the SDKPiL, and Dzierżyński was one of its most important organizers. Eluding the Tsarist police, Dzierżyński crossed the Austrian border in 1903 and made his way to Cracow in order to organize a new headquarters for the SDKPiL and to found a newspaper to express the group's antinationalist views.

Radek met Dzierżyński at a political meeting at the Jagellonian University in Cracow, and was drawn to the organizer at once.[22] Dzierżyński, a man who had come from a privileged and chauvinistic class, sought to subordinate the Polish socialist movement to the Russian movement. If Radek had rejected his own background, how much more had Dzierżyński rejected his! In 1903 Radek was not yet quite ready to accept Dzierżyński's total renunciation of Polish independence, but he had begun to seriously doubt the effectiveness of the PPSD as a revolutionary organization. His doubts grew, and it was clear that his interests were separating from those of *Naprzód*.[23] But while Radek was too unsure of Haecker's political philosophy to continue at *Naprzód*, he was by no means completely convinced of the soundness of Dzierżyński's approach.

Upon his graduation from the gymnasium, he apparently decided
to put some distance between himself and Poland in order to get a
proper perspective on the matter.
Late in 1903, Radek emigrated to Zurich—traditionally a haven
for uprooted socialists—and took a job as a librarian.[24] He soon
found himself caught up in political meetings, debates, and other
activities. His participation was voluble and forceful; it was at this
time that he first began to display some of the verbal irresponsibility that was to mar much of his later career. The few glimpses we
have of Radek in the memoirs of people who knew him in Zurich
depict him as an articulate activist, not always aware of the consequences of what he said. Max Nomad has written of one occasion
when Radek taunted an anarchist speaker with the empty yet hu-
miliating charge that the speaker could be bought by the bourgeoisie; for his maliciousness, he received a beating from the angry
audience and was physically ejected from the hall.[25] Fritz Brupbacher has noted that during a wildcat bricklayers' strike in Zurich,
he was rudely denounced by Radek, who was totally unknown to
him.[26]

Unfortunately, we have no record of the impressions of Radek's
most important contact in Zurich, the veteran Polish socialist Adolf
Warszawski (Warski).[27] Warszawski was one of the writers Radek
most admired, and of course he sought Warszawski out when he
arrived in Switzerland. Warszawski apparently overlooked the
volatile young man's less appealing side, and within a short time
he had replaced Haecker as Radek's political mentor. Radek's
youthful flirtation with Polish nationalism implied a commitment
to revolutionary action, since no other path to Polish liberation was
possible. His contacts with Dzierżyński in Cracow had served to
initiate the transfer of this latent revolutionary commitment from
Polish nationalism to Polish socialism. Now he was ready for a total
commitment to revolutionary socialism. Warszawski successfully
exploited this receptivity, and in 1904, under his sponsorship,
Radek joined the SDKPiL as an émigré member.[28]

Perhaps the most important aspect of Radek's socialist education
under Warszawski was his introduction to socialism as an interna-

tional force rather than a tactic for the achievement of Polish independence. He became increasingly aware of the activities of the Second International, a worldwide organization of socialist parties ostensibly dedicated to world revolution against the capitalist order —a goal that was to form the basis of a split in the organization.

Radek's introduction to the Second International came at a time when the organization was dividing into two camps over the basic issues of revolutionary strategy and goals. The International's *raison d'être* was to rally the working class for the struggle against capitalism. Nevertheless, from its very inception in 1889, the Second International had equivocated about the revolutionary aspects of its program. The working class of the 1890's was better paid, better protected by labor legislation, and in general far less alienated from society than the proletariat of fifty years before. The International was aware that in some countries, notably Germany, much of the socialist strength and support came from the trade unions, who were little inclined to revolutionary activities. The compromises between ideology and day-to-day reality had produced a substantial and constantly growing force in the Second International that sought a negotiated position within capitalist society rather than a showdown at the barricades.

This so-called revisionist or reformist movement challenged the preeminent position of revolution in Marxist ideology.[29] Eduard Bernstein, the leading theorist of revisionism, denied the inevitability of a showdown between the proletarian and capitalist classes and advised socialists to concentrate their efforts on achieving maximum benefits for the workers through peaceful democratic methods. He summed up his views with the pithy comment: "What is generally called the goal of socialism [the revolution of the working class] is nothing to me; the movement, everything."[30]

The widespread appeal of revisionism was undeniable. Many Social Democrats preferred to work for tangible reforms rather than an uncertain revolution in the future; some frankly feared the violence and chaos of revolution and were content to seek an amelioration of the condition of the working class. The growth of the revisionist movement reflected the peculiar circumstances of each country: many French socialists, particularly after the Dreyfus Affair, felt that their first responsibility was the survival of the Third Republic; and the German trade unions saw revisionism as a movement that emphasized their role and their goals over political goals.

Many of the leaders of the International found revisionism ideologically repugnant and did not hesitate to say so. Karl Kautsky, whose authority as an interpreter of orthodox Marxism was virtually unchallenged in 1900, derided Bernstein's new theories. Even more vociferous, although not as influential as Kautsky and the established leaders of the International, were a radical group of Social Democrats generally known as the Left. Reaffirming their faith in Marx's predictions of the impending doom of capitalist society, the Left strove to commit the Second International to the active pursuit of revolution. The most formidable spokesman of the Left was Rosa Luxemburg, a highly articulate advocate of revolutionary action and Bernstein's equal as a theoretician. Luxemburg did not enjoy the prestige or influence of Kautsky in the International—she herself recognized Kautsky's ideological authority at this time—but she was in many ways a more capable and more effective critic of revisionism than he. A charter member of the SDKPiL, she had long since left Poland to wage her antirevisionist struggle in the ranks of the German Social Democratic Party (SPD).

Radek's sympathies were almost entirely with the Left and with Rosa Luxemburg. Through Warszawski, he began a correspondence with this formidable woman, who was impressed by his writing ability and arranged for him to publish some articles in the newspapers of the German Social Democratic Left.[31] By now Radek had made contact with most of the major figures of East European socialism;[32] none, however, had as prolonged and profound an influence on him as Rosa Luxemburg did.

Radek was not the only socialist to be impressed or, for that matter, overwhelmed by Luxemburg. She was a woman of extraordinary magnetism, intelligence, and sensitivity. She was dedicated to the cause of proletarian revolution and believed that revolutionary socialism must adhere to democratic principles in order to be truly effective.[33] As J. P. Nettl, her most important biographer, has noted: "Insofar as revolutionary Marxism can be democratic, Rosa Luxemburg stands at its apex."[34] No one could be a member of the Second International and not have some special feeling for Rosa Luxemburg. She had her enemies, but most socialists, revisionist as well as revolutionary, respected and admired her even when they disagreed with her.[35]

Radek's budding acquaintance with Rosa Luxemburg and the socialist Left was suddenly interrupted by the outbreak of revolution in 1905 in Russia—a breath of fresh air for all socialists. Tsarist Russia, since Marx's day the symbol of historical regression, had at last felt the wrath of the proletariat in a wave of politically motivated strikes. For Rosa Luxemburg, the revolution was particularly exhilarating and challenging—did not the mass strike of the poorly organized Russian workers point to the viability of the democratic revolution? But some personal enemies, including trade union leaders, seized the opportunity of the annual SPD conference to accuse her of cowardice for remaining in Germany to preach mass strike tactics while a revolution spearheaded by mass strikes was spreading throughout Poland and the rest of the Russian empire.* She subsequently proved them wrong by slipping across the border and making her way to Warsaw.

Radek felt that as Luxemburg's disciple he had no choice but to emulate her example. In December 1905 he crossed the Austro-Russian border and headed for Warsaw. Once there, he reported to SDKPiL headquarters for orders.[36] By this time the Revolution of 1905 was all but over, despite the false optimism of the Western socialist press. Radek, however, acted as if it had just begun. He set to work writing for clandestine newspapers and agitating among the workers for a revival of militant activities. His actions soon came to the attention of the Tsarist police, and he was arrested in March 1906.

Jail proved no handicap to Radek's career. In fact, by providing

---

* There were few trade union leaders among Rosa Luxemburg's admirers; she had once referred to their efforts as a "labor of Sisyphus." At all events, the charge of cowardice was belied by Luxemburg's entire career; her belief that revolutionaries belonged at the scene of action was ultimately to cost her her life.

tangible proof of his commitment to the revolutionary movement, it gave him respectability among the Polish revolutionaries. His incarceration seems to have been marked more by uninterrupted leisure than by harassment or ill-treatment. Utilizing his unusual aptitude for languages, he developed some proficiency in Russian while imprisoned.[37] More importantly, he was able to continue writing for the socialist press abroad. In 1906 Radek placed his first major article in the German socialist periodical *Die Neue Zeit*. Unremarkable in itself, the article presented a conventional SDKPiL approach to the Polish labor movement and called for more politically oriented trade unions in Poland.[38] But the mere fact that Radek had published in *Die Neue Zeit* was of the utmost importance to his career. Not only was *Die Neue Zeit* the official organ of the German Social Democratic Party, it was the unofficial journal of the Second International, and the debates between Bernstein, Kautsky, and Luxemburg had taken place in its pages. Every European socialist who sought an international audience was eager to present his views there. Radek's ability to place an article in *Die Neue Zeit* augured well for his future in the SDKPiL.

When Radek emerged from prison in early 1907, he was immediately given tasks that suggested his new importance in the SDKPiL. In May 1907 he became the editor of *Czerwony Sztandar* (*Red Flag*), a newspaper whose former editors included Rosa Luxemburg and Adolf Warszawski.[39] He also involved himself in trade union work in Warsaw, an activity in line with much of his previous writing, which had been concerned with defining the proper role of Polish trade unions.

Yet neither his newspaper work nor his trade union activities satisfied him. *Czerwony Sztandar* was a newspaper of revolution; against the distinctly nonrevolutionary background of 1907 and 1908, it seemed out of place. The trade union work was equally frustrating. Radek found the Warsaw trade union movement basically unsympathetic to the purely nonnationalist doctrines he had espoused in *Die Neue Zeit*, where he had denounced the PPS-dominated unions for chasing the chimera of Polish independence and urged that the unions become centers of socialist indoctrination and agitation.[40] In fact, the unions shunned overtly socialist activities and militant tactics.

What was even more distressing was that the SDKPiL was losing its vitality in Poland, and was increasingly regarded as an extremist movement with relatively few followers.[41] The Stolypin government in Russia had increased police harassment of party members. Membership had dropped off, and the old, dynamic leadership— Rosa Luxemburg, Leo Jogiches, Julian Marchlewski, and Adolf Warszawski—had returned to Germany, where they continued to exercise considerable influence in the Left of the Second International. Of the old leaders, only Feliks Dzierżyński, who had never developed the cosmopolitan outlook of his comrades, had chosen to remain in Poland. For his efforts he had once again been exiled to Siberia. This was the kind of reward that came with SDKPiL prominence in Poland, and it could hardly have seemed attractive to Radek.

Thus in 1908 Radek faced a major decision in the shaping of his career: should he continue as a trade union agitator in Poland and risk prison or exile, or should he emigrate abroad, where he could work freely? The elite of the SDKPiL were in Germany, and Radek found those who were left behind uninspiring. There was little point in risking one's liberty while the workers remained indifferent. Martyrdom, political or intellectual, made little sense to Radek; he was eager to fling himself into the mainstream of socialist activity.

There was yet another spur to emigration. In 1908, Radek had become the target of a whispering campaign among party members in Warsaw. He was charged—although never formally—with embezzling several hundred rubles in trade union funds. The issue was whether Radek had transferred some funds to a certain Comrade Stanislawski or had kept the funds for himself. Radek, of course, claimed that he had turned the funds over to Stanislawski; Stanislawski denied that he ever received the money.[42] The fact that Radek could not produce a receipt was not in itself damning; the loosely run Polish party had nothing like the refined bookkeeping technique of its German counterpart. The case became a matter of Radek's word against Stanislawski's. Whatever may have been the truth of the matter, it is worth noting that at the time the charges originated, the party leadership seemed not to believe them or else not to assign much importance to them; several years later, when Radek was at odds with the SDKPiL leadership over other issues, the charges were revived, but with no more proof than had existed in 1908. At all events, Radek was glad enough to leave Warsaw for Berlin in 1908.

When Radek arrived in Berlin, he received a warm welcome from his SDKPiL comrades there. Warszawski made Radek a contributing editor to *Przegląd Socjaldemokratyczny* (*The Social Democratic Review*), the theoretical journal of the SDKPiL. Radek also began to write articles regularly for the *Leipziger Volkszeitung*, one of the most prominent socialist newspapers, and soon became a regular reviewer and frequent contributor to *Die Neue Zeit*. His immediate acceptance into the top socialist circles in Germany in 1908 could only have been accomplished through the intervention of leaders like Warszawski, Luxemburg, Marchlewski, and Jogiches. It would seem that the emigrant leadership gave little credence to the embezzlement charges that were lodged against Radek in Warsaw, or that if they did believe the charges, they did not regard them as serious enough to offset Radek's value as a revolutionary journalist and agitator. After a year or so in Germany, he was considered by the SDKPiL leadership to be the most effective journalist among the émigrés.[48] A prolific writer equally at home in German and Polish, Radek now began in earnest to build his international reputation.

2. The End of the Apprenticeship

In the first decade of the twentieth century, the German Social Democratic Party (SPD) was in the process of undergoing a profound change. To the outsider, the party seemed a dynamic and cohesive force; its impressive electoral strength masked the fundamental discord that was threatening to disrupt it. The source of the discord was the party's commitment to proletarian revolution— an issue forced into the open in the 1890's when Eduard Bernstein advanced his theories of revisionism in the pages of *Die Neue Zeit*. Bernstein's challenge had forced the party theoreticians to choose between reaffirming their belief in proletarian revolution and accepting Bernstein's views on the mellowing of capitalism. Fearing that the latter choice would call into question the very need for a Marxist party, the leadership officially repudiated Bernstein. Karl Kautsky even went so far as to urge Bernstein, his friend for many years, to resign from the SPD.[1]

The official attack on Bernstein gave considerable encouragement to the loose-knit group within the SPD known as the Left, which included virtually all the SDKPiL members who had emigrated to Germany. At the 1903 Congress of the SPD in Dresden, the Left, led by Rosa Luxemburg, easily secured an official condemnation of revisionism and a reaffirmation of the revolutionary goals of the party. Two years later at a Party Congress in Jena, the Left displayed startling power in matters of ideology and tactics; it successfully exploited the excitement generated by the Russian Revolution of 1905 to secure the SPD's formal approval of the tactical use of the mass strike* as a weapon against capitalism.[2]

Yet the eminence of the Left, and particularly of the Polish émigrés, was largely illusory. For Rosa Luxemburg and her followers, the choice was simply reformism or revolution, but the SPD leadership—Kautsky, Bebel, and most of their colleagues—were more concerned with party unity and discipline, and with protecting the favored position of the SPD within the Second International, than with revolutionary goals. Bebel saw the insistence of Luxemburg and the other Polish émigrés on militant action as evidence of their failure to appreciate the realities of conditions in Germany.[3]

In 1906 Friedrich Ebert, a rising party organizer from Bremen who had recently been elected to the Executive Committee, launched a reorganization of the SPD that tended away from the revolutionary doctrines espoused by Luxemburg. By its very nature, his new and complex bureaucracy was better adapted to a parliamentary party than to a revolutionary conspiracy. (Ebert was no champion of revolution; after World War I, he became the president of a decidedly capitalist Germany.) It became increasingly evident after 1905 that German Social Democracy was losing its earlier militancy and placing more and more emphasis on revisionist tactics; there was more interest in winning parliamentary elections than in organizing mass strikes.[4] On the eve of the SPD Congress of 1908, the revisionists emerged as a party power by outvoting the Left on several regional issues.[5]

Such was the situation of German Social Democracy when Radek came to Berlin in 1908. As soon as he arrived, he sought out the SDKPiL group and offered them his services. Though the group welcomed Radek, it was soon apparent that they considered him an apprentice, not a peer. The émigré group was run by the triumvirate of Rosa Luxemburg, Leo Jogiches, and Julian Marchlewski, all of whom were acknowledged leaders of the Left long before Radek appeared on the scene. The triumvirate jealously guarded their domination of the SDKPiL, reserved all de-

---

* The Left disliked the term "general strike" because of its association with syndicalism and anarchism.

cisions on political theory and strategy to themselves, and relegated the minor tasks to younger members and newcomers like Radek.

In 1908 Rosa Luxemburg still enjoyed enormous prestige among her fellow revolutionaries; her reputation had been enhanced by her active participation in the Polish sector of the Russian Revolution of 1905. In matters of theory, she virtually dictated the Left's goals and tactics. Radek unreservedly accepted Luxemburg's authority. He was quite content to be accepted into the inner circle and to serve as the voice, if not the brain, of the Left. At that time he had nothing of any great consequence to offer in the way of Marxist theory or new tactics, but he did have a flair for getting his point across verbally and was especially effective when deprecating opponents, particularly revisionists. He was well aware that in virtually all his articles he echoed Luxemburg's views, but he had no interest in doing otherwise.

In spite of Radek's open admiration for Rosa Luxemburg, he was unable to establish rapport with her. In 1908 Luxemburg was a lecturer at the SPD's *Parteischule* (Party School) in Berlin, offering instruction in political economy and what must have been an extraordinary course in the history of socialism. It was common for young militants to study with Luxemburg at the school and then to involve themselves in political work.[6] It was strange indeed that Radek was not one of those included in her classes at the *Parteischule*.

From all contemporary accounts, it appears that whatever she may have thought of his journalistic skills, Luxemburg found Radek personally unacceptable. Under the best of circumstances it would have been unlikely that an older, well-established leader of the socialist Left would have found a person like Radek politically desirable. He was obviously brash, with an apparently compulsive need to call attention to himself, which Rosa Luxemburg might have found unattractive in anyone at any time. In fact, 1908 was a difficult year for Luxemburg on several counts, and Radek was an irritant she simply was not prepared to tolerate. She had suffered through several personal and political crises and had served a jail term on a charge of sedition. As her love affair with Leo Jogiches came to a stormy end, she became more aloof than ever and seemed wary of offering her friendship to anyone, least of all to the loud-mouthed and irresponsible Radek.[7]

The distaste that Luxemburg evinced for Radek was open and total. As one socialist, Friedrich Stampfer, was to learn, mere association with Radek imperiled one's relationship with Luxemburg. For some time Stampfer had been puzzled about why Luxemburg consistently refused to be seated at the same table with him at the Café Josty, a place frequented by socialists. After a while Stampfer realized that Luxemburg had nothing against him, but would not be seated with Radek, who was usually at the same table. In Stampfer's words, "She hated Radek like the plague."[8]

Paul Frölich, a close friend of both Luxemburg and Radek, was distressed and puzzled by the extent of Luxemburg's hostility. In his biography of Luxemburg, Frölich wrote: "Karl Radek was perhaps the most talented of her pupils, but she never became friendly with him, and deliberately held him at a distance because a certain frivolity, not of word, but of political character, made her suspicious of him."[9] During the several months that Radek spent in Berlin in 1908, he was on consistently bad terms with Luxemburg, a situation that must have distressed him a great deal, in view of his consistent efforts to support her policies.

Leaving Berlin, Radek moved to Leipzig and became a staff writer for the *Leipziger Volkszeitung*, a socialist newspaper that Luxemburg had once edited and that still supported her position on most issues. At the same time, he continued to write for the SDKPiL journals, always praising Luxemburg and attempting to demonstrate that her analysis of the world situation and of socialist tactics was essentially correct. He wrote innumerable articles, all of them offering the same solutions to political and social problems as Luxemburg did, and in some cases asking the SPD to take a "Luxemburg approach" to socialist tactics.[10]

Radek's political tracts were simple and unsophisticated and had little to say in matters of revolutionary theory that Luxemburg had not already said, and said more profoundly; but they did serve the important purpose of disseminating the Left's views throughout the Social-Democratic press. Luxemburg had neither the time nor the inclination to write daily columns; Radek wrote literally hundreds of articles, first in the *Leipziger Volkszeitung*, then after 1910 in the *Bremer Bürgerzeitung* as well. By placing fewer intellectual demands on the reader than Luxemburg did, Radek reached the party member who was not well grounded in Marxist theory but could be swayed by simple argument. Radek had a genius for getting directly to the essence of the matter and establishing the cogency of his arguments. More than one German socialist writer envied this Polish émigré his forceful use of the German language.[11] They were less envious of his clever but sarcastic commentaries, which often exceeded the bounds of good taste.

By 1910 Radek was well known in German socialist circles. Most accounts describe him as a sloppy and irresponsible bohemian, carelessly dressed and given to scurrilous small talk—a man not above telling a dirty joke about his own mother.[12] This characterization is misleading. Radek was a complex person capable of moving in a variety of social milieux and adapting himself to whatever role the occasion seemed to demand. A photograph of Radek taken sometime between 1908 and 1914 shows him as a sensitive young man, impeccably dressed and groomed, striking the kind of reflective pose that might well be assumed by a new barrister seeking to attract clients—an image quite unlike that of the uncouth revolutionary of later years.[13] Radek did appear often in the role of the unkempt bohemian, especially during his later years, but it would seem that he did so largely for effect. Many young Social Democrats adopted a slovenly appearance and easy morals to underscore their protest against the mores of bourgeois society; as Konrad Haenisch notes, Radek simply overdid it.[14]

Some time between 1909 and 1911 Karl Radek married or at least began to live with a young German girl, Rosa, who was involved in the socialist movement. It is difficult to determine just when this association began, since Radek makes no mention of it anywhere, not even in his autobiography, and no record has been found of Rosa's maiden name. It is highly unlikely that he met the girl prior to his emigration to Germany in 1908, but certain that he began to live with her no later than 1911. Perhaps there never was a formal wedding ceremony; many socialists, particularly revolutionaries, scorned marriage ceremonies, even civil ones, as rites of bourgeois society, and entered into informal arrangements that over the years became de facto common-law marriages. It is highly probable that this was the case with the Radeks.[15]

Rosa Radek remained in the background of Radek's life; only rarely did she intrude into his political career. She must have understood that there was a high price to be paid for marriage to the volatile revolutionary, and she appeared ready to pay that price. At times he could be tender toward her. In 1919 he wrote her from a German prison: "I have your little photograph . . . and every day, until we see each other once again, I will think of you, you wonderful and beloved one. I embrace you heartily and kiss you many times."[16] At other times, he seemed to ignore her feelings. He was often unfaithful, and his love affairs were not conducted discreetly—particularly his long affair with Larissa Reissner in the 1920's. Perhaps Rosa consoled herself with the belief that Radek would always come back to her. In fact, the marriage lasted all his life.[17]

In the summer of 1910, at the World Congress of the Second International in Copenhagen, the mercurial Radek finally was given an opportunity to acquire some international attention. When a resolution was introduced calling upon Social Democrats to work for international and national agreements on arms reductions, Radek, although not one of the scheduled speakers, intruded himself into the debate and criticized the resolution as a utopian illusion. It was his first appearance before an international audience, and he tried to make the most of it—so much so that the presiding officer had to ask him to end his talk and give others a chance to speak.[18] The motion was carried despite Radek's opposition, but he had at least gained a moment in the limelight.

It was at the Copenhagen Congress that Radek first met V. I. Lenin, the leader of the Bolshevik faction of Russian Social Democracy and a man with a substantial reputation for antirevisionism. Lenin's only important action at this Congress demonstrated that his reputation was deserved. When consumer cooperatives were described in a resolution as a force that could teach the workers democracy and socialism, Lenin sought to reword the resolution to state that this function could be developed by cooperatives only after the expropriation of the property held by capitalists.[19] Lenin's amendment was roundly defeated and the resolution passed easily, in keeping with the prevailing revisionist mood of the Congress.

Lenin may have failed to impress the Congress with his attempt to radicalize the debate on cooperatives, but he did impress Radek, who now began to develop his own views on whether consumers' cooperatives, which were popular in some European countries, had any revolutionary potential. Prior to the Copenhagen Congress, Radek had held a low opinion of the revolutionary utility of the cooperatives; just a few years earlier, he had written derisively of the cooperative movement:

Shops for the cheaper purchase of merchandise will liberate mankind from the calamity of capitalism, and thus in an orderly manner the greatest revolution in history will be accomplished; not in the midst of the clanging noise of arms, not after a long and troublesome civil war, and not with weapons in their hands will the people raise the red flag of socialism over the bastion of capitalism. No, with their scales, with their meters, with their chalk, and with their glasses on their noses, the "cooperativists" will overthrow capitalism.[20]

After Copenhagen, Radek realized that perhaps he had been too hasty in his dismissal of the cooperative movement. Although Lenin's remarks were meant to warn the Congress of the limitations of the movement, they had shown Radek its potential utility. He revised his views, and sent his new analysis to *Sotsial-Demokrat*, the journal of the Bolsheviks. His article was clearly an answer to the argument presented by Lenin at Copenhagen. In it he insisted that cooperatives could and should be exploited by revolutionary socialists, and that the time had come for developing the cooperatives' revolutionary potential.[21] The cooperative movement was of passing interest to Radek, and he paid it little note after 1910; what was important was the contact with Lenin, which was to be

of crucial importance to Radek a few years hence. After Radek's
analysis was published, the two men began corresponding. Radek
solicited Lenin's views on the disarmament problem, particularly
as expounded by Radek at Copenhagen and in later newspaper articles; Lenin's reply was more equivocal than substantial.[22] Cordial
if sporadic, the correspondence dealt chiefly with matters of translation and publication; Lenin several times asked Radek's help in
placing articles with the German socialist press.[23]

There were important areas of disagreement between the two
men at this time. As a follower of Rosa Luxemburg, Radek came
into opposition with Lenin on several issues, particularly revolutionary organization, the role of leadership, and the question of
self-determination of nationalities.[24] Whereas Lenin in his famous
work *What Is to Be Done?* had stressed the importance of a highly
disciplined select leadership, Radek and Luxemburg denied the
necessity for such an elite. They felt that the proletariat itself was
capable of developing a revolutionary consciousness and employ-
ing revolutionary tactics,[25] while Lenin quite bluntly stated that
left to their own devices, the members of the proletariat were incapable of rising above a trade-union mentality.[26] Finally, Radek
and Lenin were in complete disagreement about the self-determination of nationalities, which Lenin believed possible and Radek
believed impossible under the capitalist system.[27]

After Copenhagen, Radek returned to Leipzig, where he became
engrossed in the subject he had debated at the International Congress: the socialist view of disarmament. He opposed socialist support of international agreements to regulate arms and international
courts to arbitrate international disputes. He frankly feared that
conceding either to be feasible or even desirable in a capitalist society would also be conceding the possibility of achieving social
reform without the overthrow of capitalism. Such a revisionistic
hypothesis was anathema to him. For this reason, Radek resolutely
opposed the quest of many Social Democrats for an agreement on
arms reductions and for the establishment of international courts
of arbitration.

Radek was not happy in Leipzig; perhaps his extreme views on disarmament were not well received by his comrades there. In any event, at the end of 1910 he moved back to Berlin for a brief stay, then went on to Bremen. There he continued to harangue his readers on the disarmament issue in a long series of articles, all of which hinged on the same point: "Within the framework of capitalism, the problem of a general disarmament, as well as the problem of a general arms limitation, is insoluble, chiefly because the solution does not exist within capitalist society."[28]

Some time in 1911, Radek reached a final parting of ways with his old associates in the SDKPiL. Exactly what caused this falling out is difficult to determine; neither Radek nor any of the others involved has ever offered a satisfactory explanation. The cause can perhaps be found in the party split that took place that same year. The émigré clique had for some time been quarreling with the Warsaw membership over party organization and leadership. As Russian subjects, SDKPiL members had a voice in the affairs of the Russian Social Democratic Labor Party, a group that had undergone a basic split in its own camp. The SDKPiL members now had the opportunity to "play politics" with their Russian comrades and use SDKPiL votes to tip the balance in the Bolshevik-Menshevik schism. Luxemburg, often suspicious of Lenin's motives, was not above using these votes as a threat.[29] Many of the SDKPiL members, particularly those still in Warsaw, were reluctant to see their party support the Mensheviks—whose moderate policies smacked of revisionism to them—and protested this use of votes by the émigré leadership. The Warsaw members also resented the tightly controlled organization that Jogiches had established with Luxemburg's tacit consent. As a result, in 1911 the SDKPiL split into two feuding factions, one based in Berlin and the other in Warsaw.[30]

Although Radek used this split to explain his estrangement from the Luxemburg group, it would seem that there was a more personal reason for his switchover to the Warsaw faction.[31] His ties with Hanecki (Fürstenburg), Unszlicht, and others of the faction were cordial but not close; certainly his ties to the Luxemburg group were a great deal closer. What is likely is that Radek had no option; the Luxemburg group simply refused to have him any longer, at least on his terms.

Originally admitted to the Luxemburg circle because of his abilities as a journalist, Radek had never really been accepted as an equal; by 1911 he may well have believed that he had long since passed the apprenticeship stage and deserved admission to the select group of SDKPiL leaders. In April 1911 he had the bad grace to challenge the leadership in public by denouncing Marchlewski for equivocation on the disarmament issue.[32] It was not so much Radek's disagreement with Marchlewski that offended the leadership as the manner in which it was aired and the stridency of Radek's tone. If Radek was ready to challenge the leadership so openly, with no regard for Marchlewski's senior position in the SDKPiL, he was obviously no longer content to restrict himself to the role prescribed for him, and therefore his usefulness to the SDKPiL in Germany was seriously curtailed. Luxemburg had never liked Radek, but she had tolerated him because of his usefulness and because of Warszawski's continued support of him.[*] Now Marchlewski refused to tolerate Radek any longer and joined with Luxemburg to expel him from the SDKPiL, denouncing him in terms that shocked even the German radicals.[33] Gossip about the old embezzlement charges of 1908 became so widespread that Radek felt compelled to issue a belated defense against the charges.[34]

While distressing to Radek, his expulsion from the SDKPiL did not terminate his activities in Germany. He had for some time been gravitating toward a new group, whose members were ready to accept him as a leader and to wink at his personal foibles. This group, which later became known as the Bremen Left-Radicals, had become by 1911 the *enfant terrible* of German Social Democracy. Until 1905 the Bremen organization was led by Friedrich Ebert, and was a well-disciplined sector of the SPD. After 1905, however, Ebert moved on to the Executive Committee in Berlin, and the Bremen organization drifted into a struggle between revisionists and radicals. The struggle was eventually won by the radi-

---

[*] Warszawski's support of Radek never did falter, from their encounters in Switzerland in 1904 to Radek's troubles in 1924.

cals under the young Wilhelm Pieck,* who had come to Bremen in 1908 full of revolutionary zeal instilled by Rosa Luxemburg at the *Parteischule* in Berlin.[35] The Bremen organization became synonymous with the extreme Left in German Social Democracy. At various times its membership included the Dutch socialist Anton Pannekoek, the journalist Johannes Knief, and Luxemburg's friend and biographer Paul Frölich.[36]

Radek began at this time to cultivate close friendships with other German radical journalists, notably August Thalheimer, editor of the Göppingen *Freie Volkszeitung* and Konrad Haenisch, editor of the Dortmund *Arbeiterzeitung* (he had long been friendly with Paul Lensch, the editor of the *Leipziger Volkszeitung*). With this new circle of comrades, Radek no longer needed favors from the SDKPiL. He still sympathized with the ideological views of Luxemburg and her associates, but he could not work as a subordinate any longer. His new colleagues in Bremen, who were more concerned with his talents than his idiosyncrasies, made him an editor of the *Bremer Bürgerzeitung*, the most radical and outspoken antirevisionist newspaper in Germany.†

Radek began to use the *Bremer Bürgerzeitung* as his vehicle for an all-out attack on the revisionist influences in the German Social Democratic Party. In the past, the personal nature of his attacks usually had been restrained by editorial censorship, but now the older SDKPiL comrades were no longer around to inhibit him. The Executive Committee of the SPD, constantly at war with the opinions of the Left, took particular exception to Radek's irresponsible and sometimes vicious attacks.

Radek might have remained just an outspoken radical journalist if it had not been for his involvement in 1912 with the problems of his friend August Thalheimer, who by some rather naïve financial dealings had brought his newspaper, the Göppingen *Freie Volkszeitung*, to the verge of bankruptcy. Thalheimer appealed to the

---

* Pieck later served as President of Communist East Germany (from 1949 to 1960).

† Johannes Knief was technically editor-in-chief, but in these years most of the lead editorials on major issues were written by Radek.

regional SPD officials for financial assistance, but they were willing to help only if the radical tone of the newspaper were changed. In late May of 1912, in the midst of the dispute, Thalheimer took a short leave of absence and asked Radek to act in his stead as editor of the Göppingen paper. Radek used this opportunity to publish defamatory attacks against revisionist socialists. He did not confine his attack to the regional officials in Stuttgart, but with characteristic irresponsibility accused the Executive Committee in Berlin, and Ebert in particular, of instigating a campaign to eliminate the leftist organization in Göppingen. Not content with this, he repeated his charges in the *Leipziger Volkszeitung,* and in so doing created a party scandal.[37]

Radek was perhaps unaware of just how much his position in the SPD was damaged by this affair, but during the summer of 1912 he received the first warning that he was about to be read out of the SPD. In the spring of that year, Radek had participated in a new party debate on the nature of imperialism. The major articles in the debate were published in *Die Neue Zeit,* then under the editorship of Karl Kautsky. Kautsky himself was the innovator of a new view of imperialism, but in line with what he considered to be his obligation as the editor of a socialist journal, he maintained a neutral stance and printed divergent views on the subject, including direct attacks on his own position.

Kautsky's new approach to imperialism could hardly have been expected to please Radek, Luxemburg, or any other member of the Left. Kautsky offered the thesis that capitalist society contained pacifist elements opposed to undesirable consequences of imperialism such as the arms race and the dangers of war, and that Social Democrats should cooperate with these elements in order to tame imperialism from within.[38]

Kautsky had long been one of the giants of the Second International and an outstanding foe of revisionism. Radek had been deferential toward him in his earlier writings, and usually spoke of him as one of those truly concerned with socialist revolution. But Radek, along with other members of the Left, believed that Kautsky should be challenged on this "revisionist" solution to the problem of imperialism. Radek's first attack on Kautsky's new views, written before the Göppingen Affair, was dutifully printed by Kautsky in *Die Neue Zeit*.[39] The article was fairly mild by Radek's standards; although he ridiculed Kautsky's views, he did not indulge in personal invective. Radek did point out, however, that in view of the international crises caused by imperialism in the past decade, the pacifistic elements of the bourgeoisie had wasted many opportunities to voice their protests—if in fact such elements did exist.[40]

During the spring of 1912 the argument grew more heated. Kautsky continued to defend his views, while Radek became increasingly critical of anyone who deviated from the revolutionary line. In July Radek submitted an article to *Die Neue Zeit* as the definitive refutation of Kautsky's new theories of imperialism.[41] In this article, Radek abandoned his former polite references to certain misinformed comrades, and aimed his attack directly at Kautsky. He pointed out that earlier Kautsky had unequivocally denounced imperialism, and demanded to know which had changed, imperialism or Kautsky? To Radek, the answer was obvious. Imperialism had not become less of a thrust; on the contrary, it was a greater danger than ever. Kautsky, by retreating from his earlier stand and creating a myth of pacifistic factions in imperialism, was aiding the revisionist cause and denying the necessity for revolutionary struggle. Radek summed up his lengthy castigation of Kautsky with the comment: "Out of fantasies, one can create poetry; out of speculation, inferior philosophy; but the struggle demands a sword, and iron is to be found only in the black soil of reality."[42]

The editors of *Die Neue Zeit* had Radek's article set in type, but in view of his rapidly deteriorating position in the party, they decided to postpone publication.[43] Radek chafed at the delay and suspected Kautsky of trying to censor the article.[44] It was typical of Radek to ascribe the delay in publication to censorship, a tactic quite inconsistent with Kautsky's past activities, and to ignore the rising demand in the SPD for his own expulsion. After two more inquiries, Radek served notice: the article must be published or returned to him at once.[45]

The editorial board was probably relieved at the ultimatum;

they certainly did not wish to act as political censors, but Radek's future as a member of the SPD was becoming a matter for speculation. The Göppingen Affair had been revived; various party newspapers were carrying notices of his earlier expulsion from the SDKPiL, and it seemed certain that further action would be taken against him at the annual SPD Congress.[46] In addition, Rosa Luxemburg had just published a long statement attacking his credentials as a member of the Left of the SPD and of the SDKPiL, and criticizing the Bremen organization for being so "misinformed" as to side with Radek.[47] Thus, by the beginning of September 1912 there was every indication that Radek would soon be ousted from the SPD. With this in mind, the editors of *Die Neue Zeit* returned the article to Radek, who forthwith published it as a special supplement to the *Bremer Bürgerzeitung*.[48]

When the annual SPD Congress opened in Chemnitz on September 15, 1912, the Göppingen Affair was on the agenda and received an extraordinary amount of attention. Speaking for the Executive Committee, Friedrich Ebert stated that what should have been at worst a comradely disagreement had become a disagreeable scandal solely because of Radek's malicious intervention. Ebert's speech was enthusiastically received by the Congress. He then went a step further and challenged Radek's credentials as a member of the German Social Democratic Party, maintaining that Radek had never properly applied for membership and certainly had never paid any dues. These charges were met with "boisterous merriment that lasted several minutes."[49] The delegates may have been more amused by the contrast between the two men than by Radek's delinquencies: Ebert, the "bookkeeper" of the SPD and the man who reorganized party finances; Radek, the irresponsible bohemian who could not be bothered with minor obligations like paying his party dues.

It was evident from the way in which Ebert was applauded and Radek's few defenders were shouted down that Radek's irresponsible behavior had made him far more enemies than anyone had realized. Some socialists, however, felt that Radek was being unfairly treated. Konrad Haenisch—who may well have believed some of the charges against Radek—summed up the views of a minority in the SPD when he referred to the revival of the old embezzlement charges of 1908 and asked: "If R[adek] has behaved like a swine, why is it being revealed only now, after so many years?"[50] Others were even more disturbed to see eminent leftists, particularly the SDKPiL leaders, collaborate with the Executive Committee in its vendetta against Radek.[51]

The Chemnitz Congress appointed a grievance committee to investigate the Göppingen Affair, as well as Radek's status, and to report its findings at the next annual SPD Congress. Some of Radek's friends, including Knief and Haenisch, tried to persuade SPD leaders to let Radek remain in the party. Haenisch, who wrote letters in support of Radek to Social Democrats throughout Germany, was shocked by the vehemence of some of the replies he received.[52] Radek himself did not seem alarmed by the feeling against him, and did little to salvage his position. He still had at least one major outlet in the socialist press, the *Bremer Bürgerzeitung*, which openly sided with him and claimed that he was the victim of a trend toward revisionism on the part of the Executive Committee. On the other hand, some German socialists normally identified with the Left, for example, Radek's old friend Paul Lensch, declined to back him.[53] In the final analysis, SDKPiL's involvement in the anti-Radek movement was the decisive factor. When the annual SPD Congress assembled in Jena in September 1913, the grievance committee had long since decided against Radek. The only problem was to find an acceptable reason for expelling him.

Herman Müller, an associate of Ebert and a member of the Executive Committee, presented the report of the grievance committee to the Congress. Although he made much of Radek's irregular record in paying his party dues, Müller was well aware that in itself this was not sufficient justification for expelling Radek. For this reason, he placed emphasis on the old embezzlement charges and Radek's expulsion from the SDKPiL.[54] The actual mechanics of expulsion were contained in the following resolution: "Persons [i.e., Radek] who have been expelled from a fraternal Party of the International Socialist Bureau [the secretariat of the

Second International] because of dishonorable actions cannot acquire membership in the German Social Democratic Party without the consent of the Party that has excluded them."[55]

By this resolution, the Executive Committee declared in effect that Radek had never been a member of the German Social Democratic Party, and thus spared the Congress the necessity of voting to expel him. The resolution embarrassed the SDKPiL, since it put the onus for the expulsion on them and clearly implied that only by their petition could Radek be granted continued membership in the SPD. Since Rosa Luxemburg had no desire at this time to help Radek, she did nothing and the ex-post-facto statute automatically brought about his expulsion from the SPD.[56]

Radek's expulsion was a serious setback to his career. Fortunately for him, the Bremen organization protested the decision of the Party Congress and continued to provide him with an outlet for his writings in their newspaper.[57] Two months later, Haenisch observed: "I see Radek from time to time. Things are quite well with him. Hopefully, this Polish judgment is now over."[58]

The case was never officially closed, and echoes of it continued to be heard in the socialist press.[59] For about a year, Radek was definitely in eclipse. Outside of Bremen he was no longer widely read, and various rumors about him circulated. By the spring of 1914, however, there were some signs that the Executive Committee was ready to backtrack on the harsh judgment of the 1913 Congress. This softening of attitude did not result from sympathy for Radek but rather from a growing concern that the expulsion had compromised the integrity of the SPD and had involved the Party in maneuvers of dubious legality.[60] But the assassination of the Austrian Archduke Francis Ferdinand occurred in the summer of 1914, and within a few weeks most of Europe was at war. The Radek case faded into obscurity before the greater issues at hand.

3. Radek and Lenin:
   Collaboration and Conflict

Since the earliest days of the socialist movement, its members, whether revisionist or revolutionary, had been united in their opposition to war, though they were often in disagreement over what steps to take against the forces of militarism. At the Stuttgart Congress of 1907, the Second International passed a resolution committing all socialists to take action to prevent the outbreak of war—though the kind of action remained unspecified. At a special antiwar congress held in Basel in November 1912, the International went a step further and threatened the Great Powers with proletarian revolution should war break out.[1] Even revisionist leaders backed the Basel statement and promised to work for a socialist strategy that would prevent war.

Developments during July 1914—the month between the assassination of the Austrian archduke and the outbreak of hostilities—demonstrated all too plainly the limitations of the socialist antiwar opposition. While socialists organized demonstrations, generals mobilized armies. More important, opposition to the war was a tenet of the socialist leadership, but not of the rank and file: patriotic rallies were as well attended by workers as antiwar demonstrations were. Nevertheless, the leadership continued its efforts to spread antiwar sentiment. France's most respected socialist, Jean Jaurès, seeking to allay his comrades' fears that there was no alternative to war, went so far as to argue that Germany's statements were not as bellicose as they sounded in French translation.[2] As a reward for his antiwar activities, he was assassinated by a nationalist fanatic. In Germany, the SPD issued a dramatic and uncompromising manifesto against the war on July 25, 1914, demanding unequivocally that the German government restrain Austria in her demands on Serbia.[3] Throughout Europe, Social Democratic leaders urged their national governments to exercise restraint and to avoid war. Perhaps if they could have exerted pressure on generals as well as cabinet ministers, they would have been able to exercise some influence; as it was, the Social Democrats expended their efforts on those who had no ability or no inclination to restrain the forces ready to plunge Europe into war.

By the end of July, the international situation had deteriorated so badly that the problem of the Social Democrats was no longer how to stop the war—it was too late for that—but what tactics to adopt during the war. The Second International had threatened proletarian action if war broke out, but no coherent plans had been formulated, and it is highly improbable that a protest could have been implemented at this time.[4] On August 1, the moment of decision for German socialists arrived: their government retaliated against Russian mobilization with a declaration of war; and two days later, uncertain of the efficacy of the Franco-Russian alliance, Germany also declared war on France. The proletarian "wrath against war" failed utterly to materialize; on the contrary, workers universally pledged solidarity to their homelands (in Germany, the trade unions called off all strikes, planned or in progress). Confronted with this situation, the SPD had but two options: to accept the war, or to use the sizable socialist vote in the Reichstag to block or at least oppose war credits, thus forcing the German government to reconsider the feasibility of its war effort. Since the government had already declared war, such opposition might well have been regarded as an act of rebellion, and the Reichstag socialists were not ready to take this risk. By a caucus vote of 78 to 14, the socialist members decided to support their government. The workers whom these men represented had already indicated their support for their country; now their elected representatives followed suit.[5] On August 4, 1914, much to the consternation of revolutionaries everywhere, the socialists in the Reichstag voted unanimously to grant the Imperial German Government the requested war credits.[6] Only in the Russian Duma and in the Serbian Skupschtina—both parliamentary bodies with negligible socialist representation—was any socialist opposition to war credits encountered. Faced with a choice between their countries and the Second International, the vast majority of socialists chose the former.

In Bremen, the SPD delegation's support of the war credits shocked Radek as much as it did other socialists. Although for obvious reasons he was not an admirer of the SPD leadership, he had not expected them to identify so openly with government aims.[7] For several weeks he pondered his own future course of action. The imposition of wartime censorship made it impossible for him to continue his career as a polemical journalist for the *Bremer Bürgerzeitung;*[8] after several halfhearted attempts to help organize a war opposition movement, he moved to Berlin, hoping that the leaders of the Left there might be able to rally socialists to an antiwar crusade.[9] Though it seemed that the entire edifice of German socialism was crumbling, Radek still hoped that the Left would act as a leaven for the whole.

The approval of the war credits bill was not the only reason for Radek's disillusionment with German socialism. Although he had always doubted the revolutionary loyalty of the SPD's Reichstag delegation, a group with substantial trade union and revisionist membership, he had had no doubts about the radicals of the German Left. What hurt him more than the voting of war credits was the defection of men he had believed to be devoted revolutionaries. Paul Lensch, former editor of the *Leipziger Volkszeitung,* was perhaps the most prominent example of a radical who under pressure proved to be more concerned with his fatherland than with revolutionary socialism. Yet it was not Lensch's defection but that of Konrad Haenisch that was the bitterest disappointment to Radek. For years Haenisch had been one of the German radicals whom Radek most admired. In 1912 and 1913, during the Göppingen Affair, Haenisch was one of the few who came to Radek's

defense. It was quite logical that at this moment of crisis for the
German Left Radek would turn to Haenisch for advice and encouragement. He received a rude shock when Haenisch not only
defended the vote for the war credits bill but also said: "If [Social
Democracy] had not chosen to side with the nation, then it would
have been utterly lost. . . . We would again become what we have
been for decades, an impotent sect without influence."[10] As if that
were not bad enough, Haenisch made a public proclamation of
his conversion to the cause of national defense, celebrating his
gratification that "one could, for the first time in almost a quarter
of a century, join with a full heart, a clean conscience, and without a sense of treason in the sweeping stormy song *"Deutschland,
Deutschland, über alles!"*[11] It was several months before Radek
could bring himself to reply to Haenisch; the transformation of this
erstwhile radical had shown him that even the most ardent be-
liever in international socialism might find it impossible to reject
his country in time of war.[12]

The mobilization of troops presented Radek with another problem. In 1914, he was still legally an Austrian citizen and as such
liable for military service. The conscription into the German army
of several of his Bremen comrades demonstrated that the German
government was not fussy about the political affiliations of potential soldiers. The threat of conscription and his feeling of political
impotence combined to make him once again consider emigration.
After several weeks of indecision, he finally left Germany for
Berne, Switzerland, ostensibly to act as liaison between the German Left and the Italian socialists (there is no evidence that Radek had any significant contact with the Italian socialists there, but
the pretext served to get him to a neutral country.[13] Free from the
harassment of the censor and worries about conscription, he was
able to resume political work and to propound his own version of
the proper strategy for socialists in war time.

The socialist newspaper, the *Berner Tagwacht*, was the most
important and widely read socialist publication in Switzerland.
Robert Grimm, the editor, was firmly against the war and sympathetic to the Left of the Second International. He quickly recruited

Radek as a regular contributor on problems of international social-ism; but in view of Radek's dubious status in the Second International and his many enemies on the Left, Grimm decided that Radek must use a pseudonym. Thus for the next two years Radek published regularly in the *Berner Tagwacht* under the name of Parabellum. By the time the public realized that Parabellum and Radek were the same person, few socialists still cared about Radek's earlier ostracism.

It was during these years that Radek for the first time came into close contact with the large group of Russian socialists—Bolshe-viks, Mensheviks, and Social Revolutionaries—living in Switzer-land. Radek had met some of these people during his brief stay in Switzerland in 1904 and 1905, but at that time he spoke no Rus-sian, and was in any case caught up in SDKPiL activities. Although the details of the Göppingen Affair were well known in Berne, most of the Russian socialists cared little about Radek's past. Some of them found him interesting company, others considered him rude and boisterous; but all seem to have formed their judgment of him without regard to his reputation in Germany.[14]

Radek's feelings about the Russian émigrés were ambivalent. Ideologically and politically, there were many points of difference between Radek and the various Russian socialist groups. He felt the least sympathy for the Social Revolutionaries. This group did not profess to be Marxist, and their political program was peasant-oriented. Radek's contacts with them were minimal. Radek consid-ered the Mensheviks, who made up the moderate faction of Rus-sian Social Democracy, to be lacking in revolutionary dedication; he had long attributed the split in the Russian Social Democratic Labor Party to Menshevik obdurateness rather than to Lenin's efforts.[15] He made friends with several of the Mensheviks, how-ever, and in 1915 he had a short affair with the sister of one of the Menshevik émigrés.[16]

Serious ideological obstacles kept Radek from a rapprochement with the Bolsheviks. In earlier years, the Lenin-Luxemburg dis-pute over revolutionary organization, the role of party leadership, and the question of national self-determination had prevented any

close association between Lenin and Radek. Even after the outbreak of the war, Radek still held to the Luxemburg point of view
on these issues and regarded Lenin's revolutionary tactics with
considerable suspicion. Now there was another issue on which
Lenin and Radek could not agree: the future of the Second International and the SPD. In September 1914, shortly after his arrival
in Switzerland, Lenin had issued a series of theses condemning
both organizations and proclaiming the demise of the Second International.[17] Although Radek found himself substantially in agreement with the spirit of Lenin's theses, he had not given up hope
for a revival of either group.

Lenin had never belonged to the German Social Democratic
Party (though he had often sought to publish his polemics in its
press), nor had he been an enthusiastic supporter of the Second
International, whose members had often accused him of per-
petuating an unnecessary division in Russian Social Democracy.[18]
Hence the collapse of both groups in the face of war had not
distressed him as much as it had Radek, although even Lenin had
not expected the German socialists to vote for war credits. Radek's
experience was different. Though he damned all socialists who
supported their country's war effort, he was not ready to write off
the SPD, and still nursed the hope that the SPD Left could raise
an effective opposition and reverse the decision of August 4.[19]

Radek's ambivalent feelings about German Social Democracy
were strong enough to induce him to risk a trip back to Berlin at
the end of November. He was again unsuccessful in establishing
rapport with Luxemburg, so he devoted his major attention to Karl
Liebknecht, who was then emerging as the voice of opposition in
the SPD's Reichstag delegation.[20] In the name of party unity Liebknecht had reluctantly cast his vote for war credits in August, but
since then he had worked hard to organize an international socialist antiwar movement.[21] Radek had hoped that Liebknecht would
be successful in turning the tide within the SPD; instead, he was
shocked to see that even the Reichstag delegates who had opposed
the credits were unwilling to break party discipline. On December
3, 1914, the second war credits bill was passed, with Liebknecht

casting the sole dissenting vote. Radek returned to Switzerland disillusioned with the SPD.

Radek finally admitted to himself that there was little hope of mounting an antiwar effort within the structure of the party, though he still hoped for a radical revival. Even when a third war credits bill passed in March 1915 he did not give up, although he commented bitterly on continued SPD support for such bills.[22] The following month a new journal, *Die Internationale*, appeared under the editorship of Rosa Luxemburg and Franz Mehring. Radek stretched his imagination to see in this journal an indication that the Left had gained new prominence in the SPD.[23] *Die Internationale* survived for only one issue, and that hope was gone. During the spring of 1915 Radek wrote less and less of the prospects of the German Social Democratic Party and virtually nothing at all about the Second International or its executive body, the International Socialist Bureau. Although he did not explicitly say so in the pages of the *Berner Tagwacht*, by the summer of 1915 he was essentially in agreement with Lenin that neither the SPD nor the International Socialist Bureau had any prospects of rallying the proletariat against the war.

Coming around to Lenin's viewpoint was one matter; becoming Lenin's political ally was another. Radek had no great hopes for the Bolsheviks' future, in Russia or in the international socialist movement. But though unwilling to join the Bolsheviks, Radek saw no reason not to work with them if it would help him advance the cause of revolutionary socialism. In spite of the ideological disputes he had had with Lenin, he respected him as a revolutionary.

Lenin lived in Berne during the winter and spring of 1914–1915, and on at least one occasion he asked Radek's advice on how various European socialists, particularly Rosa Luxemburg, might react to the slogan "A United States of Europe."[24] Other than that, the two men seem to have had little contact before this time. What made Lenin increasingly important to Radek was Radek's indeterminate status as a socialist. For all practical purposes, he was a man without a party.[25] True, he still belonged to the Warsaw Committee, but that was scarcely an impressive organization; in fact, it was not an organization at all, but merely a splinter group of Polish socialists opposed to the émigré leadership in Germany. Radek soon realized that it was difficult for a socialist—particularly one with as many political enemies as he had acquired—to work independently and have any impact on the movement.

In 1915 Berne was a center for many forms of socialist protest against the war. The Third International Socialist Women's Conference was held at Berne in March. Several Bolshevik women, including Nadezhda Krupskaia (Lenin's wife) and Inessa Armand, tried to substitute a radical revolutionary spirit for the pacifism of the Conference manifesto.[26] A week later, the International Socialist Youth Conference voiced strong pacifist sentiments.[27] These conferences, the first international meetings of socialists to take place since the outbreak of the war, demonstrated to Radek that there remained among some socialists a willingness to organize on an international basis against the "defensist" majorities of most socialist parties. He identified with the Youth Conference and became an early contributor to *Jugend-Internationale*, an antiwar journal emanating from it.[28]

The momentum of these first conferences was continued when, on the initiative of socialists from neutral countries, an international conference of socialists was planned for Berne. Radek realized that since he did not belong to any group recognized by the International Socialist Bureau, he would be unable to attend. He was most anxious that radical groups be represented there, and he was horrified to learn from Grimm, who was in charge of organizing the conference, that the Bolsheviks had not been invited. Hastily he wrote to Lenin, who had by now moved from Berne, that there would be a "preliminary conference" on July 11, 1915, and that there ought to be Bolshevik representation.[29] Perhaps Radek hoped that Lenin, busy with other matters, would ask him to act as the Bolsheviks' proxy; if so, Lenin missed the hint. His reply indicated that he appreciated the importance of the "preliminary conference," and that he suspected Grimm of deliberately overlooking the Bolsheviks. Instead of deputizing Radek, however,

Lenin sent Grigory Zinoviev, a long-time associate of his, to the preliminary conference. Zinoviev presented Lenin's view that what was needed was not pacifism but an effort to turn the war into a civil war against capitalism.[30] These were becoming Radek's sentiments as well, and he undoubtedly agreed with Zinoviev, but his position as an outsider without party status kept him from being admitted to the meetings and offering his support.

The most important single result of the preliminary conference was the decision to hold a full-scale meeting of socialists opposed to the war as soon as possible. Though all those present at the preliminary conference had agreed that such a meeting should take place, there was no agreement on who should be invited. Radek, of course, was unhappy about the criteria established for admittance to the first conference, whereby he had been summarily excluded. Robert Grimm was organizing the forthcoming meeting, and Radek did not feel confident that Grimm could arrange to have him admitted.[31] Lenin, on the other hand, had made it clear repeatedly that he favored as criteria for attendance not the credentials of the International Socialist Bureau but active identification with the antiwar Left.[32] This made him useful to Radek and thus provided the basis for a working relationship between the two men—a relationship that Radek began to cultivate assiduously. So openly did he pursue Lenin that the Menshevik leader Pavel Axelrod wrote to Grimm that Radek was now merely Lenin's "channel or instrument."[33]

Lenin's decision to work with Radek was no less opportunistic. He had always favored Radek's Warsaw Committee over the SDKPiL leadership and valued—or perhaps overvalued—Radek's influence with the German Left.[34] One of the German Left factions that interested Lenin most was the group around Julian Borchardt, the editor of the opposition journal *Lichtstrahlen*.[35] Since Radek wrote occasional articles for *Lichtstrahlen*, Lenin assumed that he could be a conduit to this group. The new collaboration did not indicate a desire for friendship, at least not on Lenin's part, but both men recognized their common goals and were willing to cooperate in achieving them.[36]

During the summer of 1915 Lenin bombarded Radek with requests for translations and information on the German Left and
other subjects. Radek found him a stern taskmaster who, oddly
enough, berated him for being "too academic" and not showing
enough enthusiasm in his polemics.[37] This was scarcely the kind of
criticism Radek was used to receiving, but he accepted it and constantly sought to impress Lenin with improved drafts and resolutions. In his new writing, Radek moved closer to Lenin's view of
the major goal of socialism—the formation of a new international
organization purged of the revisionist forces and opportunistic
leaders of the Second International. Echoing Lenin, Radek now
wrote:

When the World War emerged out of the contradictions of capitalism,
the complete impotence of the Second International was demonstrated.
Without opposition it surrendered its position, rolled up its banners, and,
with a few exceptions, undertook nationalist tasks. How can it ever be
resurrected? On the basis of mutual "forgiveness"? ... The Third International must begin where the Second [International] broke down—on
the problem of extra-parliamentary tactics.[38]

Lenin's and Radek's hopes that the forthcoming conference
would be a conference of the Left were not realized; the invitations
to the conference were distributed to a broad spectrum of socialists
that included so-called moderates whose pacifism sprang from
their basic lack of enthusiasm for revolutionary tactics. Yet the
broad range of invitations did make it possible for Radek to become
a delegate, and for that he was quite willing to tolerate the presence of moderates like Georg Ledebour, a German socialist who
occupied a position midway between the SPD's Executive Committee and the opposition forming around Liebknecht.[39]

Radek himself attended the conference as a delegate from the
Regional Presidium (Warsaw Committee) of the SDKPiL, whereas
the regular SDKPiL organization was represented by Adolf Warszawski, who had taken up wartime residence in Switzerland. Warszawski's presence was fortunate for Radek. During his difficulties
with the SDKPiL from 1911 to 1913, Radek had not fallen in Warszawski's esteem; on the contrary, Warszawski always fondly re-

membered that it was he who had introduced Radek to social democracy. Had Luxemburg or Marchlewski been able to come to
Switzerland, Radek might well have had a rough time of it.[40] If
nothing else, they probably would have objected to his representing the SDKPiL in any capacity. Warszawski, however, was not interested in resurrecting old quarrels; instead, he appeared ready to
form a common front of Polish socialists with Radek and his
friends.[41]

At the beginning of September, the delegates to the antiwar
conference began to arrive in Berne. Neither their numbers nor
their reputations would have encouraged Radek or anyone else to
believe that the conference would signal the rebirth of socialist
militancy. Liebknecht could not come; the only avowed radical in
the ten-man German delegation was Julian Borchardt, whose influence was nothing like that of Liebknecht.[42] Only the Russians
around Lenin seemed anxious to turn the conference into a Left
socialist demonstration. Although Radek and Lenin were nominally allies, Radek was wary of committing himself irretrievably to
Lenin.[43] He admired the other's zeal in rallying the leftists, but he
had no intention of being Lenin's errand boy; Lenin still had Zinoviev for that. So it was that once he had been accredited as a delegate to the conference, Radek restricted his contact with Lenin and
sought in every way to create his own identity.

As soon as the delegates were assembled in Berne, Grimm arranged for four motor vehicles to transport them to the nearby Al-
pine village of Zimmerwald, where privacy could be ensured. It
was a bitter joke among the delegates en route to Zimmerwald that
after a half century of international socialism, "it was still possible
to seat all the internationalists in four coaches."[44]

Although all the delegates were opposed to the war effort, few
were ready to adopt as revolutionary a stance as Radek's or Lenin's.[45] After lengthy debate, a manifesto was issued calling upon
the workers of all countries to take immediate action to end the
war on the basis of a peace without annexations or indemnities.[46]
In spite of the desires of the Left, however, the manifesto did
not call for civil war or social revolution. But inadequate as Radek

and other members of the Left may have thought it, the Zimmerwald Manifesto was in fact a step forward out of the inertia of the Second International.

Any hopes Radek may have had for rehabilitation were shortlived. The German delegation, insisting on the validity of Radek's expulsion from the SPD in 1913, refused to sign the Manifesto if he were allowed to do so. Regardless of personal inclinations, the members of the conference had little choice but to sacrifice Radek; any manifesto not signed by the German Social Democrats was unlikely to have a major impact on socialists in other countries. For this reason, Jakob Hanecki—who may or may not have been present at the conference itself—had his name substituted for Radek's on the declaration.[47]

Radek gave his grudging consent to the substitution of Hanecki's name for his own,[48] but he was deeply hurt by the German delegation's intransigence and by the failure of the Zimmerwald Conference to protest his exclusion from the signatories. Any lingering hopes for a future in the SPD were shattered. The whole business demonstrated to Radek that he needed the Bolsheviks more than he had realized at first.

At the Zimmerwald Conference, Radek's first act of open identification with the Bolsheviks consisted of joining them and a few scattered delegates from neutral countries in the formation of a "left bloc" that sought to impose a dramatic revolutionary character upon the conference. Radek prepared a draft resolution that condemned all Social Democrats who supported their countries' war efforts and listed several of them by name. He even urged "the organization of anti-government demonstrations, the propaganda of international solidarity in the trenches; concurrence with economic strikes, and attempts to turn them into political strikes under favorable conditions. Civil war, not civil peace, between the classes—that is our slogan."[49] The rhetoric of Radek's resolution so caught the imagination of the Left Bloc that they supported it over a similar resolution prepared by Lenin.[50] Radek's resolution was too radical for the majority of the delegates at Zimmerwald, however; the pacifist program offered by the Zimmerwald Manifesto had much greater appeal.

The rejection of his draft resolution was of minor consequence to Radek. Far more important was the creation of the Left Bloc—the so-called Zimmerwald Left—which he envisioned as the nucleus of a new international organization openly dedicated to revolutionary socialism. Since the German delegation had made it quite clear that Radek was not welcome to participate openly in the parent Zimmerwald Movement, he was forced to seek a new channel for his political activities. The Left Bloc seemed to offer him what he needed—and he knew he had much to offer it in return.

The summary manner in which the Zimmerwald Conference had rejected the Left's resolution convinced the radicals that the newly organized International Socialist Committee—the official executive group of the Zimmerwald Movement—would be unsympathetic to a revolutionary approach. Therefore, despite the small number of socialists identified with the Zimmerwald Left, the decision was made to produce journals and brochures reflecting the Left's viewpoint. Radek's experience as a journalist, his indisputable talents as a writer, and above all his facility in the German language suddenly increased his value to the Bolsheviks who made up the majority of the Zimmerwald Left. The Left could not hope to reach an international audience with a Russian-language publication. Although few socialists outside Russia could read Russian, virtually all continental socialists could read German, which had served as a semiofficial language for the Second International. Lenin and Zinoviev had some facility with German as a second language, but both wrote in German with difficulty. Radek's combination of literary talent and facility in German assured him editorship of any publication sponsored by the Zimmerwald Left.

The first of the Left's publications, a journal entitled *Internationales Flugblatt*, appeared in the fall of 1915. It disappeared after the first issue, however, probably because of a lack of funds. The journal reprinted the various documents presented by the Left to the Zimmerwald Conference as well as a long introductory article by Radek announcing the complete separation of revolutionary socialists from those who chose to tolerate the continued existence of capitalism.[51] Radek must have been greatly annoyed when the Zimmerwald Left decided that his article must be published anonymously.[52] Lenin perhaps believed that Radek's by-line might antagonize those members of the Left in Germany who had participated in Radek's exclusion from the SPD and had served notice again at Zimmerwald that Radek was no longer to be considered a socialist in good standing.

Early in 1916 the Zimmerwald Left brought out a new and more impressive journal, *Vorbote*. After the demise of *Internationales Flugblatt*, the Zimmerwald Left had managed to persuade two members of the Dutch Social Democratic Party, Henriette Roland-Holst and Anton Pannekoek, to raise money for a new publication.[53] Lenin undoubtedly regretted the necessity of giving the Dutch Social Democrats more control. What he overlooked was that the Dutch patronage placed Radek in a particularly advantageous position: Pannekoek had once been active in the Bremen organization of the SPD and had fairly strong prewar ties with Radek. It may well have been Radek's presence in the Zimmerwald Left, not Lenin's, that induced Pannekoek to raise funds for *Vorbote*.

Soon the issue of financial support became more serious than it might have been. Lenin and Radek were agreed on the general revolutionary orientation of the Left, but not on some of the specific issues and tactics involved. Their most serious difference of opinion concerned the self-determination of nationalities. Lenin recognized the dangers of nationalism and of various claims to self-determination, but he also believed that socialism could not condone the oppression of subject peoples by the capitalist powers: if socialism did not support legitimate aspirations to self-determination, it would be guilty of aiding and abetting imperialist oppression. He also recognized that opposition to self-determination might arouse considerable hostility to the socialist cause among the people of subjugated nations. Lenin hoped that once the socialist order had been introduced, such nations would be discreet about pressing their demands; in the era of capitalist hegemony, however, revolutionary socialists were duty-bound to support any struggle for self-determination.[54] For years Lenin had disputed the nationality problem with Rosa Luxemburg; more recently, he had argued it with his fellow Bolsheviks Nikolai Bukharin and Georgy Piatakov. Now Lenin was challenged to argue the matter once more—this time with Luxemburg's disciple Karl Radek.

Radek opened the dispute with a two-part article in the *Berner Tagwacht* proclaiming the importance of economic over ethnic considerations in the fixing of national boundaries.[55] Radek held that if the map of Europe were to be redrawn to coincide with national aspirations, serious economic dislocations would result. He noted that the mixed population of Austria-Hungary had prospered far more than it could have if each of the component nationalities had been a separate state. Radek saw any attempt to return to historical boundaries merely for the sake of satisfying national aspirations as historical regression.

It cannot be to the interests of the proletariat to turn back the wheel of history and thus to limit the economy which has outgrown these national borders. It is to the interest of the proletariat that the productive power shall develop as fully as possible, that the whole world become one economic organization. But if this is to be accomplished . . . it must be made clear that the proletariat cannot set as its goal the resurrection of its fatherland intact [in its former boundaries] . . . as this can only be done at the expense of someone else's fatherland.[56]

Radek denied that the possibility of self-determination could exist in a capitalist society. He declared his complete opposition to new annexations and to any sort of nationalistic oppression, and contended that the way to end these evils was by hastening social revolution, not by encouraging the masses in fruitless struggles.[57]

Lenin could not allow Radek's views to go unchallenged. Reiterating his own stand on self-determination, he accused Radek of ignoring the coming national struggles in Asia and Africa.[58] This criticism was not, strictly speaking, pertinent, for Radek had specifically limited his argument to subjugated peoples living within capitalist societies. To be sure, he had failed to deal with the problems of the peoples of precapitalist lands, but this failure did not destroy the validity of his argument concerning capitalist society. More important was Lenin's accusation that Radek had failed to acknowledge that the primary goal of socialism was to overthrow capitalism, and that democratic goals like the self-determination of peoples were in consonance with the struggle to overthrow capitalism. Lenin remarked further that although Radek had repeatedly affirmed his opposition to annexations, by renouncing self-determination he had sanctioned existing annexations and the oppression practiced by various European powers.[59]

Radek was in no way deterred by Lenin's attack and continued to pursue the fight against self-determination. Quoting Rosa Luxemburg, he held that "the right of self-determination . . . is a petty-bourgeois formula that has nothing in common with Marxism."[60] After contending that self-determination was meaningless in capitalist society and contrary to Marxist laws of history, he continued: "We do not reject the slogan of self-determination merely because it is historically false. From a practical viewpoint, it can also mislead the proletariat. It encourages the proletariat to believe that it possesses the right of self-determination . . . and that it is the duty of Social Democrats to support every struggle for independence."[61]

Lenin, of course, did not accept Radek's arguments; he angrily scribbled in the margin of Radek's article "nicht richtig" (incorrect).[62] Soon afterward, Radek angered Lenin even further by publishing in full in the pages of *Vorbote* the theses against self-determination that had been adopted by the Warsaw Committee of the SDKPiL[63] Here Radek spelled out in great detail his reasons for repudiating self-determination.

We know that socialism will abolish all national oppression because it abolishes all class interests which drive toward this oppression. Nor have we any reason to assume that in a capitalist society a nation would acquire the character of an economic-political unit. In all probability it would possess only the character of a cultural and linguistic unit, since the territorial subdivision of the socialist cultural sphere, insofar as the latter might exist, can result only by virtue of the demands of production, and then, of course, instead of individual nations having to decide separately about subdivision on the basis of their own supremacy (as *"the right of self-determination"* demands) all citizens concerned would *participate in that decision.* The assigning of the formula of the *"right of self-determination"* to socialism is due to a complete misunderstanding of the character of a socialist community. [Radek's italics.]

In the same place Radek also assailed the tactical utility of the formula of self-determination in the struggle for world revolution. Self-determination, Radek asserted, was in essence a formula compatible only with revisionism, for it deluded the masses into thinking that capitalism was "capable of adjusting itself to the interests of weak peoples."[64]

The increasing bitterness of the debate brought the two men to swords' points. Radek wrote to his old friend Pannekoek of Lenin's obduracy, and Pannekoek replied by removing Lenin and Zinoviev from the editorial board of *Vorbote* and demoting them to the status of "contributors."[65] Lenin, who apparently had never understood the nature of the ties between Radek and Pannekoek, was unable to understand how Radek had outmaneuvered him.[66]

Since the editorial board had originally consisted of the Dutch patrons, Radek, Zinoviev, and Lenin, the net effect of the change was to make Radek the sole editor. He was not able to savor his triumph long, however, since Pannekoek apparently failed to forward enough funds to keep the journal going and Radek was completely devoid of funds himself.[67] *Vorbote* never appeared again after its second issue in the spring of 1916.

Lenin held Radek guilty of a personal betrayal. In February 1916 he sent Radek the curtest of notes, virtually breaking off all relations between them: "I personally consider that from the time of receipt of *Gazeta Robotnicza* (II. 1916), our common struggle in Russian and Polish affairs is *finished*" (Lenin's emphasis).[68]

For the rest of the year, Lenin engaged in no direct correspondence with Radek, yet he was constantly concerned about Radek's activities and fearful lest Radek further undermine his position in the Zimmerwald Left. In letters to Zinoviev and other Bolsheviks, Lenin alternately condemned Radek and asked for copies of his newspaper articles.[69]

There was one occasion on which the two men could not avoid direct contact: the April 1916 meeting of the Zimmerwald Movement, held at the Swiss village of Kienthal. Despite their differences, Lenin and Radek both considered themselves part of the Zimmerwald Left and both signed various statements issued by that faction.[70] Radek's position was somewhat stronger than it had been the previous year, for he no longer needed Lenin to supply him with credentials: Pannekoek had arranged for him to serve as proxy delegate for the Dutch Social Democrats, who had been unable to send a representative.[71]

Radek's feelings against Lenin were made plain at Kienthal when he interrupted a speech by Solomon Grumbach to object to the speaker's "praise" of Lenin; in fact, Grumbach had merely mentioned Lenin's acceptance of the right of self-determination.[72] For the most part, however, Radek restrained his antagonism and concentrated on radicalizing the conference, a tactic in which he received Lenin's cooperation. When in response to a mild rebuff from Grimm Radek led a brief walkout of the Polish delegates, Lenin and his comrades walked out too.[73] Everyone returned to the hall after a few minutes, but the demonstration of the outward solidarity of the Zimmerwald Left had been impressive.

The Kienthal meeting had a considerably more radical composition than its Zimmerwald predecessor, and the prospects of the Zimmerwald Left were accordingly stronger than they had been at the first conference. The Left tried to force the Conference to adopt a revolutionary stand, and Radek, on at least one occasion, and with Lenin's consent, acted as spokesman and addressed the group on the necessity for revolutionary tactics.[74] The Left still could not command a full majority, however, and the resolutions and manifestos of the Kienthal Conference evaded the issue of whether pacifism or revolution was the course for socialists to follow.[75] A stronger resolution offered by the Left secured the backing of only a third of the delegates—more than the previous meeting at Zimmerwald, but still not enough for effective action. Kienthal represented at best but one step forward for the Left.[76]

At Kienthal the common cause of the Zimmerwald Left brought Lenin and Radek closer together, but Lenin could not forgive the embarrassment Radek had caused him in the *Vorbote* episode. The appearance of a second issue of *Vorbote* with a continuation of Radek's views on self-determination revived Lenin's anger.[77] He refused to have anything more to do with Radek and continued to denounce him. He told Shliapnikov that Radek had attempted to use the Kienthal Conference to split the Zimmerwald Left, and he complained to Inessa Armand that she had been too restrained in her criticism of Radek.[78] As late as January 1917, Lenin referred in his correspondence to Radek as "the half-wit Radek."[79]

If Radek was disturbed by Lenin's hostility, he gave no immediate evidence of it.[80] The exchange of recriminations with Lenin had become unimportant in comparison to recent events in Germany. There the opposition in the SPD had finally burst the restraints imposed by party unity and formed a revolutionary socialist organization that repudiated the commitments made by the socialist members of the wartime government. Liebknecht, of course, had openly opposed party policy ever since the vote on war credits in December 1914. Throughout 1915 he had stepped up the tempo of his opposition, invoking his famous slogan "Der Hauptfeind steht in eigener Land!" (The chief enemy is at home!) Even less radical socialists like Bernstein and Kautsky were concerned over what appeared to be annexationist goals on the part of the German government. Yet Liebknecht and his friends spurned the "centrist" approach of the anti-annexation socialists and demanded open opposition to the SPD. When the Executive Committee of the SPD expelled Liebknecht from the Reichstag delegation in January 1916, the Left regarded this act as a direct challenge. Although they still considered themselves part of the SPD, at least in a broad sense, the Left began the organization of an opposition group known as the Spartacists, a name derived from the "Spartacus Letters" of Rosa Luxemburg and others.[81]

To Radek, the formation of the Spartacist group seemed the most important event in German socialism since the outbreak of the war. This was the rebirth he had called for two years earlier in the pages of the *Berner Tagwacht*.[82] He was still persona non grata with many members of the German Left, however, and any attempts he might have made to join the Spartacists would probably have been rebuffed by Luxemburg's circle. In view of this, he fell back once again on his connection in Bremen. The Bremen Social Democrats had remained one of the most radical activist groups in Germany,

and had even been represented at the Kienthal Conference.* They
had responded to the emergence of the Spartacists by launching a
new radical weekly, *Arbeiterpolitik,* and now they opened its pages
to their old comrade Karl Radek.

Radek welcomed *Arbeiterpolitik* as his new entrée to German
socialism. Recognizing that his name would still be an embarrassment to many in the Left, he agreed to have his articles published
anonymously.[83] He also adopted a more moderate approach, avoid-
ing the irresponsible name-calling that had marred so much of his
earlier writing for the *Bremer Bürgerzeitung.* Concealing his identity as author of the articles was in some ways to Radek's advantage: unsigned articles implied a consensus of editorial opinion.
In addition, anonymity allowed Radek to publish more articles in a
single issue than he might have if he had signed each one: indeed,
some issues of *Arbeiterpolitik* carry more writing by Radek than
by all the other contributors combined.

The overriding concern to which Radek addressed himself in
Arbeiterpolitik was the necessity for the Spartacists to drop the
SPD completely and form a separate socialist party. Under no circumstances, Radek argued, would the Executive Committee accept
the Left's viewpoint—not even if it were shown to be the viewpoint
of a majority of the membership. There were no grounds, therefore,
for common action with the SPD leadership, whom he dismissed as
"social imperialists." The Centrists, with their pacifist illusions,
were just as bad, he declared, though there was some hope for the
"Left Centrists." The most important thing was for the Left not to
be frightened by the impending split with the SPD, but to welcome
it as "not only historically necessary, but directly useful to the proletarian cause."[84]

Arbeiterpolitik now became the chief outlet through which
Radek attempted to influence the affairs of the German Left. In its
pages he criticized a pamphlet published in Zurich in 1916 entitled
"The Crisis of Social Democracy" and signed by "Junius." Unin-

* Paul Frölich, an old friend of Radek's, represented the Bremen group at
Kienthal.

tentionally, Radek had involved himself in a most awkward situation, for it turned out that Junius was none other than Rosa Luxemburg, who early in 1915 had formulated her own views on the wartime dilemma of socialism, and had finally succeeded in smuggling the manuscript out of her prison cell and sending it to Switzerland for publication.[85] If Radek had known the identity of Junius, he undoubtedly would have been more circumspect in his criticism.

In his article Radek conceded that Junius understood the class character of the origins of the war; his mistake, Radek said, was in calling for a revival of Jacobinism as an antidote.[86] Jacobinism was suitable to the French Revolution, but inappropriate for the crisis of 1916. Radek argued that what socialists needed was strong radical leadership, not illusory hopes of spontaneous mass radical action: "Junius has overlooked the fact that one doesn't build a worker movement on historical reminiscences, but only on the basis of hard facts."[87] Without realizing it, Radek had finally broken with Luxemburg on the important issue of revolutionary leadership and more or less come around to Lenin's concept of a vanguard.

As Radek's influence grew in Bremen, it waned in Berne. He now began to have difficulties with Grimm, who no longer seemed willing to give him free rein in the pages of the *Berner Tagwacht.*[88] Grimm's relations with Radek and the rest of the Zimmerwald Left had been deteriorating since Kienthal as Grimm began a gradual drift toward the center of the Swiss Social Democratic Party.[89] An article by Radek criticizing the center for acceptance of the right of "self-defense of country" only served to widen the gulf between him and Grimm.[90] Cut off from the *Berner Tagwacht,* Radek moved to the mountain town of Davos, where he continued to write weekly articles for *Arbeiterpolitik.* (With his renewed interest in German socialism, Radek may well have contemplated a return to Germany in 1916; if he had any such plans, however, the imprisonment of Liebknecht and Luxemburg no doubt served as a deterrent.)

Radek's articles in *Arbeiterpolitik* had begun to draw considerable attention, and he was undoubtedly annoyed that he could not publicly identify himself as their author. In the fall of 1916 he began to sign his articles with the newly invented pseudonym of Arnold Struthahn. In this way, all his articles could be identified as coming from the pen of one man.[91]

An unforeseen effect of Radek's articles in *Arbeiterpolitik* was to help repair his relations with Lenin. After Kienthal, Radek had played down the issue of self-determination and had concentrated most of his energies on the problem of revolutionary action in Germany. Lenin had always been intrigued by Radek's potential as a contact with the German Left, and was impressed now by his apparent influence on the Bremen Left-Radicals. Inessa Armand was surprised by Lenin's sudden change of attitude. In a letter to her dated January 19, 1917, Lenin had written derisively of Radek's views on Poland.[92] Such derogatory references to Radek had been common in Lenin's letters for almost a year and Armand probably paid this one little heed. She was amazed, however, when less than a week later Lenin informed her that he had asked Radek to write a pamphlet against Grimm and his support of the Swiss Center.[93]

On January 30, 1917, Lenin gave her the news that "he [Radek] is still here and—surprise?—we are the *closest* friends."[94] Somehow Radek's new connection with the German Left and Lenin's desire for allies against Grimm (whom he had never trusted) had blotted out a year of mutual recriminations. Early in February, Lenin sent Radek a warm letter in which he proposed that they join forces against Grimm and persuade Grimm's own party to repudiate the "defense of country" approach.[95] At Lenin's request, Radek joined him at a special conference on Swiss affairs and challenged Grimm's right to call himself a socialist.[96]

At the beginning of March, Radek went to Basel to confer with Paul Levi, one of the few associates of Rosa Luxemburg who was not antagonistic toward him. At dinner one evening, their waiter brought them news of the uncontrolled riots in the streets of Petrograd and the abdication of Tsar Nicholas II. Radek returned to his room not knowing what to believe—extraordinary rumors were rife in Basel at that time. There he found a message that Lenin had called in his absence and wanted to see him at once. With revolution a reality in Russia, cooperation with Lenin was more important to Radek than ever before. He took the first train to Zurich, and Lenin met him at the railway station.[97] The old bitterness between the two men was forgotten now—a revolution was at stake.

4. The Years of Revolution: Russia

The overthrow of the Tsarist regime in Russia in March 1917 was greeted with joy by socialists all over Europe; no Social Democrat, regardless of national or ideological allegiance, could feel any sympathy for Tsar Nicholas or for the regime he represented. To the members of the Zimmerwald Left, however, the March Revolution meant much more than the end of the House of Romanov; it meant that the center of world revolution had suddenly shifted. Their most immediate objective, then, was to get to Petrograd, where they could directly affect the course of the Russian Revolution.

One had to be a very pallid revolutionary indeed not to want to go to Russia in 1917. Unfortunately for Radek and the other émigrés in Berne, Switzerland was surrounded on all sides by belligerents, none of whom initially seemed disposed to allow them passage. It was logically assumed that under no circumstances would England or France extend transit rights to homeward-bound Russian émigrés.[1] A disintegration of the Russian front would have been disastrous to the French: although it was not public knowledge, large segments of the French army were on the brink of mutiny. Nothing could have persuaded the French to allow a Russian antiwar group free passage across their country at this time.

The likelihood that the French would refuse to grant them transit rights was gloomily accepted by most of the exiles as a permanent barrier to their reaching Russia. Lenin especially was frustrated by his inability to return: for the first time, Russia had become ripe for the kind of program he espoused, yet he was unable to take action. When word came from Petrograd that the Mensheviks had assumed control of the most important socialist group in Russia, the Petrograd Soviet, Lenin exploded with rage and gave vent to one of his rare outbursts of obscenity.[2]

Radek was less pessimistic and far more imaginative than the Bolsheviks. Why should the request for transit rights be restricted to England and France? Certainly the Bolsheviks were not bound by the terms of the Franco-Russian Alliance! His first step was to persuade the Swiss correspondent of the *Frankfurter Zeitung* to sound out the German authorities on the idea of allowing the exiles transit rights across Germany.[3] The Germans were receptive to the idea, and negotiations were soon begun, although not by Radek himself, since his reputation was still tarnished. Radek's former editor Robert Grimm handled the negotiations at first, but Bolshevik indiscretion so compromised him* that he found it necessary to allow Fritz Platten, another Swiss socialist, to represent the exiles.[4]

The tentative agreement that resulted from the negotiations granted transit rights to "Russian political émigrés." Lenin hastened to point out to Platten that the Austrian-born Radek would be excluded by this wording. Platten had no objections to including Radek in the group, but he was unwilling to jeopardize the entire effort for the sake of one man, particularly one who had such an unsavory reputation in Germany. Lenin insisted, however, and Platten finally agreed to change the provision to read simply "political émigrés."[5] Radek himself doubted that he would be allowed to pass unmolested through Germany, regardless of the wording of the agreement; his wife had been arrested as soon as she had entered Germany, simply because of her connection with him.[6] As a precautionary measure, therefore, he borrowed the passport of a lesser-known comrade, Peter Voikov,[7] but refrained from signing the final agreement at all, either with his own name or with Voikov's.[8] By April, the plans had been completed and Lenin's party

---

* Lenin and Zinoviev had issued a circular in which they mentioned by name a Swiss official being contacted by Grimm.

set out in a sealed train across Germany. The tedium of the trip was periodically relieved by Radek's antics, such as heckling German soldiers through the train windows. In more serious moments, Radek observed that the Germany through which he was now passing bore little resemblance to the country he had known a few years earlier. There was a marked absence of young men, and the three years of war had seemingly lowered a pall on the country.[9] The gloomy atmosphere of the trip was a sobering education in the consequences of war.

After an uneventful passage through Denmark, the group arrived in Sweden on April 12, 1917, and was met by Jakob Hanecki (Fürstenburg), who during the past two years had been the Bolsheviks' key agent in Scandinavia, operating under the cover of a medical and contraceptive supply house.[10] Lenin arranged passage to Petrograd and prepared to leave Stockholm at once. To his disappointment, Radek soon found that he would not be able to accompany Lenin to Petrograd; as an Austrian citizen, he could not demand the right of entry from the Russian government. It was some consolation, however, for him to discover that he could serve the revolutionary cause outside Russia. Soon he was involved in an intrigue with one of the most fascinating and mysterious men on the European political scene, Alexander Helphand.

Helphand, a Russian Jew, had been active in the Russian Revolution of 1905, and under the pseudonym of Parvus had collaborated with Trotsky in formulating the theory of "permanent revolution." Later he moved to Germany, where he joined the SPD and, paradoxically enough, made a fortune speculating in munitions stocks. During the war he supported the patriotic segment of the SPD, but unknown to the party he also served as a sort of special agent for the German Foreign Office. It is doubtful that Radek had met Helphand before this time, but he had long been intrigued by the man's audacity, his success with women, and his wealth. (In the cafés of Berne during the war Radek had often told "Helphand stories," most of which were probably fabrications.)[11]

On April 13, 1917, Radek spent the entire day with Helphand. There is, unfortunately, no record of what was discussed by the two men, but Helphand's biographers have suggested, with good cause, that he promised the Bolsheviks massive financial assistance from Germany.[12] At all events, Helphand reported the details of the meeting directly to the State Secretary in Berlin a few days later.[13]

Lenin knew of the meeting between Helphand and Radek. He himself had declined to meet with Helphand in Stockholm, fearing that any direct contact might compromise the Bolsheviks' position; he risked nothing by allowing Radek to meet Helphand, however, and he was apparently quite pleased to have the contact established.[14] Perceiving that Radek could be of greater use to the Bolshevik cause in Stockholm than in Petrograd, he directed him to stay in Sweden and work with Hanecki until it was possible for both men to enter Russia.

Hanecki and Radek had been associates for some years in the SDKPiL, but had never been particularly close. Radek had chosen to work with the SDKPiL in Germany, whereas Hanecki had performed most of his prewar activities in Russian Poland. The two men had been out of touch with each other for some time, and Radek had no idea of the magnitude of Hanecki's operation in Scandinavia. Once in Stockholm, however, he could not help but observe that a great deal of money passed through Hanecki's hands. Hanecki had been the chairman of a large export firm in Copenhagen until his deportation in January 1917 for shady business dealings.[15] He and Radek, the Bolshevik with business talent and the clever journalist, made an unusual team. Radek quickly derived one tangible benefit from his association with the affluent Hanecki; he and his wife, who had made her own way to Stockholm, joined the Haneckis in new quarters in a fashionable section of Stockholm.[16] A third Bolshevik, V. V. Vorovsky (Orlowski), completed the group, which soon began to call itself "The Overseas Bureau of the Bolshevik Central Committee." The activities of the Bureau during its short existence seem to have been almost entirely the work of Radek and Hanecki; Vorovsky appears to have been assigned relatively minor tasks, and his name was occasionally omitted from the official dispatches sent out by the Bureau.[17]

Little is known of Hanecki's other activities in Stockholm during his work with the Bureau, but he seems to have renewed his financial dealings in order to meet Lenin's repeated demands for funds to be sent to Petrograd.[18] The most immediate service Radek could render the Bolsheviks in Stockholm was to create a press to disseminate the Bolshevik viewpoint to potential sympathizers among Western socialists. No attempt was made to publish a Swedish-language newspaper: German was still the language of socialism.

At first, Radek contented himself with an unimpressive mimeographed publication called *Russische Korrespondenz "Prawda,"* which largely confined itself to publishing translations of the Bolshevik press in Petrograd and Moscow and occasional statements of the Stockholm group. The publication was also utilized by the Stockholm group to deny the complicity of the Bolsheviks in the intrigues of the German Foreign Office.[19]

Radek did not have much opportunity to use his journalistic abilities in *Russische Korrespondenz "Prawda."* Only the most essential articles were printed, and news from Russia preempted most of the space. Prior to moving to Stockholm, Radek had been doing most of his serious writing for *Arbeiterpolitik*; he had conscientiously preserved his contacts with Bremen despite the difficulties occasioned by his move from Switzerland to Sweden. The events in German socialism had been encouraging enough to keep him hoping that Russia was not the only country with a potential for socialist revolution.

In February 1917, while he was still in Switzerland, he had observed with considerable satisfaction that the SPD had finally split —a step he had been urging all along.[20] Then the news from Russia had temporarily overshadowed the situation in Germany. By the time Radek had organized his activities in Stockholm, the nature of the German split had become clearer and a new party, the Independent Socialist Party of Germany (USPD), had emerged. As it was constituted in 1917, however, the new party was not the sort of Left revolutionary group Radek had hoped for. It included both the Spartacists and various "centrist" groups that had challenged the old party on the issue of support of the German government's war policy. With such leaders as Bernstein and Kautsky in the USPD, it was unlikely that the party would adopt an openly revolutionary platform.[21] Radek felt that the German Left would have to draw its lines much more sharply to achieve the kind of revolutionary élan needed. He therefore turned his fire as much against the centrists in the new party as against the pro-government leaders of the SPD, reminding his readers of Kautsky's prewar views on the nature of imperialism.[22] As much as he wanted a new party in Germany, Radek was not ready to tolerate non-revolutionaries as party members. When Johannes Knief slipped into Sweden for a secret meeting with Radek, Radek persuaded him to have *Arbeiterpolitik* withhold full support for the USPD and call instead for a rallying of radicals at the local level as a prelude to forming a new party uncompromised by centrists.[23]

More and more, Radek was forced to turn his attention from German affairs to the events in Russia. He did send *Arbeiterpolitik* a five-part article in which he attempted to identify the cause of the Bolsheviks with that of radical socialists everywhere. He stressed what he considered most significant about the events in Russia, that is, the stimulus they provided to the revolutionary movement in the West. Radek had never set foot in Russia proper, and did not share in the excitement of the nationalistic aspects of the revolution that so inspired some of his comrades. The details of the overthrow of the monarchy and its replacement by a Provisional Government interested him very little; to him, the importance of the events in Russia lay in their value as a contribution to the overthrow of world capitalism.[24] It is interesting that although Radek did not directly involve himself in the Bolshevik subversion of the Provisional Government, he was able to convince Lenin of his devotion and usefulness to the Bolshevik cause.

Above all else, Radek was a skilled political agitator, and his talents proved useful at this time. Together with Hanecki, Radek attempted to create a Swedish Left Social Democratic Party. In May 1917 he appeared before the founding congress of this group and pleaded for support of the Bolshevik revolution in Russia.[25] There was a limit, however, to the amount of influence Radek could

wield in Swedish socialism, determined as he was, and even the
donning of full evening dress for the occasion did not help him convince the congress of the importance of his cause.[26] The Swedish
socialists who attended this congress were more concerned with the
threat of Sweden's entry into World War I than with the revolutionary struggle in Russia. Lenin's correspondence at this time indicates that he had a strong interest in the development of the
Swedish Left. Because Radek spoke no Swedish, Lenin relied more
and more on Alexandra Kollontai, who did speak the language, to
rally Swedish support, and assigned Radek tasks for which he was
better suited.[27]

Radek's chief usefulness to Lenin was as the Stockholm representative of the Zimmerwald Left. Since its first meeting in 1915,
the Zimmerwald Movement had steadily become more radical, and
the forces that had sought to exclude Radek in 1915 were no longer
so powerful. The executive body of the Zimmerwald Movement,
the International Socialist Committee, now contained many who
were sympathetic to the Bolsheviks, including its secretary, Angelica Balabanoff.[28] In 1917 the committee decided, in spite of the
many difficulties involved, to move its headquarters from Switzerland to Sweden, the neutral country closest to Petrograd—an indication of the committee's interest in the Russian Revolution.

Balabanoff, a Russian citizen, returned from a short trip to Petrograd convinced that the Bolsheviks were the party worthy of
support.[29] The price Balabanoff had to pay for a tie with the Bolsheviks was acceptance of Lenin's chief deputy in Stockholm, Karl
Radek, as the voice of Bolshevism in Sweden. The prospect of having to work with Radek was far from pleasing to her, but the association was unavoidable: "Even though we despised Radek personally and considered him a vulgar politician, we knew that the Russian Revolution was at stake, and at this moment that revolution
offered the only spark of light on a black horizon."[30] Giving the success of the Revolution first priority, the Zimmerwald Movement
tacitly agreed to forget their old antagonism toward Radek and to
accept him as the fully empowered delegate of the Bolsheviks. Thus
the movement that in 1915 had gone to great lengths to conceal

Radek's presence at its initial congress now accepted him as one of its most influential members.

Radek's first duty as a member of the International Socialist Committee was to sit in judgment on his old friend and patron Robert Grimm. Grimm, who had secretly entered Russia, had been charged with being a German agent. This charge reflected discredit on the entire Zimmerwald Movement and therefore could hardly be ignored by the International Socialist Committee. The special investigating committee, of which Radek was a member, cleared Grimm of the charge of spying but asked for his removal from the International Socialist Committee.[31] Radek does not appear to have felt obligated to help Grimm at this juncture; moreover, he was quick to fill Grimm's empty place as second in command of the Committee.

By the summer of 1917, Stockholm had become a center of socialist activity. Some of the erstwhile leaders of the Second International, particularly those from neutral countries, gave their support to a Stockholm meeting of all socialists seeking to end the war. The conference never got beyond the planning stage, since the belligerent countries would not allow their socialist delegates to attend, but the mere possibility of such a conference was enough to galvanize the Zimmerwald Left into action of its own.

Lenin had written off the Zimmerwald Movement as a whole after his return to Russia in 1917. In one of his first meetings with his fellow Bolsheviks, he had demanded a complete break with the Zimmerwald Movement, which he considered too closely tied to "pacifists and Kautskyites."[32] The Bolsheviks in Petrograd had rejected Lenin's demands and adopted the more cautious approach of remaining within the Zimmerwald Movement and seeking to enhance the position of the Bolshevik-dominated Zimmerwald Left.[33] But Radek, the Bolshevik representative in Stockholm, who had few ties with the Bolshevik Party itself, had developed strong personal ties with Lenin, and he concurred now in Lenin's approach to the Zimmerwald Movement.[34] Both men felt that the prime goal of the Zimmerwald Left should be to detach itself from the movement and form the nucleus of a new international organization openly committed to world revolution. On May 29, 1917, Lenin wrote to Radek: "I am fully in agreement with you that Zimmerwald has become a decisive obstacle—that it is necessary to break with it (you know that I disagreed with the conference on this point). It is necessary to accelerate a conference of Left internationalists, but *only* Lefts. Write and tell me what you can do about this."[35] Thus Lenin gave Radek a virtual mandate to sabotage the movement (a mandate of which Balabanoff seems to have been unaware), and Radek was quick to carry out Lenin's will.

During the summer of 1917, Radek's activities in the International Socialist Committee consisted largely of being difficult. When on the initiative of the Petrograd Soviet, still under Menshevik domination, a call was issued for a general meeting in Stockholm of all antiwar socialists, Radek threatened a Bolshevik withdrawal from the Zimmerwald Movement if it agreed to participate in the conference. Balabanoff, who shared Radek's misgivings about the conference, nevertheless thought that the issue of participation should be settled by the full Zimmerwald Movement, not just the International Socialist Committee. She accordingly dispatched invitations for a Third Conference of the Zimmerwald Movement, which was to meet in Stockholm on August 1st (the date was destined to be pushed back several times). Radek, who would have preferred that the International Socialist Committee simply renounce the Menshevik-inspired conference altogether, had to content himself with having managed to avert an outright commitment to the conference.

While Balabanoff busied herself in making arrangements for the meeting of the Zimmerwald Movement, Radek engaged in some interesting activities of his own. At the beginning of August, he and his wife entertained the Gustav Mayers in their home.[36] Mayer was a German socialist who had remained in the SPD and shunned opposition movements. He had met Radek many times throughout the years, and was awestruck by what he considered Radek's extraordinary perception of world affairs.[37] Since Mayer was openly loyal to both the SPD and Germany, Radek's reason for receiving him—and he did so more than once—must have been tactical; he probably knew that Mayer would report their conversations to both the SPD and the German Foreign Office.[38] Consequently Radek deliberately let drop the remark that he would not be needing his Stockholm apartment for the winter of 1917–1918—information that Mayer interpreted to his superiors as an indication that a Bolshevik coup was imminent. More important, Radek assured Mayer that the Bolsheviks had no special animosity toward Germany—at least no more than toward any other capitalist power.[39] All in all, Radek seemed to be trying to give Mayer the impression that it was not in Germany's interest to stand in the way of a Bolshevik seizure of power. Presumably Mayer reported this to the German Foreign Office. It should be emphasized here that there is no evidence that Radek was specifically authorized, either by Lenin or by the Bolshevik Party, to convey this attitude to the German Foreign Office.

During August Radek left suddenly for Copenhagen. His purposes were not explained, either by him or by the German legation, which dutifully reported his presence to Berlin.[40] There is some reason to believe that he had gone to take care of financial business left unfinished by Hanecki, who had just been refused permission to reenter Denmark.[41] Meanwhile Balabanoff had finished arrangements for the long-deferred Third Zimmerwald Conference, which finally convened in Stockholm on September 5. Radek attended as a representative of the Regional Presidium of the SDKPiL, but in fact he acted as a Bolshevik delegate, casting his votes in accordance with Lenin's views. The Stockholm meeting was far and away the most radical of all the Zimmerwald Conferences, and during the week of sessions the radical outlook prevailed. In its general manifesto, the Conference came out against the war and advocated mass strikes in support of the Russian Revolution.[42] The call to revolutionary action was hailed by the Zimmerwald Left, but some delegates complained that the manifesto was so radical that it would lead to governmental suppression of socialists, particularly in Germany. Radek applauded such confrontations between socialists and their governments and demanded that the manifesto be published immediately, lest it lose its impact.[43] Balabanoff also agreed that the manifesto should be published, but as secretary of the International Socialist Committee she felt obliged to obey the mandate of the Conference and keep the manifesto secret until the delegates could consult with their respective parties.[44] For the moment, Radek failed to prevail.

Immediately following the Third Zimmerwald Conference, Radek busied himself with launching a new journal, *Bote der Russischen Revolution.* This journal, unlike *Russische Korrespondenz "Prawda,"* had an attractive format. Although it was printed in German, it purported to be the theoretical and analytical journal of the Swedish Left, and listed a Swedish socialist, Otto Grimlund, as associate editor. In fact, most of the articles were by Radek and Hanecki, and the remainder were imports from Russia, including pieces by Trotsky, Lenin, and Zinoviev. The new journal unashamedly championed the cause of the Russian Bolsheviks and seemed to be preparing Western socialism for the overthrow of the Russian Provisional Government. In his articles, Radek openly stated that the logical conclusion of the Russian Revolution was the establishment of a proletarian regime and, more important, the launching of the international proletarian revolution. Only a seizure of power by the Bolsheviks, he insisted, could bring this about.[45] In effect, Radek was able to say publicly in *Bote der Russischen Revolution* what he had been saying privately for some time.

Surprisingly, Radek did not use the pages of *Bote der Russischen Revolution* to publish the manifesto of the Third Zimmerwald Conference, although he had strong feelings that it should be published. It was not that Radek felt bound, as Balabanoff did, by loyalty to the Zimmerwald Movement, but rather that he hesitated to endanger his Bureau and cause trouble for Lenin by publishing the manifesto prematurely or without official sanction in a Bolshevik publication; although publication of the manifesto presented a superb opportunity to sabotage the Zimmerwald Conference, he restrained himself. Finally, when Balabanoff refused to be moved by Radek's argument that publication was vital to the success of the Russian Revolution, Radek "leaked" a copy of the manifesto to the local newspaper.[46] This breach of security could have caused a major party scandal, but fortunately for Radek, his action was eclipsed on November 7 by the news that the Bolsheviks had seized power in Petrograd and proclaimed a government of soviets for all of Russia.

Radek had known that the Bolsheviks intended to seize power soon, but apparently he had not been told the exact date. He shared the surprise and excitement of the Left Bloc in Stockholm when they received the news, and acted as their contact with Petrograd throughout that fateful day.[47] He asked the International Socialist Committee to issue a statement of support for the Bolshevik take-over, but the most they would do was to send a telegram of congratulations to the Petrograd Soviet.[48]

With the Bolsheviks in power, Radek's work in Stockholm ended. He had not succeeded in destroying the Zimmerwald Movement, but he had hampered it enough so that it could not offer serious competition to Lenin's plans. It was obvious now that the place for Radek was in revolutionary Petrograd. In a final article for *Bote der Russischen Revolution,* he offered his Western audience a strong argument that the Bolshevik seizure of power was a necessary prerequisite for peace and a warning that the proletarian awakening had just begun.[49]

Just as Radek was preparing to leave for Petrograd, Alexander Helphand arrived in Stockholm with the request that Radek intercede with Lenin for him and get permission for Helphand to return to Russia.[50] Radek agreed, and when he left with Hanecki for Petrograd on November 18, he sent advance word to Lenin that he must see him at once, presumably to discuss the Helphand matter. The trip to Petrograd proved more eventful than Radek had anticipated; at Tornio, on the Russo-Finnish border, Radek and Hanecki had some difficulty persuading the guards to let them into Russia.[51] As soon as he reached Petrograd, Radek brought Helphand's request to Lenin's attention. Apparently Radek was convinced that Helphand's original revolutionary fervor had been rekindled by the Bolsheviks' success, and that he was ready to place part of his enormous financial resources at their disposal.[52]

Lenin had reason to be cautious in the matter of Helphand's return: in July, the Bolsheviks had been accused by the Provisional

Government of being German agents, and Helphand had been named as Lenin's financial backer. Although the Bolsheviks had survived the charges, they had been severely embarrassed by them. Even after the Bolshevik seizure of power, Lenin was forced to justify Hanecki's business connections with Helphand to the party.[53] Consequently Radek was sent back to Stockholm to tell Helphand in person that his appearance in Russia now would compromise the Bolsheviks and resurrect the charges that they were German agents. Lenin put it bluntly: "It is forbidden to contaminate the Revolution with dirty hands!"[54] Radek delivered the message—probably with regret, for he had always admired Helphand—then quickly returned to Russia. Helphand was extremely bitter over the rebuff and always blamed Radek; for years he asserted that it was Radek, the "political harlequin," who had sabotaged his association with the new revolutionary regime in Russia.[55]

Whatever regrets Radek had over the Helphand affair, they were quickly submerged by his involvement in the Bolshevik Revolution. For Radek, the Revolution meant nothing less than a complete metamorphosis of his career. Hitherto he had been an outcast revolutionary, expelled from two of the parties of the Second International, and scorned even by fellow radicals as irresponsible. Now, for the first time in history, there existed a regime openly committed to the goal of world revolution—and this regime needed his talents.

There appears to have been some confusion over what post to give Radek in the new regime. He would never do as a diplomat or government official, but he was far too talented to be wasted as a mere polemicist. A post was created for him—Assistant People's Commissar of Foreign Affairs. In this role he headed the international propaganda bureau of the Foreign Affairs Department. He wrote, edited, and distributed appeals to the European working class to emulate the example of the Russians and join in the international revolution.[56] Because of his facility with languages, his quick wit, and his droll appearance, he soon became a favorite contact for foreigners living in Petrograd and Moscow. He invariably impressed them with his grasp of world affairs and his clever use of journalism as an ideological weapon: one British observer even paid him the compliment of calling him "the Russian Lord Beaverbrook."[57]

Despite his varied career, Radek was still a political newcomer in 1917. His views were by no means set, and he was still highly impressionable. In the past, his actions had often been determined by those who had served as his political mentors—Haecker, Dzierżyński, Warszawski, Luxemburg, and Lenin. Now he found himself in close daily contact with a new giant, Leon Trotsky, head of the Soviet Foreign Office.

Radek had known Trotsky for some time, but though both men had been active in the Zimmerwald Movement, they had never established close communication. Trotsky records a curious impression of the Radek he knew in Switzerland:

In those days, I came for the first time into close contact with Radek, who had come to Switzerland from Germany at the beginning of the war. In the German party he belonged to the extreme Left, and I hoped to find in him one who shared my views. Indeed, Radek condemned the ruling section of the German Social Democracy in fiercely militant tones. In this I was with him. But I was surprised to learn from our conversations that he never conceded the possibility of a proletarian revolution in connection with the war, and generally speaking, in the near future. "No," he replied, "for this the productive forces of mankind, taken as a whole, are not sufficiently developed." I was quite used to hearing that the productive forces of Russia were not sufficient for the conquest of power by the working class. But I did not imagine that such an answer could come from a revolutionary politician of a progressive capitalist country.[58]

In his autobiography Radek defended his remarks to Trotsky; at that time, Radek insisted, he had believed that Germany had a long way to go before a war between the classes could become a reality.[59] Radek pointed out that these talks took place before the third vote on war credits, and that it was after the vote that he abandoned all hopes for German Social Democracy. Certainly Radek's published writings and actions in 1915 and 1916 point to a deep commitment to revolutionary policies. Could Trotsky have been ignorant of Parabellum's real identity? It seems unlikely. Moreover, Trotsky had attended meetings of the Zimmerwald Left (although he never joined it), including the meeting at which Radek introduced the radical resolution of the Zimmerwald Left.[60] Apparently Trotsky had made his evaluation of Radek at that first meeting and was loath to change his initial impression. As a result, the two men had little communication with each other until after the Bolshevik Revolution.

Working under Trotsky's nominal direction, Radek had a chance to impress him with his revolutionary zeal and his commitment to the international significance of the Revolution. In this commitment, Radek differed from many Bolsheviks who saw the Revolution in purely Russian terms. Late in December 1917, Trotsky decided to take part in the peace negotiations with the Germans, and brought Radek with him to the parleys at Brest-Litovsk. Trotsky wanted Radek along because of his familiarity with Central Europe; moreover, Trotsky felt that "the intransigence and élan of this energetic, passionate man [Radek] would act as a tonic for the Ioffes, Kamenevs, and other softer Russian delegates."[61] Indeed, Radek did inject a radical note into the Brest-Litovsk proceedings, much to the delight of the Bolsheviks and the chagrin of the German delegation. He evinced little interest in the diplomatic proceedings, and his actual participation in the negotiations was limited to reading a declaration accusing the Germans of violating the right of the Polish people to self-determination—a rather strange task for him, considering his earlier views on the subject.[62]

Radek's chief task at Brest-Litovsk was to propagandize among the German troops, and he did so in a brazen manner that shocked and alarmed the Germans. He prepared a special German language newspaper, *Die Fackel*, which exhorted the German troops to mutiny and revolution, and in characteristically bold fashion, he distributed it to the German troops around Brest-Litovsk under the very eyes of their officers.[63] The Germans protested this open breach of diplomatic procedure, and demanded that Radek be excluded from the conferences. General Hoffman in particular voiced serious objections to the presence at the negotiations of "this Austrian deserter."[64]

In the final analysis, Radek played an unimportant role at Brest-Litovsk; but he closely observed the proceedings and was genuinely shocked by the draconian terms laid down by the Germans. When Trotsky walked out of the conference, enunciating his famous "No war, no peace" formula, Radek gave his wholehearted approval. The Russian delegation returned to Petrograd, and the Germans submitted new and still harsher terms, which Radek insisted be rejected. At first Radek hoped that Trotsky's firm opposition would rally the Bolsheviks to a rejection of the proffered treaty; but in the end, Trotsky gave in to Lenin's insistence that the Bolsheviks accept the German terms, and Radek was forced to act on his own. Together with Nikolai Bukharin and several other prominent and outspoken Bolsheviks, he organized an opposition group of those who refused to accept the Treaty of Brest-Litovsk. He hoped to persuade Trotsky to become the leader of this new opposition, but he was unable to do so.[65]

When the opposition, known as the Left Communists, finally emerged into the open, it included some of the most brilliant Bolshevik theorists and writers, but lacked a strong leader. Radek, Bukharin, and the other Left Communists could write stirring polemics, but they could not lead a radical organization; it took a Lenin or a Trotsky to lead and organize a revolutionary party. In the final analysis, the lack of such a leader precluded the success of the Left Communists in an effort that had slender prospects at best.[66]

Radek considered acceptance of the Treaty of Brest-Litovsk tantamount to a betrayal of the world revolution. He had affirmed repeatedly that the Russian Revolution was not an isolated phenomenon; it was only the first in a series of events that would culminate in world revolution. If the Bolsheviks appeased German imperialism now for the insufficient reason of consolidating their own position in Russia, they were denying their responsibilities as international revolutionaries. Moreover, if the German proletariat was indeed on the verge of revolution, there was all the more reason to oppose the signing of the peace terms.[67]

But what were the realities of the Russian situation in 1918?

Soviet Russia had no army to put into the field against Germany. The overthrow of the Provisional Government had been largely achieved by the promise of peace, but the price had been the destruction of the discipline and morale of the Russian Army. Given the breakdown of the Russian Army and the general antipathy of the Russian people to the idea of a new war, how did Radek propose to circumvent the Treaty of Brest-Litovsk?

At no time in his life did Radek make a more unrealistic estimate of the prospects for world revolution than he did in the spring of 1918. He grossly overestimated the revolutionary propensities of both the Russian worker and the German soldier. Although he admitted that Russian troops of peasant stock (and peasants made up the vast majority of the Russian Army) could probably not be aroused to fight for world revolution, he argued that the Russian worker—the true revolutionary—understood the need for world revolution and was willing to fight for it if necessary.[68] This contempt for the revolutionary prowess of the peasant was a new element in Radek's writings. Like most Marxists of the time, Radek had heretofore assigned the peasant no particular role in the revolution; instead, he had simply ignored him. Now the peasant was brought forward and blamed for the lack of revolutionary fervor in the Russian Army. Radek demanded that the regime openly differentiate between workers and peasants as potential revolutionaries. He accused Lenin of catering to the wishes of the peasants, a nonrevolutionary class, at the expense of the revolutionary working class: "We now stand before a capitulation, and the reason for this is that the proletarian party, which has been placed in power, has not given primacy to the constant interests of the working class, and consequently the revolution has capitulated to the needs and pressures of the weary peasant masses."[69]

In grandiose phrases, Radek spoke of building a new proletarian army—a "Red Army composed of those classes in favor of Soviet power and of an international proletarian revolution."[70] He carefully differentiated between the old Tsarist army of apathetic peasants and the prospective new revolutionary army of class-conscious workers. The latter, he maintained, would understand the need for world revolution, the need for enabling the German proletariat and others to do for themselves what the Russian workers had already accomplished:

It is necessary to create a revolutionary army; it is necessary to instruct the masses in the ways of war; it is necessary to create a living force that will not allow German imperialism to achieve its goals, . . . the annihilation of all Soviet power, the annihilation of all of the goals of the revolution.

"Peace has been signed; long live the revolutionary struggle!"—here is our basic slogan. Having victoriously concluded the civil war with the Russian bourgeoisie, the next stage is a civil war with German imperialism. In this war . . . we can count on the help of the German workers.[71]

Although there was considerable feeling in the Bolshevik Party against acceptance of the German peace terms, the cause of revolutionary war had already been weakened by the fact that the Left Communists had supported it all along. The Seventh Bolshevik Party Congress repudiated the Left Communists and their plea for revolutionary war and accepted Lenin's justification of the Treaty of Brest-Litovsk.[72]

Rebuked by the congress, Radek retreated from his extreme position of advocating revolutionary war. He reluctantly accepted the Treaty of Brest-Litovsk as a fait accompli, but continued to remind the party that world revolution was absolutely necessary if the Russian Revolution were to survive. He admonished the regime to concentrate on building an army revolutionary in its class composition and spirit.[73]

Radek had indeed suffered a setback in the Left Communist episode, but he was far too clever to ruin his career by loyalty to a lost cause. He now sought to reconcile his differences with Lenin, and in May 1918 executed a complete about-face, justifying acceptance of the Treaty of Brest-Litovsk as a necessary tactic in the struggle for world revolution. In a speech to the representatives at the National Congress of Economic Councils, Radek wholeheartedly supported Lenin's contention that Russian losses through the Treaty would be ephemeral, but the "breathing space" gained by the Soviet regime would be invaluable.[74]

Radek's support of Left Communism was an aberration in his political career. Usually he had a keen perception of the political climate and advocated only such action as was prudent; in fact, he was not above abandoning his position and his colleagues if the situation seemed to demand it. Fortunately, in 1918 it was still possible to dissent within the Bolshevik Party and not suffer irreparable consequences. When Radek renounced Left Communism, Lenin gladly ushered him back into the good graces of the Bolshevik leadership. Radek's new role was that of spokesman on the problems of revolution, especially world revolution.

Never much of an original political theorist, Radek easily adopted the beliefs of others—Luxemburg, Trotsky, Lenin—and cast himself in the role of "defender of the faith." It was his job to ridicule opposing theories and to justify what he currently accepted as the true dogma. Radek's great talent lay in his pen—no Bolshevik was his peer as a journalist—and he was also a clever and audacious tactician. The year 1918, however, was the year of the theoretician, and Radek found it impossible to resist the temptation to offer his own rationalization of the events of 1917. Most Bolsheviks were obsessed with the need to explain why the first Marxist revolution had taken place in Russia—an underdeveloped country that failed to meet the Marxist criteria for a mature capitalist society ripe for proletarian revolution. Perhaps Radek thought an excursion into the labyrinth of Marxist theory might help erase the stigma of his Left Communist episode. At all events, he set about constructing his own theory of the Russian Revolution.

Radek considered the major lesson of the Russian Revolution to be the demonstration of just how small an amount of capitalist development was necessary to precipitate a proletarian revolution. The triumph of the Bolsheviks had demonstrated the falsity of the Social Democratic contention that proletarian revolution had to be deferred until the majority were ready for revolution.[75] This contention, he maintained, was a manifestation of bourgeois democratic theory that effectively endangered the cause of proletarian revolution. Successful proletarian revolution depended upon an active minority, not a convinced majority. This minority could, under the proper conditions, initiate a revolution that would eventually receive the support of the majority of the working class:

Nowhere, in any country, does the revolution begin as an action of the majority of the population. Capitalism never signifies merely the physical control of the means of production, but means the spiritual control of the masses as well—even in the most developed of capitalist lands. Under the pressure of want and misery, under the influence of such blows from the capitalist regime as war, humiliation, and enslavement, [the masses] suddenly shake off their yoke. However, at the very beginning it is only an active minority which rises up and achieves a revolution, the success of which can be determined by the standard of whether or not this revolution is in consonance with the laws of historical development. . . . It might be said that each and every revolution is begun by a minority; the majority joins in only during the process of its development and then completes its triumph.[76]

In insisting that the revolution be "in consonance with the laws of historical development," Radek raised the ticklish question of when a country (Russia or any other country) could be considered ready for a proletarian revolution. Did a country have to wait until its productive forces were fully developed by capitalism before a proletarian revolution could take place? To Radek, the experience of the Russian Revolution effectively refuted such a contention. This conception of "waiting for full development of productive forces" was in Radek's eyes a step away from revolution—a step long espoused by the German Social Democrats and now by the Russian Mensheviks as well.[77]

Radek clarified the issue by enumerating specific criteria for determining when a country is ready for proletarian revolution:

The transition from capitalism to socialism begins when capitalism has inflicted such suffering on the people . . . that they rise up against the rule of capitalism; when the masses can no longer endure the consequences of capitalist economic conditions. *When in any country the capitalist development has proceeded so far that the most important branches of industry and transport are to be found in the hands of capitalists concentrated into groups, then the rising proletariat not only can but must attempt to deliver industry, transport, and finance into the hands of the victorious self-organized state power of the proletariat.* Depending upon the capitalist penetration in the economic structure of any country, the proletariat must more or less adapt this economic structure to its own interests or organize in a socialist manner the previously concentrated areas of industry, while the remainder, as for example agriculture, should be socialized by stages determined by their dependence on socialized centers of industry and dependence on cities. This is how the matter stands in Russia today. In Russia the proletariat comprises a decided minority of the population, but the Russian mining industry, coal and oil production, railroads, and telegraphs are concentrated in the hands of a few people, who also control the few banks and dictate the economic regulations of the country. . . .

Austria and Italy are in a situation similar to that of Russia, and the experience of the Russian Revolution proves that a socialist revolution is by no means certain in that land where capitalism has had the greatest development. The strongest capitalist organization cannot protect the masses from the singularly excruciating agonies which are created by capitalist anarchy; nevertheless, it can hold these masses in obedience much more readily than the younger capitalist countries can.

The socialist revolution begins first of all in those countries where the capitalist organization is weakest. The capitalist countries with the least organized institutions of coercion are the targets for the socialist breakthrough. That is exactly where the socialist revolution begins. Confined within national boundaries, it is difficult for the revolution to gain strength, because even after it [the revolution] has triumphed over its own bourgeoisie, the bourgeoisie of other capitalist lands will still be a constant sword of Damocles over its [the revolution's] head. The socialist revolution can be triumphantly consolidated only on a continental basis. . . . When can the socialist revolution begin? _The socialist revolution can begin and does begin in any place when capitalism creates an intolerable situation for the working class._ [Radek's italics.][78]

In this statement, Radek was not being faithful to Marx, who had indicated that the proletarian revolution takes place when capitalist society has completed its development. But Radek claimed that the Russian Revolution had demonstrated an inverse ratio between capitalist development and revolutionary prospects; some capitalist development was an absolute prerequisite to revolution. Radek did not yet contemplate a socialist revolution in precapitalist societies; in fact, he continued to ignore the problem of revolution in such societies. Yet he was intrigued by the possibility of proletarian revolution in the weaker capitalist lands. The great capitalist lands of the West still had economic and political systems too highly organized to be easily overthrown. For the present, the weaker capitalist lands of Europe—Austria and Italy, for example—were more likely arenas for proletarian revolution. Indeed, a socialist takeover in a land where capitalism was relatively weak might well provide the impetus for revolution in a stronger capitalist land such as Germany.[79]

Thus Radek was able both to draw a moral lesson from the Russian Revolution and to rationalize the failure of the relatively highly organized proletariat of Western Europe to effect their own release. But this did not mean that he was ready to write off the proletarian revolution in the West. From the overthrow of the Tsar, through the Bolshevik Revolution, to Brest-Litovsk, Radek had consistently maintained that the Russian Revolution would not and could not survive without concurrent action by the international proletariat. He held that the workers of Europe, for their own sake as well as for the sake of the Russian Revolution, had to understand the dire need for immediate action. Radek claimed that he sympathized with the dilemma of the European working classes, and said on one occasion: "We do not reproach the European proletariat for not having overthrown their own bourgeoisie as yet; we know that the rate of development of the workers' struggle depends on objective conditions and not merely on the wishes of the most advanced group." Yet in the same speech he warned: "The Russian Revolution can triumph over only its own bourgeoisie; only the international proletariat can triumph over imperialism."[80]

Radek continued to uphold the theory of an inverse ratio of the degree of capitalist development to revolutionary prospects; yet he was unable to convince himself fully of the theory's validity. Although according to his theory, countries such as Austria and Italy were the most likely prospects for revolution, he kept his own eyes turned to Germany. The experience of German "social patriotism" had demolished his faith in the German Social Democratic Party but not his faith in the German proletariat.

5. The Years of Revolution: Germany

The Russians had taken the major step thus far toward world revolution—this Radek readily conceded. Yet he looked more to Germany than to Russia for future breakthroughs, wistfully envisioning an invincible combination of the "human material resources of the Russian proletariat with the organizational skills and talents of the German proletariat."[1] Having abandoned the idea of revolutionary war along with Left Communism, Radek now centered his activities around the development of a working-class revolution in Germany. During the latter part of 1918 he devoted numerous articles, brochures, and speeches to the impending revolution in Germany.

Just how strong an impression Radek's call for a German revolution made on one segment of his readers can be judged by the fear with which he was regarded by the Imperial German Government. The German Foreign Office had maintained a secret file on Radek's movements, acquaintances, and activities ever since Brest-Litovsk, when the German delegation had depicted Radek as "a most dangerous and unscrupulous radical . . . who will employ any means to injure Germany."[2]

The more material on Radek the German Foreign Office collected, the more dangerous he appeared. Of all the Bolshevik leaders, he was the one most involved in German affairs and best informed on the state of German Social Democracy. Moreover, in his articles and speeches, he made it abundantly clear that furthering the proletarian revolution in Germany was one of his prime concerns. Hence when Radek indicated to the German government that he would like to make a trip to Berlin, Count Mirbach, the German Ambassador in Moscow, strongly advised his government to refuse Radek a visa;[3] and when Radek's wife suddenly appeared in Berlin a few months later, the German police, fearing that Radek might soon follow, quickly hustled her back to the Russian border.[4]

In November 1918, as German armies capitulated on the Western front and naval mutiny broke out in Kiel, the entire Imperial German Government collapsed. Kaiser Wilhelm fled to Holland while the caretaker government sued for armistice. In the chaos, Radek's old nemesis, Friedrich Ebert, emerged as the Chancellor of Germany. Radek did not consider the replacement of Wilhelm II by the antirevolutionary Ebert as an improvement, and he denounced the new socialist-led regime in even more violent terms than he had used against the Kaiser. He was obviously disappointed that the German workers—whom he described sarcastically as "the most patient people in the world"—had failed to take advantage of the confusion created by the abdication of the Kaiser to rise up as the Russians had in 1917. In an obvious slap at Kautsky and other "centrists" in the USPD, he reiterated that socialism was the product of revolutionary action, not parliamentary votes.[5]

Radek had no illusions that the German Social Democrats would do anything for the proletariat of Germany, much less for the cause of world revolution. There were, however, other groups in Germany ready to implement the strategy of proletarian revolution—the Spartacists, for example, heirs of the prewar Left, now led by Rosa Luxemburg and Karl Liebknecht. It was this group that Radek now hailed as the new hope of the German proletariat.[6]

Radek's public praise of Luxemburg and Liebknecht notwithstanding, he was aware of the practical limitations on his own involvement in German affairs. He had been on poor terms with Rosa Luxemburg for a decade, and there was little reason to believe that she would be well disposed toward him now. Although he had always had reasonably good relations with Liebknecht, he disliked Liebknecht's emotionalism and declarations of principle. Thus he placed his faith in his old friends in Bremen, the so-called Bremen

Left Radicals. During the war he had maintained his ties to Bremen through *Arbeiterpolitik*, which was edited by his old friends Paul Frölich and Johannes Knief.[7] His high standing in the victorious Bolshevik regime undoubtedly increased Radek's already considerable influence with the Breman group. In the summer of 1918, when the Bremen Left Radicals began to charge even the Spartacists with excessive timidity on the question of forming an avowedly communist party, they may well have been acting on Radek's urging.[8] If the Breman group lacked both the numbers and the influential leadership of the Spartacists, they made up the difference in activity and volubility.

Since Radek was in the unique position of being the only Bolshevik leader with a personal following in Germany, it was only natural that he should play a disproportionately large role in Bolshevik activities there. It was only a matter of time before he would throw himself into the affairs of the nascent German communist movement.[9] When a Reich Congress of Workers' and Soldiers' Councils was scheduled to be held in Berlin in December 1918, Radek became convinced that he must attend it. If this Congress could be dissuaded from supporting Ebert and his right-hand man, Philipp Scheidemann, and persuaded to support the Spartacists and other revolutionary groups such as his own Bremen group, the German revolutionary movement would be greatly advanced.

On December 5, 1918, Radek, Ioffe, Rakovsky, Bukharin, and Ignatov were picked as a special delegation to attend the Reich Congress, now scheduled for December 16. The new German government was undoubtedly aware of the intentions of this delegation even before Radek's surprisingly indiscreet telegram to the German Social Democrat Hugo Haase.* As might be expected, the delegation was denied permission to enter Germany and turned back at the border at gunpoint.[10] Radek, however, was not one to be deterred so easily. Capitalizing on his perfect command of the German language and his ability to mimic accents, he represented

---

* In this telegram Radek openly announced his intention of propagandizing among French and British prisoners of war in Germany. *Der Zweite Kongress der Kommunist Internationale,* pp. 325–26.

himself as an Austrian prisoner of war seeking to get home from Russia and succeeded in entering Germany alone.[11] He arrived in Berlin only to find that the Congress had finished its business; under the domination of Ebert and Scheidemann, it had entrusted Germany's future to a Constituent Assembly.[12]

Berlin in December 1918 was quite different from the city Radek had left in 1914. Then the country had been swept by a patriotic euphoria that had shown all but a handful of German radicals that they were more German than they were radical. Now Germany was stunned by defeat, a defeat that seemed inexplicable since the enemy had not conquered a foot of German soil. The flight of the Emperor had created a void in authority that was at best only partially filled by the Ebert-Scheidemann forces.* Confusion and trepidation were the political mood of the capital. For many of the Spartacists and other radicals, this was a revolutionary moment that might not be repeated in German history.

Radek's own situation was remarkably different from what it had been in 1914. When the war came, Radek was on the point of losing his two-year battle to preserve his status as a German socialist. Even many of the future Spartacists considered him a political undesirable, and this reputation remained with him during the war. Now he came, not as Karl Radek, a man who had been expelled from both the SDKPiL and the SPD, but as the representative of Bolshevik Russia, the only socialist regime in the world. He was no longer a man to be shunned; at least in some quarters, he was the man of the hour.

Logically enough, he sought out the leadership of the Spartacists and presented himself as the prodigal son returned. Rosa Luxemburg greeted him coolly.[13] Quite apart from her long-standing animosity toward him, she was less enthusiastic about the Bolshevik Revolution than many of her comrades were.[14] Instead of welcom-

---

* Under Ebert and Scheidemann, the Provisional Government was by no means socialist in spirit, not even in the most conservative sense. Their very leadership depended on the acquiescence of the German military, in particular General Groener, who had pledged to support them only if they agreed to fight "Bolshevism" wherever it might be found.

ing Radek as the agent of the Russian Revolution, she complained to him of the use of terror by the Bolsheviks, and, apparently with considerable sadness, of the involvement of Dzierżyński, now Lenin's security chief.[15] Moreover, she could not have been happy about Radek's continuing influence on the Bremen Left Radicals. Whereas the Bremen group had once been the gadflies of the SPD, they were now challenging the Spartacists for being too timid about breaking away from the USPD and forming a real revolutionary party.[16] The rude references in *Arbeiterpolitik* to "Frau Luxemburg" and other Spartacists had driven a wedge between the two radical groups. Though Radek may well have been responsible for some of the content of *Arbeiterpolitik*, he now sought to mediate the differences; the Bolsheviks' interests in Germany would not be served by having their potential allies at war with each other instead of with the German government. Lenin may have specifically charged Radek with uniting the radicals and reconciling their differences regardless of his personal preferences.

The most immediate problem appeared to be that of appeasing Knief, since Frölich had just moved to Hamburg, leaving Knief in virtual control of *Arbeiterpolitik*. Radek telegraphed Knief, and Knief replied by insisting that the Bremen group was still against any reconciliation with the Spartacists.[17] The prospect was an unhappy one for Radek. While he may have sympathized with his Bremen comrades, he could not visualize a German revolutionary party that excluded Luxemburg and Liebknecht.

Radek's efforts culminated in a Christmas Eve meeting in Berlin of the "International Communists of Germany," a group sponsored by the Bremen Left Radicals. Radek lectured his old comrades on the needs of the German proletariat and insisted that these needs be given priority over minor jealousies between Spartacists and Left Radicals. Invoking the authority of the Bolshevik Revolution —just how much authority and how much leeway Lenin had delegated to Radek on this mission has never been clarified—he demanded that the Breman group drop their opposition to the Spartacists and join them in forming a new Communist Party of Germany. At Radek's insistence, Knief capitulated, and a few days later, a founding Congress of the Communist Party of Germany (KPD) was held in Berlin.[18]

The Spartacists, especially Luxemburg, were far from convinced that a communist party was what German socialists needed most at this moment. Yet the pressure of events served to overcome their reluctance to organize. Having proclaimed a separate revolutionary program and insisted that the National Congress of Workers' and Soldiers' Councils adopt it, the Spartacists' hand was forced when the Congress opted instead for elections to a Constituent Assembly.[19] An old German saying, "Wer A sagt, musst auch B sagen" (He who says A must also say B), sums up the Spartacists' dilemma. Having insisted on a revolutionary program, they had implicitly committed themselves to form a revolutionary organization if the Congress declined to accept their program.

Radek's position at this founding Congress was more difficult than it appeared. He had come to Germany to foment a communist revolution, nothing less, but such a revolution was simply not in reach. Whatever anger or bewilderment Germans felt at the sudden collapse of the Imperial Government and its war effort, they were not ready to take to the barricades. Spartacist sympathizers had been active in street demonstrations, but their numbers were pitifully small and some of their random and even senseless rioting showed how little discipline there was among them. It was obvious to Radek that this was the time for organization, not revolution.

Could Radek, emissary of the Bolsheviks and symbol of revolutionary intransigence to so many German socialists, come out flatly and tell this Congress that the time was not ripe for revolution? Rosa Luxemburg, in her speech to the Congress, did just that, detailing a long and arduous program for the Communists and telling them frankly, "I will not undertake to prophesy how long this process will take . . . suffice to say, we shall see it completed in our lifetime."[20] Luxemburg could say such things without alienating her following: despite her commitment to socialist revolution, she had a reputation for responsibility. Radek did not.

The delegates to the Congress were largely from the Spartacist and Bremen organizations, but there were sixteen outside guests as well, among whom were the so-called "revolutionary shop stewards," a group of radical Berlin trade union leaders who admired the Bolsheviks' tactics of vanguard leadership. Many of them confidently expected Radek to sound the call to revolution. But irresponsible as he was, Radek had no desire to plunge the German proletariat into a futile and bloody putsch. Being Radek, however, he could not force himself to appear as a cautious organizer of future action. In the end, he treated his audience to a bombastic speech on the future of a Soviet Germany and a Soviet Russia, and promised the aid of the Russian proletariat—not the aid of the Bolshevik regime—in the future uprising of the German proletariat.[21] He at no time issued a call for immediate action, but instead praised the revolutionary heritage of German socialism and assured his audience of the importance of a German revolution to the progress of the world revolution. He compared the situation that had confronted the Bolsheviks in April 1917 with the existing situation of the German Communists, thereby implying that the present moment was not propitious for proletarian revolution.[22]

Many of those listening to Radek, particularly the "revolutionary shop stewards," were hoping for a confrontation with the German Provisional Government. Not expecting to hear a Bolshevik enjoin them to patience and caution, they chose to interpret Radek's speech as a call to arms—and indeed the speech did contain enough vague statements and revolutionary rhetoric to convince many listeners, including the ubiquitous police spy, that Radek had in effect called on the new Communist Party of Germany to seize power.[23]

Radek was alarmed at the response to his address. He had come to Berlin to foster revolution but not to expend Communist strength in a futile putsch. He contacted Rosa Luxemburg and asked her to use her influence in keeping the party from such a disaster. He reminded her of the unhappy experience of the Bolsheviks in the abortive uprising of July 1917, which had almost ruined them.[24] Luxemburg found herself torn with conflicting feelings. The Spartacist leadership, at her behest, had in fact rejected the idea of an

Adolf Warszawski

Konrad Haenisch

The Berlin Parteischule, 1908. Rosa Luxemburg stands at left,
between Kurt Rosenfeld and August Bebel.

Karl Radek before World War I

Robert Grimm

Julian Marchlewski (Karski)

Rosa Luxemburg

Leo Jogiches

The first issue of *Die Rote Fahne*.

Karl Liebknecht in 1912

Poster offering a reward for Radek's capture, January 1919

Radek about 1918

Radek in railway station about 1919

Paul Levi

Feliks Dzierżyński

Lenin in 1922

Joseph Stalin in 1919

Zinoviev at Baku in September 1920

Trotsky in the
Caucasus, 1924

Radek in the early 1930's   Larissa Reissner

Stalin and Kirov

Radek a few years before his trial

uprising at this time, but she did not care to have Radek tell her what to do. Furthermore, whatever her misgivings about the advisability of a Communist uprising, she firmly believed that all revolutionary proletarian leaders were obliged to support the fighting proletariat in any endeavor, timely or not. Her own preference was for defensive tactics, but when the "revolutionary shop stewards" overreacted to provocation and launched an uprising in Berlin, Luxemburg went along with it.[25] As for Radek's plea for caution, she dismissed it with the arrogant comment: "He will find my answer in tomorrow's edition of *Rote Fahne!*"[26] Radek had no need to wait for the next day's newspaper; he well knew what the answer would be. *Rote Fahne*, the newspaper of the KPD, supported the uprising, albeit in defensive terms.[27]

Radek did not agree with Luxemburg's conception of the obligation of Communist leaders to support any proletarian action, no matter how futile. Even after the Spartacist uprising had begun, he begged the leaders of the KPD to call it off before the entire working-class movement in Germany was drowned in blood:

Naturally I know how difficult it is, at the present, after such sacrifices, to appear before the masses and sound retreat. I know that it will lead to moral depression. But moral depression is nothing compared to what the masses will have to tell themselves after bloodletting. And they will say that they were dragged into an unnecessary struggle by a blind leadership. . . . In July 1917, although we [the Bolsheviks] were stronger than you are now, we held back the masses with all our strength, and when that failed, we helped to avoid . . . unnecessary strife.[28]

Radek's letter further advised the workers to break off the struggle but to keep their arms for a more auspicious moment. His appeal met with little response. Even if the Spartacist leaders had been disposed to listen to his advice, the weight of his letter was vitiated by his closing statement that he spoke as an individual and was in no way empowered to express the views of his superiors in Moscow.[29] His advice was ignored, and he gloomily watched the Spartacists wage their suicidal battle against the German regime.

The Spartacist uprising was a senseless martyrdom. The German people, stunned by a sudden and unexpected defeat, by the flight of an Emperor who had sworn that he would not abdicate, and by the collapse of normal authority in Germany, were in a state of confusion. The military leaders were unenthusiastic about Ebert, but the Spartacist Liebknecht was totally unacceptable to them. After ten days of rioting, the Spartacist uprising was crushed, on January 15, 1919, and the two most prominent German Communists, Karl Liebknecht and Rosa Luxemburg, were brutally murdered, ostensibly while trying to escape from custody.[30] Had the German police been able to find Radek at this time he might well have met the same fate. He was far too prudent, however, to be caught leading a doomed putsch. He kept out of sight while the police searched for him all over Germany.[31] When he was finally found and arrested on February 12, 1919, the panic caused by the uprising had abated, and he was placed in solitary confinement instead of being summarily shot, as he might have been the month before. To offer Radek some measure of protection, the Bolshevik regime appointed him Ukrainian ambassador to Germany and seized German hostages to guarantee his safety. The German government was also warned that if any "accident" should befall Radek, or if he should be shot "while trying to escape," no one would be under any illusions as to the true nature of the situation.[32]

Murder by a *Freikorps* zealot would have been an unworthy end to Radek's career. In his own account of his arrest, written many years later, Radek claimed that he had saved himself by making melodramatic threats to his captors; the German documents, however, indicate that Radek was completely cowed and terrified at the time of his arrest and hardly likely to have been issuing threats to anyone.[33] That Radek was captured in February rather than January seems to have been fortunate, since at that time his captors were anxious to avoid a repetition of the Luxemburg-Liebknecht affair.* One of them, a Colonel Reinhard, took it upon himself to transfer Radek from a civil to a military jurisdiction so that the military could guarantee his safety.[34] In the final analysis, Radek was simply lucky. His ability to remain in hiding

---

* Jogiches, however, was not so lucky. Although he escaped the reprisals in January, he was captured in March and shot to death while in police custody.

for almost a month, while posters screamed "Where Is Radek?" and 10,000 marks were offered for his capture, was surely the most decisive factor in his survival.[35]

Radek remained a prisoner for almost a year. The first several months of his incarceration were difficult, since he was kept in an isolated cell in Moabit Prison and subjected to continued interrogation, but he was able to keep up with world affairs through newspapers, and he was even allowed to receive packages occasionally.[36] On July 1, 1918, he sent a letter to Hermann Müller, the German Minister of Foreign Affairs, in which he invoked his "diplomatic status" as an emissary of the Ukraine and reviewed the circumstances of his imprisonment.* He insisted that he had never called for an insurrection, and rather bluntly reminded Müller that Germans in Soviet Russia were being held hostage for his safety.[37] How Müller received Radek's letter is uncertain; what is known is that soon after sending it, Radek was moved out of his isolated cell and given reasonably comfortable quarters, the right to receive visitors, and the assurance that as soon as the problem of returning the hostages was worked out, he would be released.[38]

In his new quarters, Radek was allowed to work on his political writings and to receive a variety of visitors, including the German industrialist Walter Rathenau and various representatives of German Communism (Radek himself referred to the latter part of his imprisonment as the period of his "political salon" in Berlin). Although a prisoner, Radek was the only representative of the Bolshevik government in Germany—there were no accredited diplomatic representatives between the two countries until a Comrade Kopp arrived in November—and many German politicians, distressed over the depressed status of their country, were curious to sound out this unofficial spokesman for the one European power not bound by the Treaty of Versailles.

There is an understandable temptation to overestimate Radek's role in determining, from his cell in Berlin, the future of Russo-German relations. Radek was not in a position to reflect Bolshevik

---

* Interestingly enough, this was the same Hermann Müller who had been involved in the SPD's campaign against Radek in 1912–13.

policy, and could only spar with the German officials who came to see him. His talks with Rathenau did hint at future cooperation, but only as a distant event. He had some interesting talks with two émigré Turkish leaders, Talaat Pasha and Enver Pasha, who may well have been shopping for support for Turkish resistance to the peace treaty.[39]

There has been a great deal of speculation about the importance of the connections between Radek and various German military figures in 1919. Radek himself has recorded a suggestive conversation with Colonel Bauer, an aide to General Ludendorff. According to Radek, Bauer suggested a bizarre alliance between the German military, the German Communist Party, and Soviet Russia, but received an unsympathetic response from Radek.[40] There is no doubt that the German military were interested in Radek, kept an eye on him, and indirectly sounded him out on various subjects; but they were well aware that Radek was not empowered to make secret military commitments. Recent research on the German military has failed to reveal any significant conversations or other contacts between them and Radek in 1919.[41] Nevertheless, for years after Radek's release, rumors circulated that it was he who had made the basic contacts for the Russo-German rapprochement that culminated in the Treaty of Rapallo in 1922 and in various secret military agreements between the two countries.

It is worth noting which Berlin socialists failed to visit Radek's "political salon." The most conspicuous absentee was Konrad Haenisch, who by now had moved so far into the mainstream of German politics that he was serving as Minister of Education for the State of Prussia. Haenisch must have realized that the best he could expect from his old friend and comrade of prewar days was a torrent of abuse. Gustav Mayer too made no attempt to visit Radek. Since Mayer had been severely harassed by bounty hunters who accused him of hiding Radek, he could scarcely be blamed if he never wanted to see him again;[42] moreover, Mayer's usefulness to Radek as a contact had long since ended, and Radek probably had little reason to want him as a visitor. A more important absentee was the KPD leader Paul Levi, now involved in a reorganization of the KPD after the Spartacist debacle. Radek maintained constant contact with Levi through intermediaries and by letter, but a personal visit from Levi would have compromised the KPD and provided a pretext for further police harassment.[43]

Radek kept in touch with the Communist world through contacts less in the public eye than Paul Levi. One of these was Karl Moor, who was rumored to have been one of the agents running German funds to the Bolsheviks in 1917 and before.[44] (Moor did in fact send help to the Bolsheviks, but it is likely that the funds came from his own sizable fortune rather than from the coffers of the German Foreign Office.)[45] In any case, Moor made himself useful to Radek now by carrying messages in and out of prison for him and arranging visits from various socialists and Communists in the area. One such visitor was the young Austrian radical Ruth Fischer. Radek's impressions of her at that time, although mixed, have proven to be far more balanced and perhaps closer to the mark than her later impressions of him.[46] Though he had doubts about her political stability, he used her to carry messages to Levi and others in the KPD.[47]

By the fall of 1919, Radek's "political salon" had attracted guests from every part of the political spectrum. He received the British journalist M. Philips-Price (who has left an account of his visit), various German industrialists, and even SPD representatives.[48] At the end of 1919, he was removed from prison and placed under house arrest in the apartment of Baron Reibnitz. The stream of visitors increased, and even a few KPD leaders chanced interviews with him.[49]

What concerned Radek most in 1919 was the fate of the disorganized and demoralized KPD. His greatest fear was that the lessons of the Spartacist putsch had not been learned. Alfons Paquet, who had been in contact with Radek in Stockholm in 1917 and in Moscow in 1918, claimed that he received a letter from Radek on March 20, 1919, in which Radek predicted a bitter class struggle in Germany, much worse than that which had taken place in Russia, but did not imply that this struggle would or should commence at once.[50] As the year wore on, Radek's apprehensions turned into grave anxiety. When in the fall of 1919 the KPD reassembled for its second congress (the first since the Spartacist putsch), Radek sent them a word of caution: "The world revolution is a very long process during which there will be more than one setback. *Yes, I have no doubt that in each land the proletariat will establish its dictatorship several times, and will see it collapse; but finally it will be victorious* [Radek's italics]."[51]

Levi agreed with Radek that putschism was a threat to the KPD, and had already made plans to purge the KPD of "wild elements" at the Congress scheduled to open October 20, 1919. One such element was the Hamburg organization led by Dr. Heinrich Laufenberg and Fritz Wolffheim. Radek and Laufenberg had worked together in September 1914 in joint efforts by the Bremen group and leftist Hamburg socialists to issue antiwar propaganda.[52] When Radek's friend Paul Frölich moved to Hamburg in November 1918, the connection was reestablished. Radek found many of Laufenberg's ideas too heady for the realities of German political life— ideas such as a separate Communist Labor Movement and National Bolshevism, a possible collaboration with nationalists against the Ebert-led government. But he considered Laufenberg and Wolffheim energetic and dependable, if in need of some restraint, and when Ruth Fischer informed him that Levi was going to split the KPD and drive out the extremists, Radek gave her a personal letter to Levi urging him to reconsider his decision.[53]

Radek's appeal to Levi was couched in the warmest and friendliest terms. Starting from the premise that they both held the same goals for the KPD and shared the same aversion to putschism, Radek wrote: "The KP [Communist Party] has no tradition that says we must . . . throw out confused comrades, all the time beating their bottoms. The split is not necessary. If we have the majority, then the Hamburg group will yield—provided that we do not force our line on them in a rigid fashion, but adopt a flexible policy."[54] There is some doubt that Levi received the letter prior to the discussion of the matter at the KPD Congress. Ruth Fischer implies that he did, and Radek states categorically that he did, but the letter was not mentioned at the KPD Congress, and Levi proceeded to act as though he had never received it.[55] He denounced Laufenberg and Wolffheim by name, and although he did not move for their formal expulsion, he told them in effect that there was no room for them in the party, a fact that the Hamburg Communists apparently accepted, since they subsequently withdrew from the KPD altogether.[56]

For Radek, the news from the KPD Congress must have come as a rude shock. Yet the deed was done and he had to take a stand. Could he continue to back the Hamburg group, which had now formed its own party, or was he still under obligation to the KPD as the bearer of the Communist standard? Whatever anger he may have felt toward Levi for precipitating the split, he knew he must back the KPD for the sake of German Communism. He may well have believed too that the Hamburg group, now divorced from the KPD, might really go the way of putschism. He was perhaps less disturbed by Laufenberg's proposal for National Bolshevism, an alliance with the extreme Right nationalists against the German government, but loyalty to the KPD demanded that he denounce that policy as well. What convinced him that he could not simply remain silent on the subject was that Laufenberg and Wolffheim now began attacking the KPD and claiming that Radek supported them, citing Radek's speeches of a year earlier to document the claim.[57] Radek published an article in *Die Internationale*, the weekly of the KPD, denouncing National Bolshevism and castigating the Hamburg comrades for refusing to accept party discipline.[58] Did Radek double-cross the Hamburg National Bolshevists by leading them on, then turning on them when they needed him most? If Ruth Fischer is to be believed, he did. Fortunately for Radek, Miss Fischer's reputation for accuracy is no better than his own.* Her claim that Laufenberg and Wolffheim visited Radek in prison just prior to the Congress and received his blessings is com-

---

* Miss Fischer's reliability has been questioned, and with good cause, by almost every serious historian of the German Communist movement. There are so many demonstrable errors in her account that none of her assertions can be accepted at face value, yet because of her unique position in party history, she cannot be ignored. Here Miss Fischer is so anxious to show Radek as a steadfast supporter of the Hamburg group that she omits any mention of the article in *Die Internationale*, although she certainly must have read *Die Internationale* faithfully and may even have been the courier who brought Radek's article to the paper.

pletely unsupported.[59] Such an encounter would have placed Radek in an extremely vulnerable position. He had been intrigued by the tactical possibilities of National Bolshevism, but whether he backed the Hamburg group in 1919 is at best debatable, and is certainly not proved by his advice to Levi not to read them out of the KPD.

During 1919, negotiations were in progress for Radek's release. There was a stalemate while the Germans insisted that the Russians release their hostages first and the Bolsheviks were equally firm in their insistence that Radek's safe return be a precondition for the hostages' release.[60] Somehow a compromise was reached, and Radek was allowed to leave Germany for Russia in January 1920.

The Radek who came back from Germany was a far more cautious revolutionary than the man who had sneaked across the border in December 1918 to foment insurrection. He had been very deeply affected by the defeat of the Spartacists and the deaths of Luxemburg, Liebknecht, and Jogiches, and appalled by the extent of the damage caused by the Spartacists' premature action. He feared that another tragedy like the Spartacist uprising would rob the proletariat of the courage to risk revolutionary action.[61] In the future this fear was to haunt Radek and make him hesitate when other revolutionaries were ready to march forward.

6. Radek and the Comintern: The Reluctant Revolutionary

Radek's return to Russia in January 1920 could hardly be described as a triumph. Fourteen months earlier he had left Moscow to trigger the world revolution by launching a Communist revolt in Berlin. As it turned out, he had been forced to watch the near-suicide of the German Communist Party and then to spend a year in jail brooding over what had gone wrong. The situation in Russia when he returned was not one to generate new optimism in him. In 1919 the advance of the anti-Bolshevik White Armies had threatened Moscow itself. By January 1920, the struggle had apparently turned in favor of the Red Army, but there was still fighting on several fronts. A dangerous confrontation seemed about to take place between Russia and Poland, the newly resurrected nation on Russia's disputed western boundary. In 1918 the Russian economy had been on the downgrade; now things were even worse. Grain shortages threatened the country with famine, and the ruble had been devalued almost out of existence. Far from spreading, the world revolution seemed at a standstill; recent attempts to establish Soviet regimes in Hungary and Bavaria had failed. But in spite of all, the Soviet regime in Russia had survived; therein lay Radek's hope for the future.

In this situation, Radek found talk about the imminence of a world revolution inappropriate. Lenin still spoke of the need for a revolution in the West to guarantee the survival of the Soviet regime, and although Radek undoubtedly agreed in principle, he

did not see how a world revolution could be launched in the face
of the realities of international politics in 1920.

Radek now began to contribute regularly to the two major Soviet
daily newspapers, *Pravda* and *Izvestiia*. He constantly stressed
both the need for faith in an eventual world revolution and the
need for prudence in formulating and implementing present tactics.
His journalistic work, however, took second place when he was
assigned to an important post in the newly formed Third International.

The Third International, better known as the Communist International or Comintern, was Lenin's new vehicle for transforming
the Bolshevik Revolution into a world revolutionary movement. It
was based on two important premises: the belief, held by Lenin
and most Bolshevik leaders, that the survival of their own regime
was contingent on the development of an international proletarian
revolution; and the fulfillment of Lenin's long-standing desire for
an International stripped of moderates and openly dedicated to
world revolution.

Radek and Zinoviev were enthusiastic and voluble supporters of
Lenin's plan.* But most socialists, including Rosa Luxemburg,
were slow to give up on the Second International, despite its virtual
collapse in 1914.[1] In calling for a new International, Lenin's was literally a voice in the wilderness, heeded by very few. As Franz
Borkenau has said, of those who responded to Lenin, "there remained Radek, Radek, and once again Radek."[2] Radek had believed in Lenin's idea of a new International since 1915; Lenin
would have been far more gratified if Rosa Luxemburg had believed in it.

Radek was not privy to Lenin's final decision to organize a new
International, which was made in December 1918 in response to
word that there would be an International Socialist Conference in
Berne in February—presumably as a preliminary to resurrecting
the Second International. By this time, Radek had already been

* Zinoviev, who had been with Lenin prior to the war, had supported the
new International from the time Lenin issued his first call; he was not adept
at writing in German, however, and hence was less able than Radek to articulate his support in the Swiss press.

dispatched to Berlin and was unable to maintain regular contact with Moscow. Luxemburg reacted to Lenin's plans with displeasure, for she feared that any organization based in Moscow would soon become a Russian vehicle. Her long-standing disagreement with Lenin on the concept of elite leadership only served to reinforce her fears, and the presence of Radek in Berlin as Lenin's emissary did nothing to dispel them.

Luxemburg's martyrdom in January 1919 strengthened Lenin's chances for a Communist International. Although he was undoubtedly shocked by her fate, Lenin could not have failed to realize that her death had removed a major obstacle to his plans. Luxemburg's very existence had threatened Lenin's International; the Bolshevik Revolution notwithstanding, she had seemed to many revolutionaries as important a leader as Lenin himself, and no revolutionary socialist organization claiming to be international could have lasted long without her support. Her death enabled Lenin to assume unchallenged leadership of the movement for an International and cost him nothing, since he could capitalize on the martyrdom of the Spartacists, extolling the dead Luxemburg and Liebknecht as "leaders of the truly proletarian Communist International," without endangering his own position.[3]

Hugo Eberlein (Albert) arrived in Moscow at the beginning of March 1919 to represent the KPD. He stood ready to defend Luxemburg's mandate: no Third International now. The fact that most of the other delegates in Moscow were émigrés long out of touch with their native countries must have reinforced his view that Luxemburg's diagnosis was sound. But Luxemburg was a match for Lenin, and Eberlein was not. He justified his presence at the Congress on the grounds that the gathering was merely a preliminary conference, not a founding congress, and he must have been dismayed when the meetings opened on March 2 and Lenin stated flatly to the delegates: "In the name of the Central Committee of the Communist Party of Russia, I hereby open the first Congress of the Communist International."[4] For Lenin, the establishment of a new International was a fait accompli, not a subject for debate.

Eberlein refused to be cowed and expressed opposition to founding a Communist International when so few countries possessed
organized, operational Communist parties. He was not able to
stand up to the continued pressure of the Bolsheviks, however,
which increased after a highly exaggerated report of incipient revolution in the West was presented by the Austrian delegate, Karl
Steinhardt (Gruber). Finally Eberlein, and through him the KPD,
acquiesced in the founding of the Communist International by abstaining on the critical vote. Lenin was relieved of the necessity to
fight Luxemburg's ghost in order to have his International.[5]

The Third International ratified its existence by declaring de-
funct the Second International and the Zimmerwald Movement.[6]
Angelica Balabanoff, Secretary of the International Socialist Committee of the Zimmerwald Movement became the first Secretary of
the Executive Committee of the Communist International (commonly referred to by its initials, ECCI), thereby emphasizing the
replacement of Zimmerwald by the Comintern.

The circumstances under which the Comintern was founded
suggested that it would become the Russian vehicle Rosa Luxemburg had foreseen. Nevertheless, it immediately appealed to disaf-
fected revolutionary socialists everywhere as a possible base from
which international Communism could be nurtured. Lenin had
filled a political vacuum, whether or not he was aware of it. In
virtually every Western country there were radical elements, not
all of them Marxist, that saw in the new organization the means of
continuing the struggle against a capitalistic and militaristic order
that had forfeited its right to exist by its complicity in the slaugh-
ter of the First World War; the Comintern, uncompromisingly opposed to the existing social order, was therefore worthy of support.[7]

By mid-1920, the collapse of the anti-Bolshevik forces had made
it comparatively easy for radicals to enter Soviet Russia. They
came in great numbers—pacifists, anarchists, Communists, people
who thought they might be Communists, and the merely curious.[8]
If they were interested in international revolution, they were often
directed to Comintern headquarters. They were led to believe that
the Comintern was not just a tool of the Soviet Commissariat of

Foreign Affairs but a truly international revolutionary organization. Thus the Comintern became a mecca for revolutionaries: they came prepared to believe and were swallowed into its ranks.

Eager as he was to exploit the identification of revolutionaries with the Comintern, Lenin could not give the organization his undivided attention—he had enough to do in leading the Bolshevik Party and the Soviet government—so he turned for help to the two men who supported the idea originally, Grigory Zinoviev and Karl Radek. The Executive Committee of the Communist International, whose responsibility it was to operate the organization between meetings of the full membership, emerged shortly after the First Congress adjourned, with Zinoviev as chairman (a choice that might not have been well received had it been announced while the Congress was in session).[9] Radek joined the ECCI as soon as he returned to Soviet Russia from Berlin. He was quick to see that the Comintern was, for all practical purposes, embodied in the ECCI. The Comintern met only once a year, and in later years less frequently, whereas the ECCI was in virtually continuous operation. When Balabanoff was eased out of her post in March 1920, Radek replaced her as Secretary of the ECCI, nominally the second most powerful post in the Comintern.* His new position would have pleased Radek greatly if the top post had been occupied by either Lenin or Trotsky; for a variety of reasons, however, among them the need to maintain a fiction of separation between the Communist International and the hierarchy of the Soviet state, neither Lenin nor Trotsky could assume the presidency of the Comintern. Instead Grigory Zinoviev, Lenin's close comrade and Radek's *bête noire*, was given this office.

People like Radek do not go through life without making ene-

---

* Balabanoff, with characteristic egotism, suggests that she was removed from her post because her unflinching frankness jeopardized the image the Comintern wished to present to foreign delegations arriving in Moscow (see Balabanoff, *My Life as a Rebel*, pp. 237–46). The position of Secretary of the ECCI was, in some ways, only as important as the person who held it. Although Radek was Secretary for less than a year, he continued to exercise enormous influence in the ECCI after he relinquished the post; none of the lesser-known party members who held the post after 1920 was able to exploit it as he had.

mies. Radek was not unduly troubled by this fact; quite the contrary, he often went out of his way to establish social contact with people who despised him.[10] Zinoviev was the exception. Radek and Zinoviev shared a contempt for each other that far exceeded the usual rivalries in the Bolshevik camp. The mutual hostility was no secret: it has been mentioned in the memoirs of nearly all defectors from the Comintern.[11] Protocol often demanded that the two men put on an outer show of harmony and occasionally issue statements bearing their joint signatures, but this was the extent of their cooperation.

Grigory Zinoviev was hardly more popular than Radek with party members (Angelica Balabanoff, for example, considered him second only to Mussolini as a despicable person).[12] According to the British historian E. H. Carr: "No leading Bolshevik of this period incurred so much adverse personal criticism as Zinoviev, or appears to have been so widely disliked. None of them inspired so little personal respect."[13] Vain and full of illusions, Zinoviev spoke openly of inheriting the mantle of the ailing Lenin. Since Zinoviev saw Leon Trotsky as his chief competitor in this regard, Radek's open admiration for Trotsky infuriated him. It apparently never occurred to Zinoviev, or for that matter to most Bolsheviks, that Stalin and not Trotsky might be the man to frustrate Zinoviev's ambitions. Consequently Zinoviev concentrated his attack on Trotsky and Trotsky's supporters, particularly Radek, who retaliated by seizing every opportunity to harass or embarrass Zinoviev.[14] Even when mutual opposition to Stalin in later years forced both men into the same camp, no real rapprochement was achieved.

Nevertheless, Radek did not see Zinoviev as a major obstacle to his using the Comintern as an instrument for planning, supervising, organizing, and, if necessary, restraining revolutionary activities. The importance he assigned the Comintern was undoubtedly influenced by his involvement in its activities. As Secretary of the ECCI, a spokesman for international Communism, and a tactician of the world revolution, he reached the zenith of his career. His position in the Comintern gave him new stature, both in and out of the party.

Radek's talents as a journalist and as a troublemaker were well known, but few people appreciated the complexity of his character. Some saw him only as a short ugly man with oversize spectacles and ill-fitting clothes who could be seen hurrying to and from the Kremlin with a bundle of ragged newspapers under his arm. Louis Fischer, one of the very few American journalists to know Bolshevik leaders at firsthand, gives us a graphic description of Radek: "He was a witty imp and an ugly Puck. He had dense, curly disheveled black hair which looked as if he never combed it with anything but a towel; laughing, nearsighted eyes behind very thick glasses; prominent wet lips; sideburns that met under his chin; no mustache, and sickly sallow skin."[15]

Yet as Fischer and others noted, Radek's erudition, wit, and intelligence soon made one forget his shabby appearance. What was often ignored by casual acquaintances, perhaps because of his lack of formal university degrees, was Radek's familiarity with European culture. Few other Bolsheviks could match his command of European belles lettres, art, and music; perhaps Trotsky and the playwright-commissar Anatoli Lunacharsky were Radek's equals intellectually, but Trotsky was simply not as available as Radek and Lunacharsky not as involved in international Communism. Could one imagine Zinoviev or Stalin making the rounds of Moscow cafés with the basso Feodor Chaliapin and joining in singing with Cossack trios?[16] How many Bolsheviks could claim, as Radek could, to be as much at home with Kleist or Grillparzer as with Gogol?[17] To meet Radek became almost an initiation for foreigners in Moscow, Communists and non-Communists alike. Not all of Radek's traits were as attractive as his intellect. He could be mean, mendacious, vindictive, even treacherous. Paul Levi and John Reed were among the first Communists to learn this. But with his friends, and sometimes even with rivals and enemies, excepting Zinoviev, he could be generous and charming. In a movement that was a bit shy on saints, many of Radek's faults were overlooked by those who were not the targets of his verbal attacks.

Radek enjoyed the limelight his position in the Comintern afforded him. Despite some setbacks, the years Radek served in the

Comintern were perhaps his happiest years. At no time in his career was he better known in international circles, more powerful in Communist organizations, or closer to the top of the Bolshevik hierarchy. He enjoyed a substantial amount of material prosperity and a respectful audience at home and abroad for his every pronouncement.[18] When Radek spoke or wrote, his views were accepted as those of a major sector of the Soviet leadership, if not of the leadership itself.

Radek's principal task was to get the Comintern and its component parties to adopt a realistic approach to revolution, and above all to avoid the putschism that had doomed the Spartacists in 1919. He was disturbed by the idea current among some Bolsheviks that if revolutionary activity continued to decline, the Red Army might be used as a catalyst to revive the force of a proletarian revolution in Western Europe. The Spartacist failure had convinced Radek beyond all doubt that a genuine proletarian revolution could not be artifically induced by military action. In one of the last pamphlets he had smuggled out of his Berlin prison, he had warned, "The revolution cannot come any faster than it can come. To my knowledge, there is no medicine that shortens the gestation of capitalist society. In short, the result of haste can only be a trade union miscarriage."[19]

Radek's constant emphasis on the compelling need to avoid putschism and premature revolutionary action put him out of step with Lenin on one specific issue, the chronic border problem between Russia and Poland. It was almost impossible to demarcate an equitable boundary between the two countries, since there was no commonly accepted historical boundary. Neither side disputed the land west of the Bug River, which was unquestionably Polish, ethnically and historically. East of the river, however, lay a jumble of Ukranian, White Russian, and Jewish villages clustered around Polish-dominated cities. On December 8, 1919, an Allied commission attempted to demarcate the ethnic boundary of the area north of Galicia (Radek's birthplace), but the line they drew was repudiated by the Poles.[20]

During 1919, while Soviet Russia was enmeshed in civil war, the Poles, through limited military action, occupied much of the territory in dispute. The Bolsheviks reciprocated with seizures of their own, but with their forces largely tied up at home, they were at a disadvantage. If one is to accept the Russian diplomatic correspondence at face value, it seems to have been an obsession with the Soviet Foreign Office to keep peaceful relations with Poland.[21] On the day that Radek returned to Russia, the Soviet government —possibly in consultation with Radek, for he was still technically Assistant Commissar of Foreign Relations as well as an "expert" on Polish problems—sent the Poles a long message recognizing Polish independence, denying an anti-Polish plot in collusion with Germany, and offering a temporary boundary along the existing occupation lines—a boundary very favorable to Poland.[22] Radek's reaction to this first act of Soviet diplomacy is not recorded, but he must have been in accord with it. Given the situation in Soviet Russia, he was not in favor of any ventures against Poland. A few days later, Mikhail Kalinin, acting in his capacity as chairman of the Central Executive Committee of the Soviets, reaffirmed the Soviet regime's intention to refrain from using military force to intervene in or impose Communism on Poland.[23]

Yet the Bolshevik leadership had to consider the question of what to do if Poland did not accept Russian terms as well as what to do if she did accept. When two months had passed without a reply to Russia's offer from the Polish Foreign Office, the need for an alternative policy became imperative. During these two months, moreover, the anti-Bolshevik forces in the Civil War, with one exception, had collapsed, thus making possible the development of alternatives for the Bolsheviks. There is a large amount of circumstantial evidence to indicate that even in the early part of 1920, there was some Soviet preparation for a possible showdown with Poland.[24]

As a prominent member of the Central Committees of both the Comintern and the Bolshevik Party, Radek must have been aware of these developments.* During the first few months after his return, Radek avoided public discussion of the Polish problem. He

---

* While still in prison in Berlin in 1919, Radek had been elected to the Central Committee of the Bolshevik Party. He was returned to this post at each election for the next five years.

wrote very little about it, and the articles he did publish contained conventional slogans and recriminations against France and other capitalist nations for pushing Poland to a more bellicose position.[25] His trepidation concerning a military venture into Poland were understandable; as a native Pole who had been conditioned in his early youth to hate everything Russian, he knew quite well the intense Russophobia inherent in Polish nationalism.

The situation became suddenly critical on April 25, 1920, when Józef Pilsudski, the Polish commander-in-chief, launched a surprise attack to "liberate" the Ukraine. Initial Polish successes, particularly the capture of Kiev, convinced the Bolsheviks that merely repelling the invasion was not enough. There was a great deal of loose talk in the Soviet press about seizing the opportunity to establish a Soviet regime in Poland. Radek, who now began to write on the Polish problem on an almost daily basis, showed far more restraint than any of the other leading Bolsheviks in stating what Soviet Russia's war goals should be now that a Russo-Polish war had become a reality.

The Bolsheviks denounced the Polish government for its attack on the Ukraine—which was regarded in Moscow as an attack on Soviet Russia—and called for the Polish workers to overthrow their government and replace it with a proletarian regime. The point on which Radek differed from his comrades was the role assigned to the Soviet regime in promoting this overthrow. With the Poles on the offensive, the point was academic, but in late May the tide of war turned and the Red Army began systematically to drive back the Poles. The Bolshevik regime was then faced with the problem of defining its objectives. Should Soviet Russia limit itself to repelling the Polish invasion and count on the military defeat of Pilsudski to provide sufficient momentum for the overthrow of the Polish government? Apparently Radek was almost alone among his colleagues in holding this view.[26]

June was a hectic month for the Bolshevik leadership. By now the youthful Red Army commander Mikhail Tukhachevsky had completely smashed the Polish offensive and proven that the Red Army could advance almost at will to Warsaw and even beyond.

Since the Russo-Polish border was a matter for speculation, where, in fact, should the Red Army stop? For that matter, why should it stop? Tukhachevsky was certainly in favor of having the Red Army establish a Soviet regime in Poland as the first step in reviving the drive for world revolution. As he wrote at a later date when reviewing the policy discussions of June 1920: "A revolution from without was possible. Capitalist Europe had been shaken to its very foundations, and . . . perhaps the Polish War could have become the link which would have united the October Revolution [in Russia] and the revolution in Western Europe."[27]

Radek was far from enthusiastic. With the ghost of the Spartacist uprising still haunting him, he cautioned the party against carrying revolution forward on the bayonets of the Red Army.[28] Furthermore, he warned Lenin that Polish nationalism would not succumb to a call for class warfare: in the final analysis, the Polish worker was far too intoxicated with nationalism to recognize class interest. Lenin, apparently intrigued by the possibility of creating a Polish Soviet state, accused Radek of defeatism and removed him from all work dealing with the Polish question.[29] For the next several weeks, while the Red Army made an abortive attempt to overthrow the Polish government, Radek's articles were conspicuously absent from the Soviet press.

In 1920 it was still possible for a Bolshevik to disagree with the leadership and not be deposed. Lenin was certainly not pleased with Radek's pessimism, which seemed to have become a permanent feature of his outlook since his return from Germany, but Radek was far too useful to be removed simply because of his opinion on the Polish problem. His knowledge of languages and Western socialist movements was an asset that Lenin planned to exploit at the Second World Congress of the Communist International, scheduled for the summer of 1920.

In the days of the Second International, Radek had been a pariah, scorned by both Left and Right. In 1920, as the delegates streamed into Moscow from all over the world, he emerged as a powerful figure. Technically speaking, he attended the Second Congress as a representative of the Polish Communist Party (thus

enabling the Bolsheviks to increase by one their membership in the
ECCI, whose rules allowed for only five Bolshevik representatives), but actually he was there to serve as hatchet man for
Lenin.[30] As head of the credentials committee, he was in a position
to determine which delegates could legally be seated and which
could not.[31] Moreover, as the Secretary of the ECCI, he had some
control over the agenda and over the speakers. He also had the
opportunity to address the Congress on whatever subject was before it. On some occasions he simply put into his own colorful language the viewpoints already agreed upon by the Bolshevik leadership. At other times, he was able to use his forum to teach that
revolutionary struggles were serious matters, not to be launched
prematurely. Only on the cogent question of Red Army activity in
Poland (in full swing while the Congress was meeting), did Radek,
the "Polish" delegate, fail to offer an opinion.

The Second Comintern Congress was Radek's first major appearance before an international audience since his speech on disarmament at the Copenhagen Congress of the Second International in
1910. He certainly intended to make the most of the opportunity
to assert himself as a major force in international Communism,
even if he was unable to discuss the Polish situation freely. One of
his most important debates centered around the question of the
Comintern's relationship to the trade union movement. In introduc-
ing the official theses on the trade union movement, Radek offered
the notion that the economic struggle for worker benefits was a
useful revolutionary device. When the worker fought his employer
for material benefits, he received valuable experience in the tech-
niques of confrontation and perhaps sharpened his hatred for capitalism at the same time. Therefore, according to Radek, the job of
Communists was to infiltrate trade unions and transform them into
organs of revolutionary struggle.[32]

John Reed, the American delegate, was horrified by what he
considered Radek's gross misunderstanding of the dynamics of the
labor movement in the United States and England. For years Reed
had been maintaining that since Samuel Gompers had organized
the bureaucracy of the American Federation of Labor so well that

Communists had no chance to capture it, Communists should pour their strength into a radical labor movement like the Industrial Workers of the World (IWW). Now Radek was demanding that American Communists once again challenge Gompers in his own organization.[33] Reed tried to deter the Comintern from adopting this policy, but found that Radek was not even willing to entertain serious debate. In a demonstration of the viciousness that had earned him his unsavory reputation, Radek accused Reed of "sabotage," a charge clearly not consistent with Reed's arguments for fighting the AFL. Using his power as Secretary of the ECCI, Radek summarily denied Reed the right to discuss the matter further.[34] The sensitive Reed, stunned by the viciousness of Radek's attack, declined to answer in kind, but abstained from voting on Radek's motion.

Radek had his say on several other issues, and when the Congress adjourned on August 7, 1920, he had succeeded in making at least one point: in the new International, he spoke as a member of the power elite and not as an outsider. The contrast with his position in the Second International could not help but have been gratifying to him.

Shortly after the adjournment of the Comintern, Radek's judgment on another issue was vindicated. In August 1920 the Red Army lost the battle of Warsaw, and the front collapsed completely. By the end of the month, Tukhachevsky was hastily evacuating Poland, and feelers for an armistice had been sent out. Radek was able to resist carping on the fact that he had more or less predicted this; he was content that Lenin could see that his warning to go slowly in Poland had been well grounded.[35]

Radek and Zinoviev were sent to Baku in September for a hastily organized "Congress of Peoples of the East." The two men harangued delegations of Asian peoples about the mutual destiny of Soviet Russia and the colonial nations of the world. With slick oratory and little else, Radek tied the Asian peoples into the quest for world revolution:

No enemy shall terrorize you; no one can hold back the torrent of workers and peasants of Persia, Turkey, and India if only they will

unite with Soviet Russia. Soviet Russia, although surrounded by enemies, can produce weapons with which it can not only arm the Russian
worker and peasant, but can also arm the Indian, Persian, and Anatolian
peasants and lead them into common battles and to common victories.[36]

Radek, of course, could not have meant any of this. If he did not
believe that the German or Polish proletariats were ready for Communist revolution, he could scarcely expect the virtually nonexis-
tent proletariats of exotic lands to rise. For him, the Congress in
Baku was only a propaganda mission designed to stir up trouble in
Asia. John Reed, who had accompanied Radek and Zinoviev to
Baku against his better judgment was shocked by Radek's rhetoric
as well as by some equally cynical speeches by Zinoviev. When he
berated them for the dishonesty of their appeals at Baku, both
men turned on him and threatened to read him out of the Communist International. The shock may have been too much for the ideal-
istic and perhaps somewhat naïve Reed; his death the following
month was attributed by many to his disillusionment at the Baku
Congress.[37]

Whether Radek took Reed's reaction or even his death to heart is
debatable; there was too much work to be done to pause and grieve
over malcontents. Moreover, Reed's American comrades all declared that he had died with his faith in Communism unblemished.
In later years they were to change their minds, but at the time
their declarations may have sufficed to ease Radek's conscience.[38]

For Radek the center of Comintern activity had always been
Germany, and he was anxious to get back to work on the German
question. The excursion into Poland had been an unfortunate mistake; Baku had been an exercise in revolutionary bombast and
nothing more. Germany, on the other hand, was the key to the
future of international Communism. Despite his depression over
the Spartacist affair, Radek was still German-oriented. As it turned
out, his obsession with Germany and his overwhelming desire to
become the chief architect of Comintern policy there led to one of
the ugliest affairs of his career: the purge of Paul Levi.

In 1920, one of the major problems of the Comintern, especially
its German membership, was to determine who spoke for the Ger-

man Left. After the putsches of 1919 had removed all the potential leaders of German Communism—Luxemburg, Liebknecht, and Jogiches—at one stroke, the grim job of picking up the pieces of the KPD had fallen to Paul Levi, who had accepted the job reluctantly.* At first there appeared to be little reason why Radek or any other Bolshevik should object to Levi. He represented the continuation of the Luxemburg tradition, though he had not come into the group until 1914, as Luxemburg's lawyer, and had not been involved in the earlier SDKPiL politics that had pitted Luxemburg against Radek. Levi was virtually the only member of the Luxemburg group who had kept up an association with Radek over the years; he and Radek had met often in Switzerland during the war. Although Radek, if placed in a similar position, would have found Levi's concept of responsibility and political integrity totally unnecessary, if not ridiculous, he and Levi had similar intellectual tastes and were working toward the same general political goals. It is not surprising, therefore, that when Radek arrived in Berlin in December 1918 he spent much of his time with Levi rather than with the SDKPiL leaders, who had old scores to settle with him.[39]

According to Ruth Fischer, Levi relied heavily throughout the summer of 1919 on Radek's advice, for example, in reversing his own stand and allowing KPD participation in the German elections and in the trade union movement.[40] At the Heidelberg Congress of the KPD in October 1919, however, Levi disregarded Radek's warnings and purged the party of the "wild elements," that is, the Hamburg group. In a sense, the purge meant that Levi had won control of the KPD—a victory that Radek begrudged him, although he was willing to go along with Levi's leadership for the present. Levi came to visit Radek prior to Radek's departure from Berlin and reaffirmed their mutual belief that caution was the order of the day with regard to revolutionary action. Aided by Levi and Luxemburg's old friend Klara Zetkin, Radek issued a pamphlet in which he categorically denounced any form of premature activism

---

* Levi had the good fortune to escape capture and death in the aftermath of the Spartacist uprising, no one knows how; his whereabouts at the time remain a mystery.

or putschism. Echoing the view held by Levi, Radek stated: "Hopes
of a quick victory [in the West] are the result of a false assignment
of the experiences of the Russian Revolution to the world revolution. . . . The position of the Communist Party must be that while
the capitalist world cannot escape the proletarian revolution, this
revolution will be slow in developing."[41] Levi could in good conscience say Amen to Radek's sentiments, and indeed he probably
had a hand in drafting them. There is every reason to believe that
when Radek left Germany in January 1920 he was still on the best
of terms with Levi.

The two men next met at the Second Comintern Congress during
the summer of 1920. The Congress took place against the background of Tukhachevsky's march into Poland and was marked by
wildly enthusiastic Comintern demonstrations for a Red takeover
there.[42] It was an enthusiasm that Radek did not share—he
doubted that there could be a Red Poland at that time; and it can
be assumed that Levi, fearing that the march on Warsaw was leading to unrealistic expectations from the KPD, was also skeptical.[43]
But this accord was effectively shattered by the Comintern's decision to reassess Levi's purge of the KPD the previous year. The
Hamburg group had formed their own party, the Communist
Workers' Party of Germany (KAPD). To Levi's dismay, this group
was represented at the Congress, and later, over Levi's objections,
it was offered "sympathizing party" status in the Comintern.[44] The
initiative in favor of the KAPD had come from Zinoviev, but Radek
had failed to back Levi on the issue of exclusion. Levi returned to
Berlin with his confidence in Radek shaken; obviously Radek was
not willing to risk his Comintern position for a man already out of
favor with Lenin and other Bolshevik leaders.[45]

After the Congress, the recruitment of the USPD members to
German Communism became the major focus of KPD politics.
Despite the professed radicalism of the USPD, its misgivings about
the Comintern's high-handed leadership and the famous "Twenty-
One Conditions" required for Comintern membership held back
many USPD leaders. Radek agreed with the rest of the Comintern
leadership that the USPD was not useful in an independent role

and that its membership should be induced to reject its leaders and join in an amalgamated Communist Party with the KPD.[46] He was, however, equally concerned over the choice of a leader for the new party. Would it be Levi, or would other German Communists better serve the needs of the ECCI?

Radek must have been annoyed when Lenin bypassed him in favor of Zinoviev as the official Comintern representative to the USPD convention in Halle in October 1920. In view of Radek's mixed reputation in German socialist circles, however, the relatively little-known but highly placed Zinoviev was a more prudent choice. (At this time Zinoviev was Chairman of the ECCI and thus the nominal leader of the Comintern.)

Radek could not prevent Zinoviev from representing the Comintern at Halle, but he was not prepared to let Zinoviev replace him as the Comintern's leader on German affairs. Hence while Zinoviev was speaking in Halle—with considerable effectiveness, it might be added—Radek made his way secretly to Berlin, where he renewed his contacts with friends from the old Bremen group as well as other KPD leaders sympathetic to him or hostile to Zinoviev.[47] Whatever direction German Communism might take, Radek was intent on keeping his own lines of communication open and having his own cadre in Germany. He succeeded in establishing close ties with several KPD leaders, notably Heinrich Brandler, Karl Becker, and August Thalheimer. For the next several years Zinoviev and Radek maintained their own factions in the KPD, and when the two men came to an open split in 1924, many German Communists took sides according to the loyalties that had been built up between 1920 and 1924.

The Halle Congress proved to be a Bolshevik triumph, with a substantial majority of the delegates voting for affiliation with the Comintern and the KPD. But Zinoviev had very little opportunity to savor his victory, for on October 15 the German government ordered him expelled as an "undesirable alien."[48] This cleared the way for Radek to become the ECCI emissary when the converts from the USPD and the KPD assembled at a Unification Congress in Berlin during the first week of December 1920.

Radek did not come to this congress with *carte blanche*; on the contrary, it would seem that Lenin had given him a specific mandate and strict orders not to negotiate any compromises with Levi. The idea of Levi leading a party of some 350,000 members (such was the result of the acquisition of the USPD majority) worried Lenin, and presumably he ordered Radek to see to it that the Unification Congress adopted a militant program instead of the cautious program Levi preferred. Working secretly, Radek submitted a manifesto to serve as the party credo and contrived to have it adopted without debate. In brief, the manifesto stated that the German Communist Party must become a party of action rather than words.[49] It is unlikely that Radek himself devised the manifesto, though he may well have written the final draft, but its implications were completely out of keeping with the caution he had advised ever since the dark days of January 1919. The most reasonable explanation is that Radek had been given a *diktat* by the Soviet high command, probably by Lenin himself, and although he must certainly have questioned the wisdom of the manifesto, he was not ready to challenge Lenin and risk his own position in the ECCI and German Communism by open opposition.

By now, the friendship and cooperation that had once existed between Levi and Radek had virtually disappeared, yet both men continued to share enough of a sincere interest in the fate of German Communism to make possible one final collaborative effort in its behalf. On January 8, 1921, *Die Rote Fahne* featured on its front page an open unsigned letter from Zentrale.[50] The letter was addressed not only to the party faithful but to outside elements as well, ranging from the KAPD to the distinctly non-Communist German General Trade Union Alliance. It soon became public knowledge that Levi was one of the authors, but it was not known until many years later that Radek was the coauthor, and that it was he who had persuaded Lenin to override Zinoviev's objections to its publication.[51]

The Open Letter was far more in keeping with Radek's ideas for German Communism than the manifesto of the Unification Congress had been. Eventually the strategy outlined in the Open Letter was given a broader application than the situation for which it had been designed; in fact, it formed the basis for the Comintern strategy popularly known as the united front. As such, it called for Bolshevik cooperation with worker organizations, including the hated Social Democrats, in order to present a solid working-class front against the capitalist offensive. The very adoption of such a strategy was a tacit confession of weakness on the part of the Communist International, but Communist weakness was a postulate on which Radek had based most of his reasoning since 1919. He conceived of the united front strategy as a necessary concession during a period of revolutionary decline and believed it could be converted into a valuable weapon when the revolutionary climate became more auspicious.

The Open Letter marked the last instance of cooperation between Radek and Levi. However reluctant Radek may have been to purge Levi, when Lenin gave him orders to destroy Levi's position in the KPD, he accepted them without question.

The first public clash between Radek and Levi took place in January 1921. Radek, using the alias "Comrade Max" to fool the police, had come to Berlin as a special emissary of the ECCI charged with correcting Levi's interpretation of recent events in the Italian socialist movement. At the beginning of the month there had been a meeting of Italian socialists at the city of Leghorn; Levi had attended as an outside observer (as had a Comintern delegation that did not include Radek). The center of the dispute was Giacinto Serrati, an outspoken radical who had attended the Second Comintern Congress, presumably as a preliminary step toward forming an Italian Communist Party. Serrati had balked at the "Twenty-One Conditions" for membership adopted by the Comintern and had thus incurred Lenin's enmity. He had further antagonized Lenin by refusing to expel the Italian anti-Comintern faction led by Filippo Turati. The Comintern's delegation to Leghorn had openly opposed Serrati and horrified Levi by their crude and coercive actions. Levi's report to the KPD criticized the Comintern's attack on Serrati as self-defeating; such tactics, he said, would only alienate Serrati and his sizable following.[52] Radek disagreed with Levi as to

Serrati's usefulness, but more important, he accused Levi of activity contrary to the wishes of the ECCI, which had already written off Serrati; such activity on the part of a KPD official, Radek warned, was intolerable.[53] In the ensuing debate, Radek made it clear that in the eyes of the ECCI, Levi had outlived his usefulness.

The Executive [of the Comintern] will never try to influence the choice of leaders of Communist parties, so long as the party does not transgress against the tactics of the International. I have spoken only to give Levi some food for thought on these matters. But I am certain that Levi can retain his chairmanship as long as he does not differ from the party on essential matters. I personally consider it very expedient that he continue as chairman, but I do think that it is harmful that he writes articles on the basis of incorrect information and facts.[54]

Levi understood Radek's intention. He was not willing to hold his post at Radek's sufferance, and within the month, in response to continued Comintern pressure, he resigned from the leadership of the KPD. Radek's hatchet job on Levi appeared to be complete; there was, however, more dirty work to be done.

In the early spring of 1921, strikes broke out in the mines of Prussian Saxony. Some Comintern leaders took this as a sign that the German proletariat was ready for action. Over Levi's objections, and apparently without Radek's knowledge, Béla Kun and several other Comintern functionaries sought to make the mine strikes the basis for antigovernment riots. The government reacted to violence with violence, and in March 1921 the KPD suffered a setback almost as grave as the Spartacus debacle. Levi was furious with the Comintern adventurers who had callously sacrificed the party in the March Action and made no bones about saying so. Technically he was speaking out of order, since he had already resigned from the Zentrale.

Radek's activities during the March Action are puzzling. For reasons that still remain unclear, he apparently was not told of Kun's intentions in Germany. He may well have agreed privately with Levi's estimate of the situation but could not condone his open criticism of the Comintern. Certainly he grasped the possibility that the affair could be used to rid the KPD permanently of

Levi and make it more amenable to his own influence. In a number of letters to his contacts in Germany, he indicated that he welcomed the situation as a chance to settle the score with Levi once and for all.[55]

Levi certainly expected to be attacked by the Comintern for his challenge, but he may have been surprised to see Radek leading the attack. After all, he believed that he and Radek were basically after the same goals in Germany—had they not collaborated on the Open Letter only two months earlier? At this juncture, Levi made a grave mistake: he issued a statement defending his position and exposing the differences within the Comintern.[56] As if to emphasize the consistency of his position with Radek's, he included an earlier article of Radek's on the evils of putschism.[57]

When the Third Congress of the Comintern met in June 1921, Levi was not in attendance, but he and his policies were in the dock, and his erstwhile friend Karl Radek was chief prosecutor. The nature of the charges had been pretty well detailed the previous month in a long denunciatory article Radek wrote for the Comintern's official journal.[58] There was no doubt now that Radek would see to Levi's expulsion from the Comintern—a symbolic sequel to Levi's exclusion from the KPD. In his long report to the Comintern, Radek repeatedly deprecated Levi and called for his removal.[59] There was a spirited defense of Levi by some of the lesser delegations and by a few individual delegates—Klara Zetkin felt that Radek's attacks on Levi exceeded the bounds of good taste and veracity and did not mince words in saying so[60]—but no one of Radek's stature argued Levi's case before the Comintern. In the end, Radek scored as complete a triumph as he could have wished —he secured both Levi's expulsion from the Comintern and the Congress's approval for the thesis that the West was not ready for revolution. Since this essentially had been Levi's view as well, it became clear that the struggle between the two men had been over command positions, not over theory. Radek had sacrificed an old friend and comrade merely to enhance his own position in the Comintern and the KPD. As it happened, his triumph was to be of short duration.

Soon after Levi's expulsion Radek once again interfered with the KPD's internal structure and reasserted the ECCI's right to control the leadership. In August 1921, the KPD held a party congress confirming the ECCI action against Levi and entrusting the leadership of the Zentrale to Ernst Friesland (Reuter), who also became general secretary of the KPD.[61] Friesland was considered much more pro-Bolshevik than Levi, had spent some time in Soviet Russia, and had even accompanied Radek on the fateful trip to Germany in December 1918; yet for all that, he was destined for the same fate Levi had met.[62] Soon after he assumed his duties as general secretary, a pro-Levi group of dissidents organized themselves into a separate faction, the Communist Labor Cooperative (KAG). Friesland was somewhat indulgent in dealing with them, and in a private letter to the Zentrale, Radek took him to task for his tolerance of the KAG and suggested that his attitude rendered him unfit for leadership. At first the KPD resisted Radek's pressuring, and Friesland even went so far as to rebuke him for meddling.[63] It was a heroic stand, but an impossible one; the controversy was not between Friesland and Radek but between the KPD's Zentrale and the ECCI, and as such, it was unequal from the start. On January 22, 1922, Friesland was expelled from the KPD just as Levi had been.[64] Once again Radek had acted as the ECCI's political executioner in Germany and had disposed of one of the KPD's ablest but least pliant leaders.

It was important for Radek to gain control of KPD affairs before attempting to transform the tactics of the united front into a Comintern strategy for worldwide application. Actually Radek had begun this work at the Third Comintern Congress in 1921: speaking for the ECCI, he had introduced the official theses on tactics and maintained that the only realistic approach for the Comintern when world revolution was in a state of "ebb," was to stress organization and agitation, and not waste its strength preparing for a class war.[65] In outlining the tactics of the united front, Radek stressed the necessity for Communists to remember that workers were traditionally organized into trade unions and Social Democratic parties, and that the chance of their abandoning their traditional organizations for Communist alternatives was remote. Citing the Open Letter as a guide to strategy, Radek called on Communists everywhere to join with proletarian organizations in a united front against capitalism. This action would serve to stress class differences and be of value in preparing the proletariat for the eventual showdown with capitalism.[66] There was no serious challenge to Radek's thesis—although there was some disagreement with his analysis of the March Action—and the united front was given the blessings of the full membership of the Comintern.

The united front was a strategy that could be implemented in various ways. Whereas Zinoviev and others emphasized a "united front from below," or an attempt to win over the Social Democratic rank and file only, Radek did not rule out a "united front from above," or an attempt to win over, or at least use, some of the leaders of European Social Democracy. Unlike most of the Bolshevik leaders, Radek was quite willing to make common cause with long-standing enemies to secure the success of the united front. He entertained no illusions about the Social Democratic leaders—he did not expect them to take forceful action against the capitalist system—but he argued that the united front would at least force them to act or be unmasked as antirevolutionaries.[67]

In January 1922 Radek was forced to interrupt his planning of united front tactics to carry out a highly important mission for the Soviet Foreign Office. With the apparent approval of both the German and Russian governments, Radek undertook a secret mission to Berlin to seek German military aid for Russia. After cooling his heels in Berlin for several weeks, he was finally received by General Hans von Seeckt, head of the German Army. According to Seeckt, Radek tried to enlist German logistic support for a Russian attack on Poland. Radek's mission does not seem to have been successful, and he temporarily let the matter drop after his interviews with Seeckt.* Whether or not Radek's work was a direct follow-up of his 1919 contacts—and this does not seem likely—he reached a dead end with Seeckt.[68]

After his futile mission to Germany had ended, Radek returned

* According to Friedrich von Rabenau in *Seeckt: Aus seinem Leben 1918–1936* (Leipzig: Hafe und Koehler, 1940), p. 309, Seeckt had no confidence in Radek's discretion and feared that he would repeat confidential information.

to his work in the Comintern and renewed his efforts to introduce a "united front from above." To this end, he led a Comintern delga-tion to Berlin in April 1922 to confer with the leaders of the Second International and the newly formed Second-and-a-Half Interna-tional.[69] The conference itself was a failure, partly because of Radek's boorish behavior toward the non-Communist delegates.[70] Yet Radek did show himself ready to make concessions to win a "united front from above." In deference to the European Social Democrats, he even promised that the Social Revolutionaries, then facing mass trials in Russia, would be spared capital punishment. Bukharin, who had accompanied Radek to Berlin, apparently ac-quiesced in this decision. (This is probably the only occasion on which Comintern representatives dared to make a decision involv-ing the internal affairs of Russia. Lenin subsequently rebuked Radek and Bukharin for their temerity.)[71]

Radek's failure to sell the Social Democrats his united front did not deter him from seeking allies. Until they could be found, the problem was to keep the united front strategy alive. Appear-ing once again in Berlin on May 10, 1922, Radek addressed a meet-ing of German Communists and urged moderation in Communist policies in Germany, particularly since the German government had just signed an entente, the Treaty of Rapallo, with Soviet Rus-sia. He defended the united front and urged German Commu-nists to persevere in their faith that the policy-makers of Soviet Russia had the welfare of the German proletariat at heart.[72]

Radek was spending almost as much time in Berlin as in Moscow during this period; the German government obviously was looking the other way and pretending that the dangerous Bolshevik was not there.[73] After all, he had come to preach a policy of moderation; and he was far too useful a contact in Russo-German relations to be excluded from the country. Some German officials eventually be-came concerned over Radek's repeated visits and advised the Ber-lin government not to grant him further visas, but from 1922 through 1923 Radek seemed to experience no difficulty in getting into Germany whenever he felt that he ought to be there.

The Comintern was scheduled to hold its fourth congress in No-vember 1922, and Radek planned to introduce once again the official ECCI resolution on the tactics of the organization. In a long-winded speech entitled "The Liquidation of the Versailles Treaty" Radek tied together the Treaty of Rapallo and the tactic of the united front. He noted that the proletariat was now on the defensive and that "for the present, the majority of the working class is not thinking of seizing power."[74] This analysis was designed to complement an article of his published in *Pravda* while the Comintern was in session. Obviously written for the benefit of the Comintern delegates, the article stated that the "Communist International must help the working class, open their eyes, *and offer the Social Democrats a joint fight against capitalism*" (italics mine). It continued, "We will encourage the working class to force the Social Democrats either to fight or to leave the working class alone forever."[75]

The formulation of the united front tactic was Radek's most important triumph. It was the one major instance where he devised a policy that set the pace for Comintern activity and, to a lesser degree, for some aspects of Soviet foreign policy. Radek's innovation had provided the Comintern with a viable policy after the collapse of the Polish campaign of 1920 had made the original revolutionary rationale of the Comintern impractical. As Jane Degras has aptly put it, "United front tactics . . . were an implicit admission that the International had been founded on a misconception."[76] The misconception, of course, was that Europe was primed for Communist revolution; that the misconception was Lenin's and not Radek's was beside the point.

The Bolshevik leadership was by no means fully convinced that united front tactics were indeed the best means to achieve their goals. Zinoviev, never enthusiastic about the policy, eventually blurted out his unhappiness over its adoption.[77] Lenin probably had his own doubts, but the policy fitted well with the so-called New Economic Policy at home and the negotiations with Germany that culminated in the Treaty of Rapallo of 1922.[78] It was probably for these reasons that he allowed Radek to persuade him that the united front was best for all concerned; certainly the policy could never have been adopted if Lenin had not concurred.

From 1922 on, the deterioration of Lenin's health severely limited his involvement in Comintern affairs. At his last Comintern Congress, Lenin, visibly exhausted, spoke of the necessity of formulating a strategy of retreat in order to prepare for revolutionary action at a more opportune moment.[79] Such a statement amounted to a de facto blessing for the continuation of the united front tactics. The Congress subsequently incorporated the united front into the Comintern's official theses—a victory for Radek and a setback for Zinoviev. Less than a month later, Lenin suffered a severe stroke and his active participation in Comintern affairs came to an end. As 1922 closed and the various Comintern delegations returned home, Radek could claim that he had firmly established Comintern policy for the era of capitalist revival: a united front with the Social Democrats and others until the time was ripe for revolution.

Barely had the year 1923 begun when the world situation underwent a serious change. On January 11, 1923, French and Belgian troops marched into the industrial areas of the Ruhr with the announced intention of forcibly collecting reparations from Germany. The German workers reacted to this action by showing solidarity with their government. Urged to meet the occupation with passive resistance, the workers refused to produce goods for the alien armies. The government in Berlin reciprocated by sending its blessing and financial aid to the embattled workers.

The Ruhr occupation challenged Communists at all levels: the Soviet regime, which had just concluded a major diplomatic and economic agreement with Germany; the Comintern, which had just proclaimed its united front strategy to cope with a presumably nonrevolutionary climate; and the KPD, which was forced to respond to the situation in order to keep their influence among the workers.

The Soviet regime sided unequivocally with Germany in the dispute. The recently signed Rapallo Treaty had provided the Soviet with access to German manufactured goods critical to the success of Soviet economic planning; moreover, the presence of a militantly anti-Soviet French force in Germany could hardly be to Soviet Russia's advantage.[80] The Comintern was in a more difficult position, for it had to provide guidance for the KPD at a very critical moment.[81] Obviously it would not advise the KPD to support the French. Could it, however, advise support for the German government? While the Comintern pondered these questions, the KPD, without guidance, found itself in the most precarious position of all.

At the beginning of 1923, the KPD presented outsiders with the appearance of a unified party. The threat to ECCI domination, first from Levi and then from Friesland, had been crudely but effectively ended. Yet all movements have the potential for factionalism, and the KPD had only recently experienced an emergence of Left and Right factions that had developed in regard to the issue of the united front. The Left, or activist faction, was led by a number of intellectuals, including Ruth Fischer and Arkady Maslow. They regarded the KPD's Zentrale as too cautious and kept urging it to adopt a more dynamic policy.[82] Although they had no patron in the ECCI, they generally expected and received a more sympathetic response from Zinoviev than from Radek. The Right (the term must be understood in a limited sense) found its leaders in Karl Becker, August Thalheimer, and Heinrich Brandler, all men with ties to Radek. After a somewhat zigzag course in 1921 and 1922, they had emerged as advocates of caution in the KPD and loyalty to the ECCI. The two factions had engaged in open dispute at the Fourth Comintern Congress in December 1922, with Ruth Fischer criticizing the united front policy—at least as interpreted by Radek—as detrimental to the revolutionary potential of the KPD.[83] Radek's reply was, in effect, that Fischer did not know what she was talking about.[84]

In no sense could this verbal exchange be considered a debate, since the winner was predetermined. As the stenographic notes record, Radek's very appearance on the platform was greeted with applause, his remarks were punctuated by cries of assent from the delegates, and the conclusion of his speech provoked "thunderous applause." The record does not show even perfunctory applause for Ruth Fischer. Directly addressing himself to Ruth Fischer's call for a "militant united front"—something that was almost a contradiction in terms—Radek reiterated his belief that the united front was the only policy possible where Communists lacked the strength for revolution.[85] When Bukharin, in another well-received oration, backed Radek against Ruth Fischer, the exchange was over.[86] The KPD was instructed to continue the cautious approach of the united front. Ruth Fischer and her friends were visibly unhappy, but in the name of party unity and discipline, they held their peace. The Left-Right split remained, but opposition was driven below the surface.

The Ruhr crisis in January 1923 reopened the question of whether united front tactics could still be used to restrain the activists in the KPD. A special congress of the KPD was convoked in Leipzig at the end of the month to determine policy on the situation in the Ruhr. Because the ECCI could not allow the KPD to choose its own course in so grave a matter, Radek, by now indisputably the Bolshevik most influential in German affairs, was assigned to travel to the meeting incognito, and once there, to instruct the German comrades on the wishes of the ECCI and the Commissariat of Foreign Affairs.[87]

Radek had no reason to be displeased with this assignment. For one thing, he appreciated the gravity of the situation, and did not trust any other Bolshevik—certainly not Zinoviev—to restrain the KPD from overzealous acts. He was also concerned lest the Left-Right alignment of factions split the KPD irreparably. Thus he went to Leipzig as both emissary of the ECCI and peacemaker for the KPD. At Leipzig, with Radek's support, Brandler and Thalheimer were able to commit the KPD to a continuation of the united front.[88] Satisfied on this account, Radek then insisted that members of the Left be admitted when the membership of the Zentrale was reshuffled.[89] Returning to Russia, he could report to the Bolsheviks that his mission had been successful: the KPD would neither split nor launch any activity that might prove embarrassing to the Soviet regime.

In April Radek became involved with the Twelfth Congress of the Communist Party in Russia, and German affairs were temporarily put aside for problems in the Bolshevik Party. Meanwhile, the situation in Germany became more acute for the KPD. The Ruhr workers remained off the job, and the problem of maintaining them financially became desperate. The government in Berlin could not finance a no-work protest indefinitely, and turned to the printing press for salvation, issuing marks far beyond the treasury's capacity. Inflation destroyed the already faltering German mark and wiped out the financial assets of millions of German citizens. As resentment swelled over the influx of foreign troops, the inflation, and the increasing misery of the people, the status of the Weimar Republic became precarious. Tempted by this opportunity, the Left of the KPD once again sought to dump the united front in favor of a revolutionary policy.[90] If 1923 was not a year for revolution in Germany, would one ever come?

Radek returned to Germany in May (legally, for once), and sought to restrain the KPD.[91] There is evidence, however, that he did not feel as secure in insisting on the traditional implementation of the united front as he had in the past. The situation in the spring of 1923 certainly demanded a fresh approach, particularly in view of the danger of a complete split in the KPD, or worse, a putsch by the Left. The KPD could not push the Social Democrats into revolution while one of their own party, Friedrich Ebert, served as president of the Republic. But if the KPD did not act, other forces would make capital out of Germany's misery.

The resolution Radek drafted in May reflected these considerations. Now he hinted that the supporters of the united front might do well to look to the ranks of German nationalists, even including the National Socialists (Nazis), for future allies. In one highly suggestive remark he referred to certain Nazis as members of a "misled nationalistic petty bourgeoisie."[92]

It is difficult to pinpoint just when Radek began to promote an alliance between the KPD and the nationalists. Ruth Fischer argues that Radek was thoroughly captivated by the idea as far back as 1919, and that only Lenin's derision forced him to drop it.[93] Gerald Freund is more persuasive in pointing to the KPD resolution of May 18, 1923, as the possible launching of Radek's flirtation with National Bolshevism.[94]

Whatever the truth of the matter, Radek was certainly intrigued by the possibilities of collaboration with the Right and began to sound out his Comintern colleagues for their reactions. Apparently he succeeded in convincing most of the ECCI that such cooperation was indeed the right tactic for the unique situation in Germany.

On June 21, 1923, before an open session of the ECCI, Radek electrified the Communist world by offering to make common cause with German fascism.* As the departure point of his long speech, Radek eulogized a recent Nazi martyr, Leo Schlageter. The spectacle of a well-known Comintern leader praising a Freikorps officer—albeit a deceased one—caused an immediate sensation in Germany, both in and out of KPD ranks.† Several nationalists accepted Radek's offer, with qualifications (not, however, Adolf Hitler, who had his own plans), and the strange phenomenon of Communists and nationalists sharing the same platform, writing in the same newspapers, and even conceding some merit to each other continued in Germany throughout the summer of 1923.

In his flirtation with National Bolshevism—the term used to designate this strange alliance of Communists and ultra-chauvinists— Radek stressed nationalism to a degree previously unknown in his writings. What did German fascists and German Communists have in common? Radek now supported the principle he had rejected in 1919: mutual opposition to foreign oppression could temporarily overcome other differences. The immediate task for both parties was to free the workers in the Ruhr:

We are not sentimental romanticists . . . nor are we diplomats who say: "If you have nothing good to say at the grave, then keep quiet." Schlageter was a courageous and brave soldier of the counterrevolution and as such deserves to receive genuine recognition from us who are soldiers of the revolution. . . .

The manner in which he [Schlageter] risked his life speaks in his behalf, and demonstrates his conviction that he thought he was serving the German people. But Schlageter thought that he served the people

---

* At this time Communists referred to all right-wing movements as "fascist," although strictly speaking the term applied only to the regime of Mussolini. The use of the term in the next several pages reflects Radek's usage in 1923.

† Schlageter was a Freikorps officer executed by the French occupation troops for attempted sabotage. His martyrdom made him a hero to various nationalist groups.

best by restoring to power the class that had hitherto led Germany into such misery. . . .

The internal enemy for Schlageter was the revolutionary working class. Schlageter could see with his own eyes the results of this policy when he returned to the Ruhr in 1923 during the occupation. . . . He could see the profound distrust of the workers toward the German government and toward the German bourgeoisie. He could see just how greatly the division of the nation hampered its ability to defend itself. He could see yet more. Those who share his views complained of the passivity of the German people. How can a defeated working class be active? How can a working class be active when they have been disarmed and when they are told that they must allow the profiteers and speculators to exploit them? . . . Schlageter read in the newspapers how the very people who pretended to be the most ardent German nationalists sent their money abroad so that they could become rich while the country became impoverished. . . .

This is what the German Communist Party and the Communist International have to say at Schlageter's graveside. . . . The German Communist Party must openly declare to the nationalist petty bourgeois masses: Whoever is working in the service of the profiteers, the speculators, the iron and coal magnates to enslave the German people and to drive them to desperate measures will meet the resistance of the German Communist Party, which will oppose violence with violence. Whoever, from lack of comprehension, allies himself with the lackeys of capitalism we shall also fight with all our power. But we do believe that the great majority of the nationalist-minded masses belong not to the camp of the capitalists but to the camp of the workers. We want to find and we shall find a way to reach these masses. We shall do all in our power to make men like Schlageter, who are prepared to die for a common cause, not wanderers into the void, but wanderers into a better future for all mankind, so that they will not spill their blood for the profits of the coal and iron barons, but in the cause of the great toiling German people, one of a family of nations fighting for emancipation. . . . Schlageter himself cannot hear this declaration now, but we are certain that there are hundreds of Schlageters who will hear it and understand it.[95]

Beneath all this rhetoric Radek was simply stating that not all fascists were anathema. He was now distinguishing between two groups of fascists: those who consciously pursued a reactionary policy calculated to enhance the position of the officer class and similar elements and those who had turned to fascism in their despair over the social ills and enslavement of their nation. The

"Schlageter line" was pitched toward the latter group with the ostensible goal of channeling the legitimate grievances of these people away from chauvinism and toward the support of proletarian objectives.

Following up his Schlageter speech, Radek cautioned that this new line did not imply Communist acceptance of fascism or its philosophy; fascism was still a danger. The goal was not to reconcile Communism and fascism, but to woo the fascist masses who had been attracted by the theme of national liberation:

Fascism is a political movement of the wide masses of the proletarianized bourgeoisie. And if one wishes to combat it [fascism], he must combat it politically. One can combat fascism only if he first opens the eyes of the suffering masses . . . to the fact that capitalism is not only responsible for their own economic distress but for all of Germany's problems. Secondly, fascism can be combatted only by showing this petty bourgeoisie the proper way to protect its own interests. Against what is it fighting? It is fighting against the insufferable misery to which it has been reduced, and it is fighting against the enslavement of Germany by the Treaty of Versailles. Should the working class support this fight? It has the obligation to do so. . . . Socialism was never a struggle merely for a crust of bread for the industrial workers.[96]

At the same time, Radek warned of the dangers implicit in an unqualified alliance with fascism:

The German Communist Party has the obligation . . . to fight . . . against a fascist revolution, which would be a calamity for Germany. However, at the same time, it has the obligation to do everything to convince the petty bourgeois elements of fascism involved in the struggle against the impoverishment and enslavement of Germany that Communism, far from being their foe, is the star that will guide them on the path to victory.[97]

For several weeks, thanks to Radek's initiative, Germany was treated to the bizarre spectacle of Communists and fascists appealing from the same platform to the innate patriotism of the German masses. In a later analysis, Radek insisted that he had cleared the "Schlageter line" through the ECCI and that even Zinoviev had approved.[98] Perhaps this was the case, but even so, the "Schlageter line" was to provide some embarrassing moments for both Radek and the KPD: some Communists, for example, all too faithfully echoing their new allies, indulged in anti-Semitic polemics.[99] At all events, such an unnatural alliance could not endure. Communists and fascists were soon fighting each other in the streets in spite of the seeming accord between their leaders. Radek's bold attempt to bridge the gap between fascism and Communism failed, and by August all semblance of cooperation had broken down.

Radek continued to ponder the problem of controlling Communist activity; how was the ECCI to prevent protest from turning into putschism? The Left, now led by Ruth Fischer and Arkady Maslow, was ready for action. Bypassing Radek, they appealed to Zinoviev to allow a demonstration in defiance of a prohibition by the Prussian state government. Zinoviev, out of Moscow "on vacation," and probably anxious to undermine Radek's position with the KPD, assented. Horrified, Radek quickly returned to Moscow and enlisted Stalin's help (one of the few occasions on which the two men collaborated prior to 1929). Together they succeeded in calling off the demonstration, which would have led to a showdown between the KPD and the Prussian police.[100] On August 1, Radek, still apprehensive, made one more public appeal against putschism:

It is necessary that we fight the battles with which we are confronted by history, but we must never forget that we are the weaker side. Not only must we not yet advance to the decisive battle, but we must avoid anything that could give our enemy the opportunity of defeating us in separate attacks. . . . An army can be easily defeated when it begins its offensive, before it has made sufficient artillery preparations. . . . We, for our part, must refrain from forcing a decision.[101]

On August 23, 1923, the Politburo, the high command of the Bolshevik Party, held a special session. Radek, not a member of the Politburo, was present in his capacity as the ECCI's German expert. An unofficial account claims that Radek expressed optimism about the chances for a German revolution;[102] this, however, seems highly doubtful, in view of his public stand on the German situation (even Zinoviev hedged on the likelihood of a German revolution). Trotsky, however, who lacked personal experience in the affairs of German Communism, was carried away by the emotional appeal of a German revolution.[103] Ultimately it became obvious that as a group, the Politburo was inclined to support revolutionary action in Germany, and Radek had no choice but to defer to the majority decision.

Radek's acceptance of the Politburo's stand was made public on September 29 in an article in which he called attention to the fact that the new German government formed by Gustav Stresemann had given up passive resistance to the French. Attacking Stresemann's "sellout," Radek broadly hinted that the time was drawing near for a showdown between the German workers and the bourgeoisie.[104] A few days later he went further and stated that if the German workers could supply the necessary will and determination, the German revolution would soon take place.[105] Clearly Radek had decided to implement and support the majority decision of the Politburo.

By the end of September, despite the misgivings of Radek and the visiting KPD leader Heinrich Brandler, the Politburo decided to schedule the German uprising for early November—by Bolshevik standards, a vintage time for revolutions. Radek and Brandler were both opposed to setting a specific date, but their opposition was overruled.[106] Brandler was sent back to Germany at the beginning of October to launch the revolution.[107] He was to lead a KPD infiltration of the Saxon state government, and from this base arm the 50,000 to 60,000 workers who were presumed to be sympathetic to a proletarian uprising.[108]

The plan for insurrection in Germany never had a chance. As one observer has demonstrated, only total miscalculation of the attitudes of the two most important elements in the German scene, the Reichswehr (German Army) and the German working class, could have led the Politiburo to think that there was any chance of success.[109] Whether or not Radek perceived these obstacles to a successful uprising, he was still bound by Politburo orders. There was a slight touch of irony in the choice of Saxony as a base for the revolution, for it was there that Radek's policy of a united front had almost worked: the Social Democratic state government had been forced to rely on Communist support.

En route to Germany, Radek stopped in Warsaw, where in secret conversations he sounded out Polish diplomats on the situation in Germany and implied that in the event of a successful German revolution, Polish neutrality would be rewarded by the gift of East Prussia.[110] Then he proceeded through Czechoslovakia to Dresden, the capital of Saxony.

In Dresden, to protect himself from the local authorities, he registered under an alias at the same hotel where the Reichswehr commander was billeted—presumably the last place government troops would look for him.[111]

The day after Radek arrived in Dresden, October 23, 1923, he found to his horror that although Brandler had persuaded most of his associates to postpone action, communications had broken down, and a putsch had been initiated in Hamburg, with disastrous results.[112] The Hamburg Communists had seized several police stations, but had been quickly dislodged by combined civil and military forces after the Hamburg workers refused to come to their aid. The Hamburg fiasco was the kind of thing Radek feared most, and he was anxious to avoid a repetition in Saxony. But his proposal to substitute a call for a general strike for the planned uprising was badly received by local Communists and largely ignored. The situation became critical when the Reichswehr, without any substantial opposition from the 50,000 to 60,000 militant Saxon proletarians counted on earlier in Moscow, moved into Dresden and deposed the socialist government of Saxony. The best Radek could do was to organize a one-day strike on October 30.[113] He was still trying to get the KPD to launch demonstrations—not uprisings—but he must have known that the cause was lost. Now it did not matter that he had never favored the German venture; what did matter was that he had been placed in charge of an insurrection in Germany and had failed. A scapegoat was needed for this new failure to generate a German revolution. Radek came back to Moscow at the end of 1923 to learn the bitter truth—that the strategy he had opposed was now to be used against him to end his influence in international Communism.

7. Radek and Trotsky:
The Revolutionary in Opposition

The year 1923 marked the high point of Radek's career. He was a leader of international Communism—one of the Comintern's most important spokesmen and tacticians, particularly with regard to German affairs. By the summer of the following year, however, he had lost his status in both the Bolshevik Party and the Comintern and had been relegated to the ranks of hack writers for the Soviet press. The ostensible cause of Radek's political downfall was his alleged responsibility for the ill-fated Communist venture in Germany in 1923.[1] The real reasons for the campaign against him, however, had little to do with his activities in Germany. Radek was, in fact, a victim of the power struggle developing within the Bolshevik Party.

Early in 1922 Lenin's health had begun to fail noticeably, and by the end of that year the leading aspirants for the leadership of the Bolshevik Party were maneuvering for position. Zinoviev openly considered himself the heir apparent. Trotsky, though not so crude in the expression of his hopes as Zinoviev, was equally ambitious. It was natural that Radek should throw his support behind Trotsky rather than Zinoviev, whom he despised. By Radek's standards, Trotsky was a true internationalist, both intellectually and politically.

It is doubtful that Trotsky regarded Radek as his peer. He was quick to detect Radek's weak points, especially the irresponsibility that had distressed Rosa Luxemburg and August Bebel in earlier years. Yet he was impressed by Radek's talents, devotion to the cause of internationalism, and boundless energy.[2] There were striking differences between the two men. Trotsky was obsessed with a feeling of noblesse oblige concerning world revolution. He cultivated a consistency of thought and action that Radek would have found incomprehensible; if a position or tactic proved untenable, Radek could easily shift to another. Moreover, there was a greatness about Trotsky that Radek did not possess. Trotsky's stern sense of revolutionary ethics made him a trusted leader, whereas Radek's opportunism and volatile nature aroused mistrust. Despite these differences, in the next few years Radek became one of Trotsky's ablest supporters.

On March 9, 1923, Lenin suffered the stroke that was to incapacitate him for the rest of his life. Five days later *Pravda* published a special edition commemorating the twenty-fifth anniversary of the founding of the Russian Social Democratic Labor Party, the parent organization of the Bolshevik Party. On page after page Zinoviev, Stalin, Bukharin, and other prominent Bolsheviks identified the success and development of the Bolshevik Party with the career of Lenin. There was, however, one discordant note, supplied by Radek. In the space allotted to him Radek published an article entitled "Leon Trotsky—the Organizer of Victory." Using the superlatives normally reserved for Lenin, Radek extravagantly praised Trotsky's military and organizational genius.[3] The article provoked immediate speculation, probably unfounded, that a Bonapartist coup by Trotsky was imminent.[4] Although Zinoviev seems to have been confident that Trotsky would not use his position as Commissar of War to seize power,[5] others were not so certain, and talk of Bonapartism was in the air in Moscow for several weeks.[6]

When the Twelfth Congress of the Russian Communist Party opened, the rumor campaign about Trotsky's "Bonapartism" was in full swing. The numerous public tributes to Trotsky that marked the beginning of the Congress added fuel to the fire. Early in the meetings, an altercation between Radek and Klimenty Voroshilov (a Stalin supporter, who as a military man may have felt particularly imperiled by Bonapartism) revealed how strained relations had become.

Voroshilov was in the chairman's seat, presiding over a session,

when Trotsky walked into the chamber, followed by Radek. Voroshilov certainly ought to have known better than to trade verbal
barbs with Radek, an acknowledged master of the art. Attempting
a pun on Trotsky's first name, Lev, the Russian word for lion, Voroshilov called out: "Well, here comes the lion—followed by his tail!"
Radek retaliated with a torrent of abuse, and ended: "In the final
analysis, I would much prefer to be the lion's tail than Stalin's
arse!"[7] This retort was, however, the only triumph Trotsky and
Radek were allowed at the Party Congress. In spite of the many
messages in favor of Trotsky sent to the meetings from worker
groups all over the country, the sessions were effectively controlled
by the recently formed triumvirate of Zinoviev, Kamenev, and
Stalin, whose mutual bond was their opposition to Trotsky.

Radek's duties in connection with the German situation prevented him from working directly with Trotsky for the next several months. Furthermore, he and Trotsky had their differences
concerning Germany: Trotsky was encouraging a far more zealous
course of action than Radek was ready to support.[8] When Radek
returned from Germany at the end of the year, however, he found
that his fate and Trotsky's were more closely connected than he had
realized.

In December 1923 Lenin still lived, though he had suffered repeated debilitating brain hemorrhages and was incapable of exer-
cising any control over the Party.[9] So long as Lenin was alive, Zinoviev was afraid to attempt a direct move against Trotsky; for the
time being, it made more sense to concentrate his attack on Radek.
If Zinoviev needed any prompting in his offensive against Radek,
he received it on December 13, 1923, when Radek delivered a
speech in which he declared that if the Russian Communist Party
were to turn against Trotsky, the majority of Polish and German
Communists would rally to his support.[10] When a letter from the
Central Committee of the Polish Communist Party seemed to con-
firm Radek's assertion, the threat of a pro-Trotsky movement
sweeping the parties of the Comintern seemed real.[11] Zinoviev decided to act quickly. On December 27, 1923, he and Stalin forced
through the Politburo a resolution condemning Radek's role in

Germany.[12] With the acceptance of this resolution, Radek was on his way down.

The next stage in Radek's downfall came at a meeting of the ECCI on January 11, 1924—a meeting apparently called for the purpose of destroying not only the pro-Radek leadership of the KPD but Radek himself. Radek attempted to justify the cancellation of the uprising in Germany and to defend himself against the charge that he had subverted the German revolution.[13] His efforts were to no avail, and Zinoviev was able to achieve passage of a resolution condemning "past mistakes" that clearly referred to Radek's alleged actions.[14] A few days later at the Thirteenth Party Conference, Zinoviev denounced Radek openly and derided his actions in Germany.[15]

Because of ill health Trotsky left Moscow about this time, and Radek was without support against Zinoviev's allegations. An unexpected ally came to his aid—Adolf Warszawski, who had originally initiated Radek into the Social Democratic Left and was now a representative of Polish Communism. Warszawski submitted a resolution to the Congress protesting the treatment being accorded Radek and praising him as one who had rendered extraordinary services to the Comintern.[16] Warszawski's avowal of faith, though probably much appreciated by Radek, was not enough to extricate him from his dilemma, and the pressure continued.

Lenin's death on January 21, 1924, gave Radek a breathing spell. Under the circumstances, an open continuation of party rivalries would not have been tactful. The members of the anti-Trotsky triumvirate, especially Stalin, took advantage of the occasion of Lenin's funeral to publicly assert their roles in the new leadership, but direct attacks on Trotsky and Radek were avoided.

Radek's troubles began again in earnest when the Thirteenth Congress of the Russian Communist Party convened in May 1924. Once more he was forced to defend his role in Germany in 1923; as before, he stoutly maintained that a full-scale uprising in 1923 would have been suicidal.[17] He was mildly heckled but allowed to present his case in some detail. Immediately upon completion of his speech, however, he was attacked by D. Z. Manuilsky, a Bolshe-

vik anxious to replace him on the ECCI and therefore eager to ingratiate himself with Zinoviev and Stalin. Then Bukharin rose and
took apart Radek's arguments item by item, to the accompaniment
of continual applause.[18] Bukharin's arguments were not substantially different from the ones Zinoviev had used several months before, but as the leader of an important faction in the Bolshevik
Party, Bukharin's opposition was symbolic of a substantial anti-
Radek alignment in the Party. The strength of this alignment was
soon demonstrated when a resolution was introduced following
Bukharin's speech. The resolution read in part:

The Thirteenth Congress is in full agreement with the work of the
representation of the RKP in the Executive Committee of the Comintern and in complete solidarity with the tactical line of the Executive
Committee of the Comintern. The Congress states that the Right devia-
tion [in Germany] defended by Comrade Radek, notwithstanding the
decision of the CC of the RKP [Central Committee of the Russian Communist Party], has *nothing in common* with the political line of the Russian Communist Party.[19]

The resolution was passed by a "unanimous" voice vote (Radek
abstaining). He apparently realized the futility of protesting the
measure when the cards were stacked against him. Radek's humiliation was complete when the Central Committee deprived him
of the membership he had held since 1918.[20] Trotsky was retained
on the Central Committee because it was too soon to move against
such a giant; for the present, the triumvirate was satisfied to punish
the more vulnerable Radek.

The Fifth Congress of the Comintern, held in June, differed in
many ways from its predecessors. The replacement of German by
Russian as the official language of the Comintern marked a significant change in leadership. Prior to 1924, most speeches at Comintern meetings were given in German, and what few were not were
translated into German; the official protocols of the meetings also
were printed in German. The choice of German as an official language was a logical one. Thanks to the former hegemony of the
Habsburgs and the Hohenzollerns, German had been the common
language of all educated persons in Central Europe. Among the

leading Bolsheviks, both Trotsky and Lenin knew German reasonably well, and Radek had spoken it since childhood. The Fifth Congress, however, marked the first major appearance of Stalin, who spoke no German. Zinoviev, at that time Stalin's ally, could speak German—as he had more than adequately demonstrated at the USPD Congress at Halle in 1921—but since he was unsure of himself in the language, he normally delivered his speeches in Russian and had an interpreter—sometimes Radek—render the German version.[21] The change in language, insignificant as it may have seemed at the time, actually reflected the change that was taking place in the Comintern leadership: Lenin was dead, Zinoviev and Stalin were in ascendance, and Trotsky and Radek were on their way out.

In his opening speech, Zinoviev once again confronted Radek with his "mistakes" in Germany in 1923.[22] His attack was followed by an even stronger denunciation from Ruth Fischer, who was maneuvering for a stronger position in the KPD and probably getting some revenge for the criticism Radek had heaped on her at the last Comintern Congress in 1922.[23] Radek defended himself, maintaining that the united front policy as he had espoused it had been completely consistent with Comintern policy and with Lenin's directives, and accusing Zinoviev of clever analysis after the fact. Radek's defense was well reasoned and devoid of the usual insulting references. He was, however, addressing an audience handpicked by Zinoviev. At the end of Radek's speech, the stenographic notation "applause in part of the hall," indicated which way things were going.[24] Zinoviev, taking the rostrum again, had the final word; he once more denounced Radek for the events of 1923, then described various instances over the years when he and Radek had differed on questions of Comintern strategy.[25] When the Congress closed, Radek's name was pointedly omitted from the new roster of the ECCI.[26] One more gratuitous insult was to come several months later when the ECCI, probably at the behest of Ruth Fischer, specifically forbade Radek to meddle in KPD affairs.[27]

Radek was stunned by his defeat and by Trotsky's inability to do anything to forestall it. He was still an admirer and supporter of

Trotsky, but this did not seem to be a very rewarding role. Expelled from the ECCI, Radek lost all power in the Communist International and became a political pariah once again.

In this difficult time, Radek was fortunate to have beside him a trusted and beloved companion, Larissa Reissner. That Radek should have taken a new mistress was not surprising; he had long been known as something of a rake. He had engaged in several brief liaisons and one longer affair in Switzerland during the war, but in recent years had lived respectably enough in his Moscow apartment with his wife and child, a daughter born while he was in prison in 1919.[28] Rosa Radek surely knew of her husband's reputation, but she either ignored or condoned his activities. Hitherto, his amorous adventures had involved no lasting commitment; with Larissa it was different.

Larissa had been married for some years to the Bolshevik diplomat Fyodor Raskolnikov, Soviet ambassador to Afghanistan. Returning to Moscow in 1923 after two years in Kabul, she became interested in the progress of the revolution in Germany. In September 1923 she asked Radek's help in getting to Germany under the auspices of the Comintern.[29] Somehow what started as a purely political association became a personal involvement; Larissa and Radek became lovers, and they remained so until her death three years later. The affair was well known and apparently bothered no one—except perhaps Comrade Raskolnikov and Rosa Radek.

We know little about Rosa Radek; most Westerners who knew her have described her as a capable and pleasant person, but apparently were not strongly impressed by her.[30] Larissa Reissner, on the other hand, was extraordinarily attractive; indeed, a quick comparison of pictures of her and of Radek gives the impression of a match between Quasimodo and Esmeralda. Moreover, she was a dynamic and intelligent woman, well known as a writer and political activist.[31] It is reasonably certain that it was Larissa who restrained Radek for over two years from throwing away what was left of his career by openly supporting Trotsky. Without doubt, her love helped him to face the humiliation of his fall from prominence.

For several months after his defeat by Zinoviev, Radek restricted his activities to journalism. His articles were as perceptive and well-written as ever, but he so carefully avoided controversial subjects that some Western observers were led to believe that his career as a Bolshevik tactician and leader had come to an end.[32] In fact, Radek was lying low to avoid political annihilation while he decided how to conduct himself in the power struggle. Although he still sympathized with Trotsky, he had taken a terrible beating in Trotsky's name. Consequently in January 1925, when Trotsky suffered a major defeat and was forced to relinquish his post as Commissar of War, Radek refrained from becoming directly involved in Trotsky's defense.

In the articles he wrote during the summer of 1924, Radek was reasonably faithful to the official Bolshevik position on international affairs, perhaps hoping to be taken back into the good graces of the Party leadership. Much of his attention was devoted to what the Bolsheviks were then describing as a temporary stabilization of capitalism in the West and the meaning of this stabilization for the prospects of world revolution. In analyzing this phenomenon, Radek turned first to the claims of certain Social Democrats in Western Europe that an era of pacifism had set in. Radek attributed the illusion, as he called it, of democratic pacifism to Social Democratic electoral triumphs in Europe. In Great Britain, Labour was for the first time forming a government, while in France a bloc of "left" parties had come to power. Nevertheless, Radek warned, democratic pacifism was no more than a reformist illusion. He dismissed it with the terse comment, "For us Marxists, there is no doubt that the democratic pacifist era cannot begin without the world revolution—that the currently ruling classes cannot achieve international democracy or peace."[33]

Following the official line established in the tactics of the Comintern in July 1924, Radek presented an "obedient" analysis of the function of this "stabilization" in the panorama of world Communism:

This era, or to be more exact, this zigzag, has a decided historical function. This function is the shattering of the last illusions which are now the basic strength of capitalism. The huge worker masses in Europe, even in Germany, are convinced that a better day is dawning, that the Conference [of 1924] means a lightening of their burden, if not [the establishment of] socialism. . . . But if this historical zigzag ends in bankruptcy, this will prove the failure of the petty bourgeois effort. And if, at the end of this zigzag, the masses take the offensive on an international scale, . . . the bourgeoisie will not be dealing with the proletariat of 1923 but with a proletariat that has experienced this period [of democratic pacifism].[34]

Radek was not abandoning Trotsky, but he was certainly flirting with the prospects of political rehabilitation and perhaps of a general realignment in the Bolshevik Party. In 1925 the Zinoviev-Kamenev-Stalin triumvirate began to crack, as Stalin maneuvered to shed his two erstwhile colleagues and chart his own course of action. Radek apparently entertained the politically unrealistic hope of coming to terms with Stalin—perhaps even reconciling Trotsky and Stalin—and then wreaking vengeance on Zinoviev.[35] He had no overwhelming animosity toward Stalin at the time; Zinoviev was still the enemy.

Radek's circumspect behavior after the Comintern Congress of 1924 was finally rewarded. In the summer of 1925, he was appointed provost of Sun Yat-sen University, a school recently founded in Moscow for the training and education of selected Chinese youths. This academic post was scarcely comparable to his former position as Secretary of the ECCI, but it did present a challenge. Furthermore, Radek was allowed to appoint Larissa Reissner as lecturer in Russian literature.[36] The only unpleasant feature of the new situation was that Pavel Mif, one of Stalin's supporters, was appointed associate provost, presumably so that he could keep an eye on Radek.

There surely could have been no better time for Radek to have held such a position than in 1925. For several years China had been pregnant with revolutionary possibilities. National resentment at the privileged position of foreigners in China had manifested itself in demonstrations, strikes, and boycotts, but at first there did not appear to be any force capable of unifying the people and rallying them to struggle for national liberation and unification. Civil war and chaos were rife, and several factions aspired to power.

Of the various warring groups in China, the Kuomintang, headed by Sun Yat-sen, impressed Moscow as possessing the greatest revolutionary potential. Enthusiastic reports by Comintern representatives who had spoken with Sun had convinced the Bolsheviks that the Kuomintang was well disposed toward the Soviet Union and followed a political program that could be reconciled with Comintern aims. Sun Yat-sen proved to be a hard bargainer, but eventually an agreement was reached in the summer of 1923 and the Chinese Communist Party was instructed to join the Kuomintang in the struggle for national unification and liberation. Since it seemed that both sides would derive genuine benefits from the alliance, few Bolsheviks objected.[37] When a new wave of xenophobia swept China in May 1925, the alliance seemed to be a well-planned stroke on the part of Soviet strategists. Sun himself had died in the winter of 1924, but his successor, Chiang Kai-shek, seemed likely to carry on the cooperative arrangement.[38] One condition called for the training of selected students, presumably the future cadre of the Kuomintang, at the Sun Yat-sen University in Moscow. As provost there, Radek was uniquely well placed to gather advance information on revolutionary activities in China.

Although the position of provost of the university was important, it offered Radek little opportunity for political action. Nevertheless, he was genuinely interested in his new duties and enthusiastically described his school as the Soviet counterpart of the missionary schools in China.[39] Within a short time he developed a fairly extensive grasp of Chinese affairs and began to comment openly on the strategy of the Chinese Revolution and what the Comintern's tactics should be with regard to it.

When Radek assumed his duties at Sun Yat-sen University in the summer of 1925, he found that the job committed him, at that time, to support the de facto alliance between the Comintern and the Kuomintang. In 1925 this was not a difficult position for a Bolshevik, regardless of his sentiments about internal party struggles, and Radek did not seem to have any quarrel with the arrangements. The association with the Kuomintang was quite in keeping with his own ideas on revolutionary strategy. Only a few years earlier,

Radek had been willing to accept the German extreme Right as an ally in the struggle against foreign imperialism. He found the Kuomintang of 1925 as palatable as the German "fascists" of 1923; moreover his admiration for the late Sun Yat-sen lent itself to a rationalization of the present alliance. In his articles in *Pravda*, Radek admitted that Sun was of a petty bourgeois background and had received most of his original backing from bourgeois sources, but he maintained that Sun had never lost his overwhelming concern for the masses and that this concern had been instrumental in convincing Sun that only in alliance with the international proletariat would the Chinese people find their salvation.[40]

What Radek particularly liked about the alliance with the Kuomintang was that it would prevent the small, weak Chinese Communist Party from wasting itself on putschism as the German party had done. The Chinese proletariat, he noted, constituted at best a minute fraction of the Chinese people, who were as yet relatively undeveloped in matters of class consciousness.[41] At the Fourth Comintern Congress in 1922, Radek had sternly warned the overzealous Chinese Communist Party that in the embryonic stage of a party's development, "socialism is not the order of the day.[42] Three years later, he readily admitted that events in China had progressed much more rapidly than had been expected—but he still remained unconvinced that China was ready for proletarian revolution. In fact, he feared that the growing animosity to foreigners in China increased the danger of putschism, since the Chinese Communists might be tempted by events to push their luck too far. Thus, shortly after assuming his post at Sun Yat-sen University, he wrote: "At the present, and in the near future, the Chinese proletariat will not be capable of independently seizing power. Should it, however, in the course of the revolutionary struggles of the forthcoming period, be faced with this necessity, together with the petty bourgeoisie it will be forced *for the time being* to develop the economic power of the land in a capitalist fashion [Radek's italics]."[43]

Radek saw the alliance with the Kuomintang as both a valuable influence on the Chinese Communists and a necessary and proper tactic for achieving the national liberation of China. That the

Kuomintang might also serve to develop the base of a proletarian revolution in China appeared to be a purely academic question to Radek in 1925. More to the point was the potential of the Kuomintang to construct a sort of united front in China by appealing to the petty bourgeois of the cities, who resented foreign control of Chinese commerce.[44] Furthermore, the Kuomintang was immensely popular with the Chinese peasants, and had even achieved among them the reputation of a revolutionary army despite the tendency of most Chinese peasants to regard all native armies as bandit hordes.[45] He viewed the development of the Chinese Communist Party with something less than satisfaction. In 1922 he had advised the Chinese Communists to get out of the Confucian study rooms and go to the masses;[46] now he found the Chinese party still more engrossed in abstract questions than in practical solutions to the problems at hand.[47] This was a serious shortcoming for a revolutionary party, and Radek used it as one more excuse for entering into a coalition with the multiclass Kuomintang.

The relative peace and security Radek enjoyed during the winter of 1925–26 was a welcome change from the harassment he had suffered after the German fiasco of 1923. Since Trotsky had not seen fit to challenge the triumvirate after his deposition as Commissar of War, Radek had been spared further attacks by the Bolshevik leadership. He was not invited to rejoin the Central Committee, but on the other hand he was no longer a target.[48] He continued to find life at the Sun Yat-sen University pleasant and challenging. Together with Larissa he was involved in the training of some six hundred Chinese students who would ultimately exercise tremendous influence in Chinese Communism.[49] Perhaps Radek hoped that the Chinese revolution would give him the opportunity to win back the prestige he had lost in Germany.

In the spring of 1926, events in China and in Moscow threatened the end of this calm interval in Radek's life. A change in Kuomintang-Comintern relations was brewing, though neither Trotsky, Radek, nor most other Bolsheviks realized it. The first major crisis occurred on March 20, 1926, when Chiang Kai-shek shocked the Bolsheviks by suddenly purging all Communists from major

posts in the Kuomintang. The resulting breach with the Comintern
was hastily closed, largely on terms dictated by Chiang.[50] Radek
was probably well aware of what had taken place, but in an article
published a week later, he made no mention of either Chiang or the
coup, and once again implied that he supported the Kuomintang.[51]
A year later, Radek attempted to explain his attitude during this
period by noting that Chiang had cleverly concealed the true nature of his coup by simultaneously acting against Communists and
rightist elements.[52] Whether Radek really had been deceived by
Chiang's ploy is a moot point; at any rate, he did not speak out
against the Kuomintang. One American correspondent who knew
Radek claims that Radek gave up on the Kuomintang at this time,
but there is no evidence to support this assertion;[53] on the contrary,
it would seem that Radek continued to support the Kuomintang
until 1927.

In the spring of 1926 there was an open renewal of party strife
in Russia, but not along the lines that Radek might have predicted.
The triumvirate had finally broken down completely at the end of
1925. Zinoviev had for some time been less and less inclined to go
along with Stalin's cautious plans, and throughout 1925 had been
making preparations to treat Stalin in the way he had treated Trotsky. At the Fourteenth Party Congress in December 1925, however,
Stalin decisively defeated Zinoviev's ambitions, and when the Congress ended, it was Stalin who spoke for the Bolshevik Party and
Zinoviev who had been forced to gather a new opposition.[54]

Radek's initial reaction to the news of Zinoviev's predicament
must have been one of *Schadenfreude*, but he managed to keep his
feelings to himself. There was no sense in risking his post at Sun
Yat-sen University just to satisfy his urge to triumph over Zinoviev.
Moreover, although he may well have rejoiced at Zinoviev's defeat,
he could not view with equanimity the virtual endorsement by the
Congress of Stalin's policy of socialism in one country. Stalin had
actually stated his theory in 1924, but only now had it emerged as
official policy. The theory itself was quite simple: since world revolution did not appear to be imminent, particularly in a period of
capitalist stabilization, it behooved the Soviet Union to proceed

with its own attempt to build a socialist society. Trotsky, Zinoviev, and others interpreted this new theory as an abandonment of world revolution in order to satisfy the national self-interest of the Soviet Union. Stalin, however, maintained that rather than doing violence to the cause of world revolution, as his opponents claimed, he had merely changed the priorities.

Their shared opposition to the theory of socialism in one country did, however, provide Trotsky and Zinoviev with a common bond. Kamenev, whose opposition to Trotsky had been less violent than Zinoviev's, undertook the task of bringing the two men together. Radek was far from enthusiastic about cooperation with Zinoviev under any circumstances. Socialism in one country notwithstanding, he urged Trotsky to seek a rapprochement with Stalin rather than with Zinoviev.[55] Trotsky also had his doubts, but nevertheless in April 1926 the United Opposition emerged. Radek could no longer remain in the background; everyone in the Bolshevik Party was choosing sides. It galled him to be aligned with Zinoviev, but the overriding consideration was that Trotsky still represented international revolution, whereas Stalin did not. At first Radek was reluctant to reveal his role in the new opposition—perhaps he still did not want to be closely identified with Zinoviev—but within a few months, he threw himself into the activities of the United Opposition with a zeal reminiscent of his early days in the Comintern.

Radek's way of assisting the United Opposition was to keep his ear to the ground at Sun Yat-sen University. Since he had no other means of influencing the Bolshevik Party, it was inevitable that he would attempt to bring Chinese policy into the Party disputes. He was careful, however, not to challenge the Stalinist leadership too boldly, for he had no desire to lose his position as provost. By the summer of 1926, Radek had accumulated certain information, perhaps from his students, which indicated that Kuomintang policies were taking a turn to the right, and that the Comintern's position in the coalition was deteriorating. After consulting with Trotsky and Zinoviev, Radek sent a letter to the Politburo expressing concern over events in China and requesting a clarification of various points of policy.[56] Receiving no reply, he sent another letter in September, stating that an answer was imperative if he were to present the correct conclusions in his lectures at Sun Yat-sen University.[57] Again silence was the Politburo's answer, and Radek suspected that his worst fears about the Chinese situation were correct; still, he hesitated to seize upon this issue to challenge Stalin.

In September 1926, Larissa Reissner became ill, and within a short time it was established that her illness, probably cancer, was terminal. Radek's situation at the University with Larissa had meant so much to him that heretofore he had restrained himself politically in order to safeguard it; now he threw caution to the winds and plunged back into the political struggle.

Radek's first target was the Stalinist doctrine of socialism in one country, which he regarded as a betrayal of world revolution in favor of the interests of the Soviet Union. On September 27, 1926, a debate took place at the Communist Academy in Moscow and Radek appeared, ready to do battle with Stalin's supporters. In the spirited discussion that day, Radek displayed his old vigor and command of the art of political debate. When hecklers shouted that the idea of socialism in one country was derived from Lenin's ideas, Radek had a ready comeback, claiming that the theory should be attributed not to Lenin but to the nineteenth-century writer Saltykov-Shchedrin. In Saltykov-Shchedrin's novel *Pompadours*, the protagonist decides to establish a liberal regime in his *uezd* (district) of Tsarist Russia; naturally, the Tsarist government learns of this liberal uezd and smashes it. Radek claimed that just as liberalism in one uezd had been impossible in Tsarist Russia, so socialism in one country was impossible in the midst of a hostile capitalist world. Only when capitalism had been destroyed could the building of a socialist society proceed.[58]

Radek's remarks were much resented by Stalin, who considered an attack on his theory an attack on himself. The debate at the Communist Academy eliminated the possibility, remote as it had been, of a reconciliation between the two men. In a speech a few weeks later, Stalin openly attacked Radek for the first time and denounced his speech at the Communist Academy as "un-Leninist."[59] This marked Radek as a member of the United Opposition. One immediate result was that his articles virtually disappeared from *Pravda, Izvestiia,* and other official party journals.

Deprived of public outlets for his opinions, Radek turned back to his duties at Sun Yat-sen University. He also began work on an exposition of his own views on the historical development of the Chinese Revolution.[60] In November Larissa Reissner died at the age of thirty-one, and any lingering inhibitions Radek had about taking risks with his position in the Party or at the University died with her.

Throughout the fall of 1926, Radek had been receiving persistent reports through his students that a troubled situation existed in China.[61] Unable to elicit any news from the Comintern or from the Politburo, Radek decided to seek his own sources of information. Acting in his capacity as provost of the University, he sent Sergei Dalin as his representative to China to make on-the-spot observations. When the Central Committee of the Communist Party found out about this action, Radek was rebuked, but inasmuch as Dalin was already on his way, nothing could be done.[62]

At the beginning of 1927 Dalin returned from China and gave Radek his report on the sorry plight of the Chinese Communist Party. He recounted at length the persecution of Communists, the dissolution of peasant and worker organizations, and the general rightist trend of Kuomintang policy. Radek was alarmed at what he heard. When he compared notes with Dalin, he was further shocked to discover that Dalin's letters to him from China had been intercepted and in at least one case confiscated.[63]

Party discipline prevented Radek from openly attacking the Comintern policy on China, but he felt that something must be done to save the Comintern's commitment there. In an article written in February 1927 he expressed his dissatisfaction with the trend to the right in China, gently rebuking the Kuomintang for not proceeding with social reforms in the areas under its control and warning that it would be remiss if it did not embark at once on a radical program to root out social evils. He pointedly reminded the Kuomintang of the role played by Communist agitation in Chiang's victorious Northern Campaign of that year and of the dependence

of the Kuomintang on good relations with the peasants and workers and with the Chinese Communists as well.[64]

Radek had hoped that Dalin's reports would provoke the Comintern to a serious reexamination of its China policy, but he was dismayed to learn that Dalin was unable to publish his findings in the
Stalin-controlled press and had to resort to innuendoes and oblique
references in feuilletons. Further investigation revealed that Dalin
was not the only observer having censorship problems. It now
seemed to Radek that the Comintern was out to preserve its ties
with the Kuomintang at any price.[65]

Dalin's experience convinced Radek that the United Opposition
should make China a central issue in its struggle with the Stalinist
leadership. He wrote to Trotsky of his grave concern over the
events in China and set forth some new radical slogans he believed
should be adopted by the Chinese Communist Party. Radek also
noted, however, that the triumphal Northern Campaign of the
Kuomintang had captured the imagination of the Chinese masses
who were as yet unaware of and would be slow to accept the
Kuomintang's dangerous shift to the right.[66] In his reply, Trotsky
expressed anxiety over the situation in China but disputed Radek's
contentions that the Chinese masses would react slowly to the
Kuomintang's "reactionary" policies.[67]

Finally Radek decided, apparently on his own, that salvaging the
Chinese Revolution took precedence over observing party discipline, and that in any case the Chinese situation presented the Opposition with too formidable an issue to be ignored. On March 18
he appeared at a debate at the Communist Academy with the
avowed purpose of criticizing Stalin for his lack of policy in China.
At the Academy he found a formidable array of Comintern special-
ists and representatives of the security police (GPU), ready to debate with him.[68] In the course of his argument Radek proposed a
new line in China—a line that completely reversed his earlier policy of caution and cooperation. Still maintaining that the Chinese
Communists should not take power by themselves, he now proposed that they join with the Left Kuomintang in wresting control
of that organization from Chiang Kai-shek and the Right.[69] Under

the circumstances of growing Stalinist control of all Soviet publications, the debate was never published, but news of it spread by word of mouth and provoked violent reactions from all sides. Radek continued to attack Stalin's blind cooperation with the Kuomintang and boldly predicted that Chiang Kai-shek would, at the first opportunity, turn on the Chinese Communists and betray the Chinese Revolution.[70] Stalin, for his part, dismissed Radek's fears with the boast that the Comintern would use Chiang as one uses a lemon—squeeze out the juice and throw away the rind.[71] On this point at least Radek was better informed than Stalin: Dalin's report, together with information gleaned from his students, had convinced him that Chiang could neither be used nor be trusted by the Comintern.

On April 12, 1927, Chiang destroyed Stalin's illusions by marching into Shanghai and slaughtering thousands of Communists and suspected Communists. In essence, this was what Radek had predicted, but rather than being praised for his insight, he was attacked more viciously than ever. Unable to defend himself in the Soviet press, he prepared a detailed analysis of his views and circulated it privately among the members of the Opposition.[72] Taking a long hard look at the situation in China, Radek came to the conclusion that the basic flaw in Comintern strategy was a misunderstanding of the nature of the Chinese Revolution and the class contradictions in China. He accused the Comintern leadership of treating the events in China as part of a bourgeois-democratic revolution bent on destroying the feudal structure of China while simultaneously delivering the land from foreign imperialism—essentially the same view he himself had held a year before. Now he conceded that significant feudal remnants did exist in China, but denied that feudalism was the predominant form of society in the country.[73]

Radek found the Comintern's attitude distressingly familiar; it seemed to echo the views the Mensheviks had held on Russia a decade earlier. The more he drew comparisons, the stronger the similarity appeared to him. How had the Bolsheviks allowed themselves to be maneuvered into adopting what was essentially a Menshevik position on such a crucial issue? To find the answer to this question, Radek turned away from theoretical considerations and explored the backgrounds of the men responsible for determining the Comintern's policy in China. He noted that Martynov and Rafes, the Comintern "experts" on China, were both onetime members of the Menshevik Party. Radek drew the conclusion that they had never ceased to be Mensheviks at heart, and that they had become Bolsheviks in order to impose Menshevik policies on the Comintern.[74] As if to support Radek's contention, Feodor Dan, a leading Menshevik émigré, wrote an article complimenting Martynov for analyzing the Chinese situation in a "Menshevik manner" and for rebutting Radek's "leftist" arguments.[75]

It was much more difficult for Radek to affix Menshevik labels to the two top leaders, Stalin and Bukharin, and in the case of Stalin, he did not even try. Bukharin, however, was a special case. In October 1926, Bukharin had replaced Zinoviev as president of the ECCI and hence, in Radek's eyes, bore much of the responsibility for the catastrophe in China. Radek had been made the scapegoat for the German failure in 1923; now he sought to blame Bukharin for the Comintern's China debacle. He accused Bukharin of losing his nerve in the face of the rising tide of worker and peasant agitation in China and, worse yet, of falling under the influence of Martynov, whom Radek dubbed the "John the Baptist of Menshevism." Radek went on to point out apparent contradictions in Bukharin's recent polemics as evidence of his ideological confusion. When Bukharin put forth a new concept of the struggle in China as a fight against feudalism rather than capitalism, Radek claimed that he was attempting to shrink from the real struggle, the struggle against imperialist-supported capitalism.[76]

Radek further accused Bukharin of deliberately ignoring the danger signs that had heralded Chiang's action in China—his hostile acts toward the Left and toward peasant and worker organizations should have warned the Comintern that the Kuomintang was not what is professed to be. History, Radek said, proves that in the moment of crisis, the bourgeoisie will abandon the revolution and go over to the side of reaction; history does not, however, require that the masses be caught off guard by this perfidy. The Chinese Communists had warned the Comintern of these dangers, but Bukharin chose to ignore them. Radek attempted to excuse his own earlier defense of the alliance with the Kuomintang with the weak plea that he had been misinformed and misled by the reports of the Comintern's Far Eastern Bureau.[77]

What could be done to save the Chinese Revolution? Despite the crushing blow dealt it by Chiang in the April 12 coup, Radek did not believe that final defeat was inevitable. In his controversial speech at the Communist Academy in March 1926, he had held that the best prospects for revolutionary action lay with the radical government of Hankow, then under the control of the Left Kuomintang.[78] It was not too late for the Comintern to support this government in its struggle against the Right Kuomintang and to encourage Hankow in revolutionary actions, particularly the formation of soviets.[79]

In advocating the establishment of soviets, Radek was proceeding in direct contradiction to Comintern policy, and he knew it. Nevertheless he continued to maintain that the establishment of soviets could save the Chinese Revolution. Still nagged by fears of putschism, he insisted that the Chinese Communists form these soviets in collaboration with the Left Kuomintang, which could command a broader base of power. As for Stalin's contention that the Chinese would regard this move as "Moscow sovietization," Radek maintained that Stalin was merely quibbling over the word soviet: what was really important was that soviets would be able to seize power on the local level from reactionary forces. Until local control had been achieved, argued Radek, it would be impossible for the Hankow government to act as a revolutionary regime.[80]

There was one point in this lengthy exposition where Radek deviated from the line being advocated by Trotsky. Since March 1927 (and according to his own claims, well before 1927), Trotsky had been pressing for a complete break with the Kuomintang. In his letter of March 4, 1927, he had expressed the fear that further cooperation with the Kuomintang would lead to a "Menshevization" of the Chinese Communist Party.[81] Radek, however, categorically denied that he himself had ever wanted the Chinese Communists to withdraw entirely from the Kuomintang. He accused Stalin of perverting his views on the subject, and went so far as to state (incorrectly) that Trotsky too was innocent of requesting such a withdrawal. Radek reiterated his demand that the Kuomintang be forced to adopt a radical program of social reform, that worker and peasant organizations be fostered and encouraged, and that even the Left Kuomintang be severely censured if it failed to cooperate. Radek ended his treatise with a bitter reference to the coup of April 12 and a restatement of his contention that the Chinese Revolution was not only a national liberation struggle but also a class struggle of peasants and workers against their exploiters.[82]

Stalin could not let this challenge go unanswered. On May 13 he appeared at a meeting of students of the Sun Yat-sen University and criticized Radek's policies at length. He accused him of failing to comprehend the peculiar nature of China's agrarian society, which allowed for feudal domination despite the existence of merchant capital: therein lay the source of Radek's mistaken analysis of the Chinese Revolution. This fundamental misreading of the nature of the anti-imperialist fight, Stalin charged, was the basis for Radek's other erroneous conclusions. Stalin once again repeated his belief that the time had not yet come to establish soviets in China, and that such a program would hinder Communist support of the Hankow government.[83]

In June 1927 a new turn of events in China brought forth a renewed attack from the United Opposition. A telegram from Moscow to the Hankow cell of the Chinese Communist Party fell into the hands of the Left Kuomintang regime. The contents of the telegram, which called for the mobilization of a Communist army, indicated how out of touch Moscow was with the realities of the situation in China. Nevertheless, the Left Kuomintang took alarm and prepared to defend itself against the Chinese Communists.[84]

The Opposition, meanwhile, had resolved its internal differences on the China problem. Radek opposed Trotsky's attempt to apply the theory of permanent revolution to China; whatever the case had been in Russia in 1917, China in 1927 was not ready for a conspiratorial coup at the national level.[85] Zinoviev bridged the gap with a new thesis on the Chinese Revolution, and in the interests of presenting a united stand by the Opposition, both Radek and Trotsky subscribed to it. This new thesis called upon the Chinese Communist Party to leave the Kuomintang at once, adopt an independent revolutionary line, and immediately begin the establishment of soviets. In addition, the Comintern was urged to end the special status of the Kuomintang as a "sympathizing member."[86]

Sometime in May, Radek was replaced by Pavel Mif as provost of Sun Yat-sen University. There is little doubt that his increasingly radical line on the Chinese situation made his continuation at the university intolerable to Stalin. Now that he no longer had access to special sources of information on China, he was of diminished value to the Opposition. In fact, without his post at the university, without access to the press outlets, and without any special status in the Bolshevik Party, he had become an oppositionist without an outlet for his views.*

In this unenviable position, Radek turned during the summer of 1927 to writing long theoretical arguments on the situation in the Soviet Union, which he typed on onionskin paper and circulated privately among members of the Opposition. In these memoranda Radek discussed Trotsky's prediction of a "Soviet Thermidor." The allusion was of course to the reaction that followed the death of Robespierre in the month of Thermidor during the French Revolution. The historical implications of the term were such that any hint by the Opposition of a Thermidorean reaction elicited a violent outburst from the Party leadership; on one occasion, Bukharin referred to the charge as "unforgivable";[87] on another, the Central Committee of the Bolshevik Party took Trotsky and Zinoviev to task for their use of the term and forced them both to accept a reprimand on the subject.[88] In his private memoranda, Radek was far from circumspect in expressing his views on the subject:

---

* Unlike Radek, Trotsky and Zinoviev were still members of the Party's Central Committee and thus were in a position to present their views to the higher echelons of the Party.

Whoever weakens the international character of our revolution, that
person [Stalin] is also inducing a Thermidorean reaction. The USSR has
been able to develop, thanks to the international crisis of capitalism
caused by imperialism and the imperialist war. We can continue to build
socialism only if there is a proletarian revolution in the West. Until then,
our primary goal is to strive to protect the dictatorship of the proletariat.

After continuing to describe possible manifestations of a Thermidorean reaction in Russia, he cited the obligation of the Opposition
to lead the masses (presumably against the Stalinist leadership),
thereby saving "the international character of our revolution."[89]

In another memorandum, Radek went still further in prescribing
the means for the Opposition's struggle: he openly urged dramatic
action to break down Stalin's undemocratic methods of retaining
control of the Bolshevik Party. In a thinly veiled threat, he warned
that if the Party wished to avoid a complete split, it should start be-
having as a "Leninist party," that is, it should respect the rights of
the Opposition, allow the Opposition to present its program, and
remain true to the goal of world revolution.[90] Radek was playing
with fire, especially since Trotsky had gone to some pains to declare the loyalty of the Opposition to the Soviet Union and to the
Bolshevik Party (although not to Stalin).[91] In pointing out that
Lenin had created the Bolshevik Party by splitting Russian Social
Democracy into two parties, Radek clearly implied that he would
not shrink from the formation of a second party. Naturally enough,
Trotsky refused to accept Radek's dangerous proposal.

The final show of force for the Opposition came on November 7,
1927, the tenth anniversary of the Bolshevik Revolution. Denied access to the press, the members of the Opposition decided to make
public appearances on this day and try to reach the working masses,
whom they were certain sympathized with their aims. Radek accompanied Zinoviev to Leningrad, until recently a city whose party
apparatus Zinoviev had controlled, but was never given a chance to
address the workers. The Leningrad police, under the guise of offering protection, kept the two men under virtual house arrest.
Opposition leaders in other cities received similar treatment, and
the November 7 demonstrations failed to materialize. The Opposi-

tion had in effect collapsed; all that remained was for the Party Congress to seal the victory Stalin had won.

Radek knew that he had lost completely. Victor Serge, the French writer and revolutionary, tells in his memoirs of visiting Radek in his Kremlin suite on November 21, 1927, and watching him destroy his papers and other effects preparatory to moving out of his offices. In a frustrated moment Radek blurted out: "We've been absolute idiots! We haven't a halfpenny, when we could have kept back some pretty spoils of war for ourselves! Today we are being killed off through lack of money. We, with our celebrated revolutionary honesty, we've just been overscrupulous sods of intellectuals."[92]

At the Bolshevik Party Congress in December, Stalin accomplished the formal humiliation of the vanquished. He had already forced the removal of Zinoviev and Trotsky from the Central Committee of the Party, thus denying the Opposition its one chance of presenting its views. Supported by Bukharin and the "Right," Stalin had no trouble inducing the Congress to expel the Opposition. Trotsky suffered an additional setback when Zinoviev deserted him and announced through Kamenev that he accepted the decisions of the Congress as correct. Radek, speaking as a follower of Trotsky, refused to capitulate, saying that although he accepted the authority of the Communist Party, he could not accept decisions that he believed to be incorrect. Together with Nikolai Muralov and Christian Rakovsky, he submitted a statement reaffirming the right and duty of the Opposition to hold to its views in spite of the decisions of the Congress.[93] It took courage to stick with Trotsky at this time, but the decision may have been made easier for Radek by Zinoviev's defection.

After the Party Congress, exile was inevitable for the intransigent members of the Opposition. Radek and Rakovsky attempted to negotiate on behalf of the Opposition, but their efforts came to nothing, and in January 1928 Stalin ordered the expelled members of the Opposition to exile in various parts of Soviet Asia.[94]

Trotsky was to have been sent to the Caspian seaport of Astrakhan, but Radek and others protested that the semitropical climate of that city would be ruinous to his health.[95] Unfortunately for

Trotsky, Stalin responded by sending him to the much more isolated city of Alma-Ata in Central Asia. Radek himself fared better;
he was sent to the West Siberian town of Tobolsk, from which he
was able to maintain some communication with the outside world.
In a letter to Trotsky written shortly after his arrival in Tobolsk,
Radek noted that he was given access to newspapers and books.[96]
After a few months, Radek was moved eastward to the Siberian city
of Tomsk, but this involved no additional hardship. Tomsk was a
city of over 100,000 on a spur of the Trans-Siberian Railroad; it
had a well-established university and offered as much opportunity
for cultural activity as could be found in central Siberia. The
weather was less than ideal, but at least the area was not so isolated
from the rest of the Soviet Union as Trotsky's place of exile.[97]

In Siberia, Radek spent much of his time corresponding with his
fellow exiles, especially Trotsky, and began work on a biography
of Lenin. The proposed scope of the book on Lenin indicated that
Radek expected to be in Siberia for some time. In a letter to Eugene
Preobrazhensky, in exile in Uralsk, Radek noted that the first volume, which was to cover Lenin's activities prior to World War I,
would take about a year to write.[98]

During the first months of his exile, Radek seemed to be as intransigent as ever. When Stalin changed his economic policies early
in 1928, initiating a "Left" approach in a crackdown on the *kulaks*
(wealthy peasants) as a prelude to massive industrialization, Radek
was far less impressed than some of the others, notably Piatakov, who used this new "Left" approach as a rationalization for
abandoning the Opposition and reconciling himself to Stalin's leadership. Radek rebuked the defectors and used the opportunity to
throw a few more verbal bricks at Zinoviev. A Zinoviev, he wrote,
might use this rationalization to improve his situation, but a true
member of the Opposition would never stoop to do so.[99] Economic
issues had never involved Radek to any great extent; for the time
being, he was willing to vegetate in Siberia rather than reconcile
with Stalin on this pretext.

Sometime during the summer of 1928, however, Radek's resolve
perceptibly weakened. It is doubtful that Radek was impressed by

Stalin's continued leftward drive in economic policies, but he began to ponder whether his support of Trotsky was worth the price of indefinite exile in Siberia. The cosmopolitan Radek could not bear the thought of remaining the rest of his life in a town thousands of miles from the mainstream of European (or even Russian) life. For Radek, devotion to principle had its limitations. Little by little, he began to back away from his total commitment to Trotsky. The first sign of this inner change came in July 1928: in a letter to one of the exiles, Radek expressed some doubts about the validity of the Opposition as a minority group in Russia.[100] In a long memorandum written at the end of the summer of 1928 and dissiminated widely, he took Trotsky to task for overlooking crucial factors in the struggle with Stalin, specifically the declining standard of living in the Soviet Union. He also criticized Trotsky's view of the role of the Opposition, but held back when it came to any more fundamental criticism.[101]

Perhaps this memorandum was a trial balloon: Radek knew that Stalin had access to all correspondence passing between the members of the Opposition.[102] If so, it failed; Stalin maintained silence. It may be that Radek realized then that rehabilitation could not be bought so cheaply. Zinoviev had been readmitted to the Party, but only at the price of total and unequivocal denunciation of the Opposition.

Soon after this, Radek took another step toward a complete ideological break with Trotsky—a disavowal of Trotsky's views on permanent revolution. Radek had never been enthusiastic, even during the heyday of the Opposition, about applying the theory of permanent revolution to China.[103] Now, seeking to impress Stalin, Radek attempted to prove that Lenin himself had disavowed Trotsky's theory and, had he lived, would have supported "socialism in one country." He even forced himself to say something reasonably polite about Zinoviev's defection from the Opposition.[104] Still Stalin did not seek a reconciliation with him.

Then in January 1929 Stalin once again moved against Trotsky, this time deporting him to Constantinople as a punishment for continuing Opposition activities. Trotsky's fate forced Radek to the realization that only two alternatives lay open to him: continued opposition, which surely meant either Siberian exile or deportation, and capitulation. Finally, in the spring of 1929, Radek made up his mind. In May an article in *Izvestiia* quoted a letter from Radek announcing his capitulation and his eagerness to participate in the building of socialism in one country.[105] The tone of the letter implied that Radek had been impressed by Stalin's leftist economic policies. In view of his earlier disregard of these policies and disdain for those who had been so impressed, however, this seems unlikely. Radek had simply had enough.

From his exile in Turkey, Trotsky expressed shock and dismay at Radek's defection. Despite their differences, Trotsky had not expected Radek to surrender as ignominiously as Zinoviev and the others.[106] Trotsky did not understand that no ideological metamorphosis was involved in Radek's decision. Given the only two existing alternatives—being his own man in Tomsk or Stalin's man in Moscow—Radek had simply opted for the latter role. If he had expected Radek to suffer exile indefinitely for the sake of loyalty, Trotsky had never really known him at all.

8. Radek and Stalin:
The Revolutionary as Epigone

As Radek rode the Trans-Siberian railroad westward in June 1929, he must have wondered what his role in the Soviet Union would be now that he had left Trotsky for Stalin. Stalin had changed the Soviet system more than any Bolshevik, Left or Right, would have imagined possible. Early in 1929 he had disposed of Bukharin and the newly formed Right Opposition with ease, thus consolidating his position as exclusive leader of the Bolshevik Party.[1] Radek may not have wasted much sorrow on Bukharin's fall—after all, Bukharin had been an eager accomplice in Radek's political destruction in 1924-27—but he must have been appalled to realize that Stalin now ruled the Bolshevik Party without any opposition whatsoever. Furthermore, those who surrounded Stalin—Molotov, Voroshilov, Yaroslavsky, Ordzhonikidze, Yagoda, and others—were men with whom Radek felt no sympathy at all. Virtually none of these men had any ties with the historical international movement; a factor that perhaps explained their commitment to socialism in one country; all were Russian-oriented and regarded the cosmopolitan Radek with deep-rooted suspicion. The chance that Radek would ever become a member of this new inner circle was remote indeed.

Whatever his shortcomings, Radek had never been a sycophant. But now he was faced with a grim choice: either to effect a total identification with Stalin and his program, or to accept political oblivion or worse. As Radek knew, rehabilitation did not necessarily mean restoration: Zinoviev, who had been readmitted to the Bol-

shevik Party a year earlier, had regained none of his old prominence. If a similar fate was in store for Radek, perhaps it was not
worthwhile for him to leave Siberia.

These thoughts may well have been in Radek's mind as his train
stopped at a small Siberian depot. Learning that Radek was on the
train, a group of local Trotskyite exiles assembled at the depot and
demanded that he explain his defection from the Opposition. They
were shocked by his vehement reply, in which he demanded that
all Opposition activity cease and that everyone rally behind Stalin.
When one of the group was indelicate enough to raise the question
of the personal relationship between Trotsky and Radek, he announced that he had completely broken with Trotsky, whom he
now considered his political enemy.[2] It would seem that even before his arrival in Moscow, Radek was trying to emphasize publicly
that his break with Trotsky was genuine and final.

In July 1929 Radek met with Stalin for the first time since the
Fifteenth Party Congress, learned the price of rehabilitation, and
decided to pay it.[*] On July 13, 1929, in company with Smilga,
Preobrazhensky, and scores of other defectors, he publicly announced his total disavowal of Trotsky and his complete acceptance of Stalin's plans for the Soviet Union.[3]

Though Radek was one of Stalin's prize catches among the hundreds of ex-Opposition members, his presence posed certain problems. His volatility and loose tongue were well known to Stalin—in
fact it was Stalin himself who once said of Radek, "Most men's
heads control their tongues; Radek's tongue controls his head."
Clearly it would never do to use Radek in a diplomatic capacity.[4]
He was still the most talented of the Soviet polemicists, however,
and Stalin knew it; moreover, he had an acquaintance with the

---

[*] According to an anecdote retold by many émigrés from the Soviet Union,
Stalin is supposed to have said on this occasion: "Comrade Radek, we are
pleased to have you back, but you must watch your jokes and gibes about me.
Do not forget that I am not only the Secretary General of the Communist
Party, I am also the leader of the world revolution." Radek is supposed to have
been unable to resist the reply: "That, Comrade Stalin, is your joke, not mine!"
The story is obviously apocryphal, and reflects undeserved credit on Radek:
he had no desire to return to Siberia, and was certainly in no position to make
sarcastic remarks about "socialism in one country."

world outside Russia that was lacking in most of Stalin's personal retinue. Finally Stalin decided there was little to lose by allowing Radek to write for the various Bolshevik journals, and soon after his rehabilitation, Radek began contributing articles to Soviet publications. The "new" Radek never questioned official policies or criticized the leadership, but his articles contained enough of the old wit and originality to add some interest to what had become an extremely monolithic and boring press.

The first test of Radek's loyalty to Stalin was not long in coming: unwillingly, Radek found himself the pivotal figure in the martyrdom of Jakob Bliumkin. Bliumkin, a supporter of the Opposition, had remained aloof from the factional struggle in the 1920's because of his position in Soviet counterintelligence, yet his heart had been with Trotsky and he was troubled that he had not been able to do anything for him. In the summer of 1929, Bliumkin, who had been on a mission abroad, met Trotsky's son, ostensibly by chance, on the streets of Constantinople.[5] A meeting with the elder Trotsky ensued, and Bliumkin left Constantinople carrying a message from Trotsky on the legitimate role of the Opposition in the Soviet Union. Looking for a former member of the Opposition who might be receptive to the message, Bliumkin went straight to Radek, a man he had long admired.[6] Radek had been known in the past to react sympathetically to those out of favor, and Bliumkin had no reason to believe that he had changed.[7]

Radek was horrified at Bliumkin's approach, for he knew that he dared not involve himself in a Trotskyite intrigue. Perhaps to demonstrate his loyalty to the Party by his "proper" actions, he advised Bliumkin to go straight to Ordzhonikidze, the head of the Party's Control Commission, tell him exactly what had happened, and throw himself on Ordzhonikidze's mercy.[8] Whether Bliumkin ever saw Ordzhonikidze is not known; what is known is that Bliumkin was arrested, charged with treason, and executed. Radek was caught in the middle: Trotsky virtually accused him of engineering Bliumkin's murder.[9] It is highly unlikely, however, that Radek could have suspected what Bliumkin's fate would be: no Bolshevik had ever been executed for political activity. Why Bliumkin? There is no proof, but it seems possible that Stalin had Bliumkin executed solely to destroy any chance of future cooperation between Radek and Trotsky.[10]

Whatever Radek's feeling about Bliumkin's fate, he could not protest without endangering himself. He continued his policy of ingratiating himself with Stalin, and in 1933 was rewarded with a post on the editorial board of *Izvestiia,* one of the major newspapers of the Soviet Union and the official press organ of the government. The editorship did not place him in a policy-making position, but it restored him to the public eye, a spot he had always enjoyed, and gave him an opportunity to renew his contacts with Western correspondents and even to travel abroad again. It may have been galling to him to be unable any longer to say what he chose, but at least his new position offered him a reasonably cosmopolitan existence and a fair amount of political activity as well as certain economic privileges.[11] Moreover, because Radek was one of the few "Old Bolsheviks" still in circulation, he once again became a great favorite of Westerners in Moscow, most of whom seemed unable to establish rapport with those who, like Ordzhonikidze and Yaroslavsky, typified the new breed of Bolshevik.

Changes in the international scene in 1933 suddenly increased Stalin's dependence on Radek, one of the few Bolsheviks who knew Europe at first hand. A few weeks after Adolf Hitler's appointment as Chancellor of Germany, he outlawed the KPD and launched a foreign policy marked by a bellicose attitude toward the Soviet Union. Stalin was alarmed by and uncertain of the purpose behind Hitler's actions. The Soviet Foreign Office was faced with the necessity of making an appropriate adjustment to the situation; in the meantime, Radek was assigned the role of unofficial herald of a new policy toward Germany. In May 1933 he published a series of articles announcing a basic change in Soviet foreign policy.[12] Since 1919, the Soviets had denounced the Treaty of Versailles as a symbol of imperialism and capitalist exploitation. Now, however, with an avowedly revisionist government in power in Germany—a government openly opposed to the Soviet Union—

the old policy could no longer serve, and Radek consequently stressed the necessity of preserving the Treaty of Versailles *faute de mieux*. If anything was to be revised, let it be the capitalist world hegemony; since this change was not imminent, let existing treaties be protected.[13]

Radek of course was not the author of this new policy, nor was he responsible for executing it, but he was certainly the primary agent in publicizing and gaining acceptance for it. Radek's articles could still command more attention outside Russia than all the sonorous official pronouncements of the Soviet government combined. His articles attracted particular notice in France, where they were hailed as the harbingers of a new anti-German policy on the part of the Soviet Union.[14]

Step by step, Radek was regaining his old influence and prestige. In 1929 he had been restricted to hack work for the Soviet press; in 1932 he had so recovered his position that he was allowed to accompany the Soviet delegation to the Geneva disarmament conference, albeit in a minor role and under heavy surveillance;[15] by 1933, he was once again a foreign policy spokesman for the regime. Now, as if to underscore his new prominence, he was assigned a highly sensitive and important mission: to induce the Poles to cooperate with Stalin rather than Hitler. Radek was received in Poland as Stalin's personal emissary and treated with appropriate deference.[16] His efforts were successful, at least temporarily, and a policy of cooperation was initiated between the two traditionally hostile states.[17] The experience of once again acting as a Kremlin emissary abroad so pleased Radek* that he took steps to prepare for a visit to the United States; for one reason or another, however, this trip never materialized.[18]

Upon his return from Poland, Radek stepped up his campaign to ingratiate himself with Stalin. Did he expect to be rewarded with a high post in the Comintern or the Foreign Office? Or did he discern omens of the violent purges to come and seek to avoid

* The trip to Poland had given Radek a chance to visit his aged mother in Tarnov and show her that her "Lolek" was now a person of consequence.

the inevitable? Whatever the reason, his campaign took on a dual approach: intensified deprecation of Trotsky, both historically and in the context of contemporary events, and intensified aggrandizement of Stalin. His first step was to omit from the 1933 edition of a selection of his previously published works[19] the controversial article "Leon Trotsky—Organizer of Victory," taking pains to explain:

The role of Trotsky in the October Revolution has proved to be no more than a transitory episode. After shining like a meteor, he fell back once again into the quagmire of the struggle against Bolshevism, and slithered into the camp of the counterrevolutionaries. The author [Radek] himself formerly made his own contribution to Trotskyism, but having broken with [Trotsky], considers it impossible to reprint in this book, dedicated to the struggle for socialism, his own historically erroneous article.[20]

During the next two years Radek stepped up his attack on Trotsky, first sticking to rather general points,[21] then directly accusing Trotsky of various crimes, including arranging the murder of Bolsheviks in Russia from his sanctuary abroad.[22] No matter what Radek's reservations, ostensibly at least the break with Trotsky was complete.

As a preliminary step toward Stalin's apotheosis, Radek prepared an article for the influential American journal *Foreign Affairs* explaining in detail the position of the Soviet Union in world affairs and commenting in somewhat more general terms on internal affairs. Radek shrewdly portrayed the Soviet Union as willing to negotiate treaties with states sharing an equal interest in the prevention of war. And the old bogey of the Communist drive for world revolution? Radek glibly explained that Stalin's policy of "socialism in one country" was derived from his belief that the achievement of world revolution would result not from violence but from the workers' desire to emulate the society being built in Russia.[23] Such pronouncements were generally regarded as harmless propaganda in the West, and Radek cleverly exploited this feeling, all the while making Stalin appear a champion of peace. Once again, Radek had illustrated his unique value to Stalin—

could Molotov or Voroshilov write anything that could command an international audience?

Radek knew he had impressed Stalin with the *Foreign Affairs* article, and continued to play on his colossal vanity. Louis Fischer, an American correspondent close to the Soviet leadership, reported that Radek's references to Stalin were "most rapturous, too rapturous for good taste in private conversation."[24] Radek did not limit his adulation of Stalin to rapturous phrases in private conversation. His articles began to contain more and more references to Stalin as the greatest leader the Party, the Soviet Union, and even the world had ever known. Such tributes first appeared on January 1, 1934, in a long article on Stalin in *Pravda* entitled "The Architect of Socialist Society." It was probably the most fatuous thing Radek had ever written, yet it was fabulously successful. The article began with a fancied lecture that might be given in 1967 on "The History of the Victory of Socialism" at the School of Interplanetary Communications, then turned to a rather simplified defense of "socialism in one country" and a designation of the motives of those, himself included, who had struggled against the program. After glorifying the role of Stalin in defeating the Opposition, Radek continued with the straight Stalinist line, utilizing Stalin's own rhetoric to describe the Leninist origin of the doctrine of "socialism in one country":

In the autumn of 1916 . . . Lenin wrote: "Capitalism develops at various speeds in various countries. *There is no alternative under commodity production.* This leads us to the inescapable conclusion that *socialism cannot win simultaneously in several countries. It will triumph initially in one or a number of countries,* while the others for some time will remain bourgeois or pre-bourgeois."

Lenin made abundantly clear what he meant by the triumph of socialism in a single country. He did not mean merely the seizure of power by the proletariat. . . .

In the last articles written before his death, Lenin most emphatically demonstrated that in the USSR there is "quite a sufficient supply of everything that is needed for a [socialist] construction." [Radek's italics.]

After several thousand words, Radek's readers might have thought that perhaps he was overdoing his salute to Stalin. If so, they must have found the concluding paragraphs even more difficult to stomach:

On Lenin's mausoleum . . . stood Stalin in his gray soldier's greatcoat. His peaceful eyes gazed thoughtfully on the hundreds of thousands of proletarians as they marched past Lenin's tomb with the firm step of the future conquerors of the capitalist world. He knew *that he had fulfilled the oath he had sworn ten years earlier at Lenin's tomb*: all the workers of the USSR knew it; all the revolutionary proletariat of the world knew it.

And toward the calm, invincible figure of our leader there rolled waves of love and confidence of the masses marching by, strengthened by the knowledge that there, on Lenin's tomb, was arrayed the General Staff of the coming victorious world revolution.[25]

Such obviously insincere idolatry was completely out of keeping with Radek's character. His tributes in past years to former heroes —Trotsky, Dzierżyński, Luxemburg, and even lesser figures like Vorovsky—had been marked by sensitivity and grace. Why then did Stalin rate such purple prose? It may have been that in writing thus Radek sought to gratify Stalin's enormous ego and at the same time create a parody for his own amusement and that of his friends. It was, of course, an enormous gamble—assuming that that was what Radek intended. In any case, Stalin chose to accept the article at face value, and had it reprinted and extensively distributed.[26]

In August 1934 Stalin gave Radek a new and unusual assignment. For more than two years Stalin had been urging Soviet writers to conform to a doctrine he called "socialist realism," a basically didactic approach to life that sought to compensate for the grim realities of the 1930's. Soviet writers were to write of the "great tomorrow" and not of the difficult present; or if they wrote of the present, it was to be in the language and outlook of the "great tomorrow." It was Radek's job to instruct those in attendance at the First Soviet Writers' Congress in this new approach. While allowing for the usefulness of some bourgeois literature such as Erich Maria Remarque's *All Quiet on the Western Front*, Radek lectured the writers on the dangers of imitating bourgeois authors indifferent to the needs of the proletariat.[27] As the prime example of such a writer, he chose the Irishman James Joyce, then of "morbid interest" to some Soviet writers:

What is the basic feature of Joyce? His basic feature is the conviction that there is nothing big in life—no big events, no big people, no big ideas; and the writer can give a picture of life by just taking "any given hero on any given day," and reproducing him with exactitude. A heap of dung, crawling with worms, photographed by a cinema apparatus through a microscope—such is Joyce's work.[28]

Stalin's message, as transmitted through Radek, was quite clear: in the building of "socialism in one country" there were big events, big ideas, and big people, and it was the job of the Soviet writer to depict them. Implied coercion would have been enough to keep Soviet writers in line, but Stalin was pleased to use the extra touch of advice from the worldly and widely read Radek.

After his speech to the Soviet writers, Radek could consider himself completely rehabilitated. While Zinoviev and other erstwhile leaders of the Opposition floundered in continued ostracism, Radek had become one of Stalin's most important advisers. The German Embassy in Moscow, reporting to Berlin, referred to Radek as "the trusted agent of the Central Committee on foreign policy" and carefully reported all suggestions by Radek that the Soviet Union was not necessarily committed to an anti-German alignment in international affairs.[29] The extraordinary notice taken of Radek's writings throughout 1935 confirmed the impression that Radek alone of the Left Opposition had managed to regain power in the Soviet Union. In his preface to a collection of articles by Radek, published in London in 1935, A. T. Cummings wrote: "I hope that Karl Radek will live long and prosper mightily, if for no other reason than that he, more than any other Soviet writer, has imparted colour and vivacity to the large and somewhat arid field of Soviet propaganda."[30] Cummings had every reason to believe that his hopes for Radek's future would be fulfilled.

The following year, Radek, along with Nikolai Bukharin and several other important Bolsheviks, was entrusted with writing a new Soviet constitution reflecting the changes wrought by socialism in one country. Constitutions, even in the Soviet Union, are usually written by the victors; the assignment seemed one more indication that Radek's star was rising. But Radek's work on the constitution of 1936 was to be his last contribution to the Soviet state. Even before the constitution was formally ratified, Radek was in a cell in Liubianka prison awaiting trial for treason. What had happened to bring about his fall from grace? Why did Radek's well-calculated plans to retrieve his position and influence collapse just when it seemed that he had achieved his goal?

To a great extent, Radek's downfall was brought about by factors beyond his control. By 1934, for reasons known only to himself, Stalin had come to the decision to purge the Bolshevik Party and to eliminate anyone who owed even the smallest amount of loyalty elsewhere—to Trotsky, to the General Staff of the Red Army, to the "conciliatory" wing of the Politburo, or to foreign states. Just when and how Stalin reached this decision has never been established. Perhaps, as some of his detractors insist, he had the idea all along, even during the intra-party struggles of the 1920's; perhaps the failures of the first Five Year Plan, climaxed by the crisis in the Politburo in 1932, had set him on this course; perhaps some of the supposed maneuvering behind the scenes at the Seventeenth Party Congress in January and February 1934—the so-called "Congress of Victors"—had convinced him that nothing short of physical liquidation of all his opponents, potential, real, and imagined, would suffice;[31] perhaps he was so impressed by Hitler's success in the "night of the long knives," June 30, 1934, that he sought to emulate him in Russia; perhaps the matter is more simply explained by Stalin's increasingly acute paranoia.[32] In any case, for the next four years the Soviet Union went through an ordeal unequaled in Russian history. Spectacular trials and wild rumors of trials held the Party in a grip of terror. Bolshevik after Bolshevik was arrested, tried, found guilty of treason, and, as often as not, executed. Prominent members of the early Bolshevik regime, men who had served on Lenin's Central Committee and on the ECCI, were executed as capitalist agents. In this grim setting, the way to survival lay in caution and servility. Outspoken persons could disappear forever; obscurity was the safest status.

In this atmosphere Radek had no chance for survival. Although he threw himself heartily into the condemnation of the accused, he himself was the perfect example of the type of Bolshevik Stalin had earmarked for liquidation. At the top level, the criteria for purging were clearcut: long-standing membership and participation in the international socialist movement was particularly dangerous; those who had been in the old Second International and had been comrades of Luxemburg, Liebknecht, and the old Left were automatically suspect. Stalin preferred to surround himself with men of his own background, men whose political experience had been largely limited to Russia. Molotov, Voroshilov, and Zhdanov filled Stalin's requirements; Radek never could.

Another disadvantage for Radek was his continued contact with Western correspondents and diplomats. One of the main reasons that Westerners sought out the garrulous Radek was that he could be expected to drop a bit of classified information now and then. In the 1920's Radek had the reputation of being careless with state secrets, and on occasion even Trotsky found it best to conceal information from him.[33] One would think that by the thirties Radek would have learned to control his tongue, yet there was at least one occasion on which he was guilty of a major breach of security.

Late in 1935, at a reception given by the Czechoslovakian Embassy in Moscow, Radek repeated verbatim to the American ambassador, William Bullitt, a recent conversation between Bullitt and Josef Beck, the Foreign Minister of Poland.[34] Bullitt's first thought was that Beck had been foolish enough to repeat the conversation to some Soviet diplomat. Radek assured him, however, that his source was a Soviet spy within the "colonels' clique" that had been running Poland since Pilsudski's death in May. Bullitt was of course astounded. He realized that Radek must be telling the truth, since Beck would reveal nothing to the Bolsheviks, whom he regarded as his country's enemies. There is no reason to disbelieve Bullitt's account; he even went so far as to seek advice from Washington on whether to inform his Polish counterpart of the situation. Bullitt noted in his covering letter to Secretary of State Cordell Hull that should this affair become known, "Radek would be on the next train to Siberia."[35] If the Soviet Union did indeed have a spy so highly placed in Warsaw, Radek had terminated the man's usefulness to Moscow by his indiscretion. This sort of carelessness made Radek a liability in spite of all his talents, and Stalin knew it if Radek did not.

The beginning of the end for Radek and for countless other Bolsheviks had come on December 1, 1934, with the assassination of Sergei Kirov, supposedly the leader of the "conciliatory" bloc in the Politburo. The circumstances of Kirov's death were highly suspicious, and they have for over thirty years given rise to a belief that Stalin himself ordered Kirov's murder in order to bring about the execution or deportation to Siberia of dozens of people he wished to get rid of—many of whom could not possibly have been involved, since they had been prisoners in Soviet jails for some time before Kirov's death.[36] Zinoviev and Kamenev, along with some lesser lights, were charged with complicity in the murder, brought to trial, found guilty, and imprisoned. In 1936, Zinoviev and Kamenev were retried, accused of more direct complicity in the murder, as well as complicity in a number of political crimes, and sentenced to death.

The implications of the Zinoviev-Kamenev trial and the appearance of his own name in the testimony must have been frightening to Radek.[37] The charges against the men, including revival of the Left Opposition and sabotage of the Five Year Plan, could just as easily have been leveled against him if Stalin had chosen to do so. To all outward appearances, however, the trials of Zinoviev and Kamenev did not affect Radek's position. He joined the jackals' chorus against the accused and did not publicly question what was going on.[38] So far as the public knew, he was still a trusted editor of *Izvestiia*, one of the chosen few engaged in the constitutional project; far from being a target, he appeared to enjoy Stalin's confidence more than ever.

Sometime in 1936 Radek was sent to the Free City of Danzig on a mysterious mission. All that can be established is that he met certain German representatives in the Danzig suburb of Oliva. The subject of discussion is unknown: was it alliance against Poland, or renewal of military cooperation with Germany?[39] Whatever mission

Radek was entrusted with, he surely hoped that it would guarantee his position and save him from a fate similar to Zinoviev's. He is supposed to have remarked to his contacts at Oliva: "Now, in the USSR anything is possible. Why, I myself might even survive!"[40]

He was wrong; the mission to Oliva was one of his last services to the regime. In September 1936 Radek's articles suddenly disappeared from the Soviet press, and on October 7, 1936, *Pravda* announced what many had suspected: Karl Radek had been arrested and would stand trial for treason. Despite the events of the year, Radek's arrest came as a surprise to those who had assessed his position at face value: Zinoviev had been out of favor when he was purged; Radek, on the contrary, had given the impression of being close to Stalin and hence secure.

Why did Stalin decide to purge a man who had been so useful to him for so long? On the other hand, since no other member of Lenin's old guard had survived the purges, why should Radek be spared?[41] Alexandrov suggests that Yagoda, the head of the security police, used a report that during the Oliva meeting Radek had admitted involvement in a conspiracy as an excuse to demand Radek's arrest, hoping thus to advance his own fortunes.[42] If so, the joke was on Yagoda, who was replaced by Yezhov in September 1936 and subsequently purged.

Radek's famed wit may have been one of the factors in his downfall. Rumor had it that every anti-Stalin joke in Russia emanated from Radek. In summarizing Stalin's role as the founder of "socialism in one country," Radek is alleged to have remarked, "Who will be the infallible commentator on Marx after Stalin's death? Comrade Budënny's mare!"[43] It did not matter whether Radek was actually the source of such gibes; the fact that he was believed to be was in itself sufficiently damning, since Stalin was surrounded by toadies who repeated every rumor. Perhaps Stalin was led to suspect that he had been lampooned in Radek's article "The Architect of Socialist Society." If so, Radek's fate was sealed, for no one was so useful to Stalin as to be allowed to assail the leader's colossal vanity and go unpunished.

There was an unusually long delay between Radek's arrest in

September 1936 and his trial in January 1937. Alexander Orlov, a former Soviet security official, has given us an interesting account of the difficulties the police experienced with Radek. According to Orlov, Radek's interrogator, Molchanov, finally brought Radek to the point of confession, but Radek was determined to have the last word even then. He insisted on adding Molchanov's name to his list of accomplices, telling the terrified inquisitor: "What does the fate of a Molchanov matter to Yezhov when the interests of the Party are at stake! In order to have at the trial one Radek, Yezhov will gladly throw into the bargain a dozen like Molchanov!"[44]

Radek's trial promised to be far more spectacular than that of Zinoviev and Kamenev. For one thing, it was to be held in an open court with non-Communist observers in attendance; with Radek as defendant, this could be a risk. He had numerous friends in the Western press and diplomatic corps; remarks of his that might pass unnoticed by Stalin's men would have a double meaning to those who knew him well. For this reason, his trial was prepared with the utmost care. Finally, on January 24, 1937, Radek stood with Georgy Piatakov and fifteen lesser defendants before the Military Collegium of the Supreme Court of the USSR. He already knew that he would not be sentenced to death, yet he may well have sensed that this would be his last public appearance.[45] Pleading innocent or repudiating the confession he had already made would be of little avail—it would only cost him his promised exemption from the death sentence—and too much sarcasm or verbal byplay in the courtroom might have a similar result. Yet Radek could not give his last performance without some attention to the impression he would make on the court, on the assembled foreign observers, and, in view of the circumstances, on history. If he was finally to be martyred, let it be in style!

For the first several hours of testimony, Radek let Andrei Vyshinsky, the State Prosecutor, lead him through a well-rehearsed confession of his alleged misdeeds. Under Vyshinsky's prompting, Radek told of learning from Trotsky in 1932 of the creation of a new bloc of opposition, and cited all the people who had been purged or were being purged as accomplices in this bloc.[46] He implicated Bukharin, who had not yet been purged, in a plot against the regime. He admitted knowledge of virtually every terrorist or terrorist group adduced by Vyshinsky, and of the formation of a plot to assassinate Kirov. He drew a marvelously detailed picture of an alleged plan by Trotsky to return to power by precipitating a disastrous war, then seizing control of the government during the chaos following Russia's defeat. Laying it on thick, he even described the postwar territorial concessions planned by the Trotskyite bloc: the Ukraine would go to Germany and Eastern Siberia to Japan.[47] As though his story to this point were not sufficiently ludicrous, Radek went on to describe a program devised by Trotsky in 1935 for a return to capitalism in the Soviet Union. As Radek summed it up:

And therefore the conclusion: restoration of capitalism in the circumstances of 1935. For nothing at all, just for the sake of Trotsky's beautiful eyes—the country was to return to capitalism. When I read this I felt as if [I were in] a madhouse. . . . We had to put up with Trotsky when he gave us directives from abroad, but in this case we were to become the agents of foreign fascist states.[48]

This last demand, Radek asserted, was too much; he broke with Trotsky, but lacked the courage to take action against the bloc or to report the matter to security officials. It was a bizarre tale—too bizarre for anyone who knew Radek or Trotsky to believe. Yet the prosecution accepted it at face value, and a surprisingly large number of knowledgeable people did the same.[49]

In *Darkness at Noon*, Arthur Koestler sought to provide an explanation for the mystery of "Old Bolsheviks" confessing to a long string of crimes that they could not possibly have committed. In Koestler's novel the protagonist is induced to confess by appeals to his sense of duty to render a last service to the Party against the capitalist world. Koestler's thesis is indeed plausible as a possible explanation of the ritual confessions in the purge trials of the 1930's. In Radek's case, however, other hypotheses should be explored. There are three possible explanations for Radek's confession: first, that he was guilty as charged and confessed to his crimes; second, that he cooperated with the prosecution in order to win a lighter sentence; third, that he deliberately told a story that he knew no well-informed person would believe.

The first explanation, that Radek's confession was based on truth, is the most easily refuted, especially with regard to the role assigned to Trotsky. The charges against Trotsky were subsequently investigated by an American committee under the noted philosopher John Dewey and easily disproved.[50] It is difficult, moreover, to believe that Radek and Trotsky could have become reconciled, if one recalls the circumstances of their political separation. Could Trotsky have forgiven Radek for his role in the Bliumkin affair? Could he have been oblivious to the attacks made on him by Radek in the 1930's? Trotsky's testimony to the Dewey Committee indicated that he was very much aware of and incensed by these attacks.[51] More important, if there really had been a neo-Trotskyite bloc operating in the Soviet Union, would Trotsky have entrusted the notoriously loose-mouthed Radek with conspiratorial responsibility? Finally, the charge that Trotsky sought a return to capitalism is simply too ludicrous to be believed by anyone other than a fanatic Stalinist. Perhaps Radek was attempting to do Trotsky a last service by including in his testimony a charge so obviously false.

The testimony of Piatakov, who claimed to have met Trotsky at an airport in Norway, was quickly disproved by reference to Norwegian aviation records.[52] The testimony of many other victims of Stalin's purges was refuted with equal ease by foreign authorities.[53] No such discrepancies were contained in Radek's testimony. Almost all the events Radek described, however, took place in Russia, and therefore could not be checked by foreign investigators. Even the mail he had allegedly received from Trotsky had been conveniently destroyed.[54]

The second hypothesis, that Radek was buying a lighter sentence for himself with his confession, is much more plausible. There is some evidence that Radek insisted on an interview with Stalin before he agreed to confess; perhaps a deal was made at this meeting.[55] Since Radek was one of the few Old Bolsheviks not sentenced to death, a pretrial bargain must be considered.

The third hypothesis may be closest to the mark. Gustav Hilger, who observed the trial for the German delegation, was convinced that Radek was deliberately putting his friends on notice by his exaggerated testimony: "I, who followed Radek's dialectics from among the audience, did not have the slightest doubt that his exaggerated confessions of repentence were not means by which he wanted to save his skin, but were appeals to comrades abroad, in whose eyes he wanted to show up the true nature of Stalin's regime by his grotesque and absurd self-accusation.[56]

At one point it certainly seemed that Radek was implying to his audience that the case against him was built of straw. Vyshinsky made the mistake of pushing Radek too far, implying that Radek's lack of frankness on some subjects cast doubts on his claim to have broken with Trotsky over the issue of a return to capitalism, and Radek retorted: "Yes, if you ignore the fact you learned about the program and about Trotsky's instructions only from me, of course, it does cast doubt on what I have said."[57] Thus Radek called attention to the complete lack of evidence outside his confession to support the charges against him. Vyshinsky dared not pursue the point. If Radek was a liar, then there was no case—only a liar's confession. It could be argued that Radek was giving public notice that had he made up the whole testimony in accord with Vyshinsky's instructions. To reiterate the point, later in his testimony Radek stated: "All the testimony of the other accused rests on our [Radek's and Piatakov's] testimony. If you are dealing with mere criminals and spies, on what can you base your conviction that what we have said is the truth, the firm truth?"[58]

Here Radek was indeed playing a dangerous game: any private agreement he might have made with the prosecution would certainly be imperiled if he deliberately embarrassed them. Having taken this risk and made it clear that there was no evidence against him outside his own testimony, he returned to the role of criminal and in his last plea reiterated his self-accusations.

Much to the surprise of foreign observers, Radek was not sentenced to death; instead, he was given ten years' imprisonment. Perhaps this was his reward for following Vyshinsky's instructions. Except for the two occasions when he had made dangerous allusions to the validity of the case against him, he had been very cooperative. He had accepted all the accusations, implicated Bukharin for good measure, and even made some cryptic although not openly damning references to Tukhachevsky. Perhaps he would not have to serve his entire term; when the purges were over, perhaps Stalin would once again find Radek useful. When Radek received his sentence, he merely shrugged his shoulders and smiled impishly at the spectators in the courtroom.[59] Did he suspect that his career was finished, or only feel that he had received another setback similar to that of his expulsion and exile in 1927? The grim fact is that Radek was never seen again by a non-Soviet observer after he was taken from the courtroom on January 30, 1937.[60]

What happened to Karl Radek? The mystery was heightened by his historical relegation to the status of what George Orwell has aptly called the "unperson." For twenty years the Soviet press avoided mentioning his name, and Soviet authors went out of their way to pretend he had never existed. The situation lent itself to all sorts of rumors, but no facts emerged. According to Alexander Orlov, Radek was not immediately imprisoned, but was used by the security police to assist in persuading Nikolai Bukharin (who was arrested in January 1937) to confess to a series of charges.[61] A Soviet defector maintained in 1956 that in 1939 he had decoded a message from a prison camp in northern Siberia telling of Radek's death in a brawl with another prisoner.[62] Throughout World War II and afterward rumors of Radek's survival persisted. Walter Duranty, the *New York Times* correspondent, gave credence to a story that Radek was back at his desk at *Izvestiia*, writing lead stories anonymously; Duranty even thought he detected Radek's inimitable style in some of the *Izvestiia* stories of 1941.[63] In 1957 some Polish Communists spread the story that Radek had actually written the famous anti-Stalin speech delivered by Khrushchev to a secret session of the Twentieth Party Congress in February 1956.[64] Other émigrés spread stories that Radek was alive and writing for the Soviet press under the pen name Evgeny. Even well-informed Soviet officials passed on stories of Radek's survival.[65]

The mystery was partially resolved in 1960 when the proceedings of the Ninth Party Congress of 1920 were reprinted and brought up to date. The text of the biographical sketch of Radek given there did not offer any new information, since it carried his career only as far as his arrest in 1936 and did not even mention his trial. Of more interest, however, were the dates given in the title of the sketch:

RADEK, K. B. (1885–1939)

This was official notice that Radek had died, presumably in prison, in 1939. Since then a few other Soviet sources have alluded to "Karl Radek, 1885–1939," and there seems to be no reason to doubt that he died in that year.[66] Whether in a prison brawl or alone, whether in Moscow or Siberia, Karl Radek had given up his place in the revolutionary arena at last.

9. The Last Internationalist

Communists of the pre-Stalin era traditionally took special pride in their roles as internationalists dedicated to the goal of a world revolution. All the socialist Internationals—First, Second, Third, and the splinter groups—were based on the supposition that socialism and internationalism were one, and Marx himself bluntly stated in the *Communist Manifesto* that the proletariat "has no fatherland."

Radek met the criteria for an internationalist as well if not better than any other Communist of his time. To some extent, his advocacy of internationalism was not so much a deliberate choice as a commitment born of the circumstances of his political career. His failure to achieve direct leadership of any major party or political organization prevented him from pursuing a primarily nationalistic policy. Had events been different, he might have gladly forsaken his ardent internationalism for the leadership of Bolshevism or German Communism. One of Radek's harshest critics, the German Communist Ruth Fischer, who often maligned him, may have inadvertently struck on an essential truth about his intense commitment to internationalism when she suggested that it was a compensation for his lack of prestige and power in Moscow.[1]

In the Soviet regime there were many rungs of power, but by far the highest echelon of command under both Lenin and Stalin was the Politburo, the executive body of the Central Committee of the Bolshevisk Party, where all major policy decisions were made. Under Lenin, the Politburo usually consisted of five men; under Stalin its membership grew somewhat, but it still remained a select group. Election to the Central Committee, which Radek achieved repeatedly under Lenin, raised one to the ranks of the major leaders of the Bolshevik Party. In elections to the Central Committee, Radek proved to be one of the most popular Bolsheviks, once polling more votes than any candidate save Lenin, but he was always denied admission to the Politburo, the true center of power. In the Comintern, on the other hand, Radek was placed at the top level of command, and in some instances, notably during the formulation of the united front tactic, wielded enormous influence. His prominence in the Comintern, of course, was only at the sufferance of the Politburo; yet in the Comintern, and specifically in the ECCI, he commanded a good deal of power.

Why was Radek never elected to the Politburo despite his prominence in the early 1920's? There is reason to suspect that the Politburo members themselves did not want him to serve on that body. Both Zinoviev and his close friend Lev Kamenev were Politburo members; both would certainly have opposed Radek's inclusion. Furthermore, it is entirely possible that Lenin believed that Radek lacked the sense of responsibility and the restraint that Politburo membership required.[2] It is even possible that Trotsky did not push Radek's candidacy; again, Trotsky and Radek were political allies at one time, but they remained personally aloof from each other, partly because of Trotsky's uncertainty about Radek's reliability.[3] Of the five Politburo members, it appears that only Stalin was reasonably well disposed toward Radek, and even he did not advocate bringing Radek into the select body.

Another reason for Radek's exclusion from the Politburo may well have been that while his credentials as a Communist were always in good order, his credentials as a Bolshevik were not. He was not a Russian, and in the early years of the Comintern he had represented Poland, not Russia, as a delegate. This had been merely a device for increasing Bolshevik membership on the ECCI while maintaining the fiction of its international character, but nevertheless it was indicative of Radek's lack of national affiliation in the eyes of his Bolshevik colleagues.

Radek's Jewish ancestry may have been another count against him. True, a great many of the Old Bolsheviks were Jews; in 1921 Lenin and Stalin were the only Gentiles in the Politburo. Yet Radek's Jewishness seemed to take on greater significance than was warranted. One rarely thinks of Zinoviev as a Jew, and even in Trotsky's case it is a matter of secondary importance. Radek, although he never identified himself as a Jew except by telling an occasional coarse Yiddish joke, was always described thus, as, for example, in a State Department memorandum of 1922, where he is referred to as a "typical Jewish type."[4] Such a remark is not unusual. One can find many references to Radek as a Jew—a Galician Jew, a Polish Jew, an Austrian Jew, more rarely a German Jew or a Russian Jew, but always a Jew. Some but not all of these references are derogatory: indeed, Fritz Brupbacher wrote, "In contrast to others, I consider Radek to be a good-hearted person who would never be so witty had he the misfortune to have been born a *goy*."[5]

What special quality did Radek have that called attention to his Jewishness? True, his appearance and mannerisms certainly fit the Jewish stereotype so popular among anti-Semites; but more importantly, it was his peculiar lack of allegiance to any national group that set him apart from others of similar origins. He may have had a lifelong fondness for Mickiewicz, but he certainly was no Pole, nor did his affinity for Kleist or Grillparzer make him a German.[6] He was perhaps least of all a Russian. During the Stalinist 1930's he ground out nationalistic clichés like "the broad plains of the socialist homeland," but obviously without any sincerity. His identification as a Jew was surely not one he cherished, but in effect he had no other national or racial affiliation.

Radek's Jewishness may well have been one of the factors that brought about his downfall. In one of the best known but least informative books of recent years, *Twenty Letters to a Friend*, Stalin's daughter, Svetlana Alliluyeva, reveals that Stalin's anti-

Semitism was not confined to the years of open persecution, 1949–53, but was an essential and long-standing part of Stalin's makeup. If this is true—and Alliluyeva makes a convincing case for it—then Radek's fate was inescapable, and his Jewishness the proverbial straw.[7] The lifelong atheist, internationalist, and Communist, who at no time identified himself with Jewry, ultimately may have met his end because of Stalin's hatred of Jews.

It is difficult to find consistent values in Radek other than his enduring commitment to internationalism. As Gerald Freund noted: "Radek was notoriously volatile; it is a mistake to ascribe logical patterns of thought or consistent opinion to him."[8] Freund's judgment is essentially correct; Radek's political values, sincere as they may have been, were subject to discard if they interfered with his political objectives. Such a lack of consistency indicated to some observers a lack of moral fiber as well. Thus Franz Borkenau, a former Comintern functionary, wrote: "The one thing this brilliant man lacked was character, that deep-rooted moral balance which draws an undefinable line between what is right and what is wrong. Radek was too clever to be either heroic or consistent."[9] Similar assessments of Radek's moral stature have been voiced by Angelica Balabanoff, Ruth Fischer, and a host of others. Yet it does not necessarily follow that a man lacking in moral stature is immoral by definition. Radek had redeeming features, including an impulsive generosity toward friend and foe. If nothing else, he lacked the vindictiveness shown by Zinoviev and other Bolsheviks. In 1922, when Zinoviev was urging the harshest measures against the Mensheviks, Radek secretly visited some of them in prison and offered encouragement.[10] A more typical story is told by Boris Souvarine, who was expelled from the Comintern in 1924, the year of Radek's exclusion: "When I was expelled from the Party by the Fifth Congress in 1924, Radek was the only one who thought of my financial predicament and, putting his hand in his pocket, inquired: 'Don't you need some money?' I managed to get along without his help, but I never forgot the gesture."[11]

The purge of Paul Levi was perhaps Radek's crudest act: he simply abandoned a friend in order to protect himself and gain the position of the Comintern's man in Germany. Unsurprisingly, Trotsky considered Radek's 1929 defection from the Opposition immoral.[12] Nor was Trotsky alone in condemning Radek's role as Stalin's henchman. According to a recent summary of Radek's career in the 1930's by Robert Conquest:

Stalin had not, since his [Radek's] recantation in the twenties, had anything to complain about from Radek. He had betrayed the Opposition on every possible occasion, and had flattered Stalin in an unprecedented fashion. He was one man who had truly burned his bridges to the Opposition; and at the same time he was nowhere regarded as a serious politician, and there was no question of his ever competing for even the lowest rung of power.[13]

This is an unfair estimate. It is not possible to say that Radek had betrayed the Opposition unless one holds—and few aside from Trotsky do—that he deliberately set Bliumkin up for execution.[14] In essence, Radek's renunciation of Trotsky was the only logical step. Trotsky had suffered irreversible defeat, and few Bolsheviks —Christian Rakovsky was a notable exception—were willing to throw away the rest of their lives on a lost cause. In any case, a substantial argument could be made that espousal of "socialism in one country" was not an abandonment of world revolution but merely a strategic deferral. For Radek, strategic deferrals had been a necessary tactic in the quest for world revolution ever since 1919. Furthermore, the reality was that Stalin was securely in power. By returning to Moscow, Radek could and did try to educate Stalin in the exigencies of world politics—no mean contribution to the Communist cause.

In many ways, the last decade of Radek's life was a sad epilogue to his revolutionary career. It was not so much that Radek had changed as a revolutionary internationalist as that the Soviet regime had changed as an instrument of revolution. Because of this change, Radek found it his fate to be written out of the political scenario. Under Stalin, Radek did not have the option of choosing what he believed to be the best path to world revolution. To survive, he was forced to adapt himself to circumstances, and for several years he succeeded. His trial in 1937 was a bitter finale to a full and energetic career.

For all his frivolity, Radek cared deeply about his place in history. Though he confessed to all sorts of exotic charges of crimes against Stalin's regime, he never confessed to any acts against the cause of world revolution. In his final plea he stated with uncharacteristic seriousness and pathos: "I have not the right to speak as a repentant Communist; nevertheless, the 35 years I worked in the labour movement, despite all the errors and crimes with which they ended, entitle me to ask you to believe one thing—that, after all, the masses of people with whom I marched do mean something to me."[15]

And there were those who believed him. Even Angelica Balabanoff, never at any time Radek's admirer, wrote after his trial: "I feel about Radek . . . that though he was capable of anything within the confines of the revolutionary movement, he would never sell himself to the enemies of the revolution. These would be his enemies too."[16]

Notes

In the case of Radek's works, complete publication data will be found in Radek's Publications, pp. 213–19. For other works cited here in short form, complete names, titles, and publication data are given in the Bibliography, pp. 221–33.

NOTES TO CHAPTER 1

1. For an interesting commentary on the nature of Germanophilism among Galician Jews, including those with a religious bent, see Deutscher, *The Non-Jewish Jew*, pp. 17–20.

2. Soviet publications have always given 1885 as Radek's date of birth, and still do, but for some reason a great many recent Polish and East German publications give 1883 (see, for example, Koszutska, I, p. 312, and Stern, IV, p. 200). Radek himself always gave 1885 as the year of his birth, and his fiftieth birthday was publicly noted in 1935.

3. Radek, "Avtobiografiia," p. 138. My description of Radek's early years is taken largely from this long autobiographical article, which describes in great detail his activities up to about the age of thirty, then briefly summarizes his life from 1914 to the middle of the 1920's. There are few sources for the first twenty years of Radek's life. A picture of the environment in which he lived during this time can be formed from reminiscences in the collection of writings entitled *Torne: Kiyum un Khurbn fun a yiddisher shtot*. A few items can be culled from Polish publications of the past several years; yet one of the most important sources for the history of socialism in Poland, the Journal *Z Pola Walki*, is singularly unhelpful. Its issues carry many vague allusions to Radek's early career, but little more. Radek's own account, cited above, is unsurprisingly selective and biased, yet it does present an interesting discussion of the formative influences of his youth—at least as he chose to remember them.

4. *Torne*, p. 318.

5. For evidence that Radek never learned to read Yiddish, see his sketch of Dzerzhinsky (Dzierżyński) in Radek, *Portraits and Pamphlets*, p. 100.

6. Radek, "Avtobiografiia," pp. 138–39.

7. Shaynfeld, pp. 318–19.

8. *Ibid.*

9. Radek, "Avtobiografiia," p. 138.

10. Radek claimed that he first discovered *Naprzód* when an illiterate workman asked him to read it aloud (see *ibid.*, p. 139).

11. *Ibid.*, p. 140.

12. Recent works from Poland have not met the need for a comprehensive study of Polish socialism prior to World War I. Although Polish historians have far more latitude than their Soviet counterparts, they must work with pre-assigned heroes and villains. For an example of an "official" work on Polish socialism, see Grünberg and Kozłowski. A well-written but cursory view of the formation and problems of early Polish socialism may be found in Dziewanowski, pp. 3–39.

13. Radek, "Avtobiografiia," p. 139.

14. Just when Radek made this change is uncertain. One veteran of Polish socialism maintains that Radek was still using the name Sobelsohn as late as 1903, but dropped it completely after leaving Poland in 1904 (see Drobner, pp. 133–34). Radek appears to have used his new name in print for the first time in a letter published in the Polish journal *Promien*, VI, No. 2 (February 1904), p. 71. After that, he rarely, if ever, used the name Sobelsohn. A fanciful account of the origins of the name Radek appears in Ruth Fischer, pp. 201–2. Miss Fischer errs on several points, particularly in her chronology of events and her interpretation of the Polish language. Unfortunately, her account has been repeated in a number of studies.

15. *Torne*, p. 319.

16. Radek, "Avtobiografiia," p. 139.

17. It is somewhat ironic that Marian Kukiel should be the one to introduce Radek to socialism in Cracow (*ibid.*, p. 140). Kukiel has been a major force in Polish politics for over half a century, but hardly as a socialist. He has had a long career as a military historian and professional soldier and holds the rank of Lieutenant-General; for the past two decades he has been active in Polish émigré affairs in England, most importantly as director of the Sikorski Institute.

18. Drobner, p. 133. That a Polish author would speak favorably of Radek in the 1960's is surprising; Soviet authorities barely mention him. A brief factual account of Radek's career in Cracow is given in Buszko.

19. Radek, "Avtobiografiia," p. 140. I have been unable to find copies of any of these early articles.

20. *Ibid.*
21. Dziewanowski, pp. 26–27.
22. Radek, "Avtobiografiia," p. 140.
23. *Ibid.*, p. 141.
24. Drobner, p. 133.
25. Nomad, pp. 35–36.
26. Brupbacher (p. 109) explains that he was unaware of the identity of his antagonist at the time, but that Radek later identified himself as the guilty party.
27. Warszawski's correspondence has not been published, and he apparently died without writing his memoirs. His printed works have been published and heavily annotated. There are no references to Radek in Switzerland in Warski (Warszawski), I.
28. Radek, "Avtobiografiia," p. 143.
29. Radical socialists often used the terms revisionism and reformism interchangeably. Radek himself rarely differentiated between the two.
30. Bernstein, p. 202.
31. Radek, "Avtobiografiia," pp. 144–45.
32. Radek heard Lenin speak for the first time in Switzerland, but the language barrier kept Radek from making personal contact with his future mentor. See *ibid.*, p. 144.
33. Perhaps the best example of this dedication to democratic revolution can be found in her critique of the Russian Revolution of 1917 and the Bolshevik terror. See Luxemburg, *The Russian Revolution*, pp. 25–80.
34. Nettl, I, p. 2.
35. Numerous former communists who completely broke with the movement still expressed admiration for Luxemburg's principles: see, for example, Bertram D. Wolfe's introduction to *The Russian Revolution*.
36. Warski, pp. 594–95.
37. Radek, "Avtobiografiia," p. 146.
38. Radek, "Die Gewerkschaftsbewegung," pp. 564–69.
39. Walecki, I, p. 317, note 32.
40. Radek, "Die Gewerkschaftsbewegung," pp. 568–69.
41. See Dziewanowski, pp. 40–54.
42. For Radek's explanation of the affair, see Radek, *Meine Abrechnung*, pp. 29–39. In later years, a special committee of the German Social Democratic Party investigated the affair but never offered any satisfactory explanation of what had actually taken place. For the committee's findings, see *Protokoll . . . 1913*, pp. 536–45. Some of the committee's correspondence is to be found in the small manuscript collection "In Sachen Radek."
43. Grünberg and Kozłowski, p. 322.

NOTES TO CHAPTER 2

1. Gay, p. 80. Gay's work contains the best analysis of Bernstein and his intellectual development.

2. *Protokoll . . . 1905*, pp. 342–43. For a good discussion of the issue of the mass strike see Schorske, pp. 28–58.

3. Note, for instance, his arguments for the judicious use of the mass strike in *Protokoll . . . 1905*, pp. 285–314.

4. The best description of this evolution is given in Schorske, *passim*.

5. Gay, pp. 233–35.

6. See Nettl, I, pp. 392–95.

7. *Ibid.*, pp. 377–88.

8. Stampfer, p. 143.

9. Frölich, p. 211.

10. Radek, "Vor dem Parteitag," *Bremer Bürgerzeitung*, No. 210 (September 8, 1911), pp. 1–2.

11. Mayer, p. 195.

12. A specific example of this unsavory side of Radek is to be found in A. Litwak, "Bletlekh zikhroynes," *Unzer Tsayt*, IV, No. 1 (January 1944), p. 33. (In Yiddish.)

13. The picture appears herein on the second page of the picture section; it originally appeared in *Archiv für Sozialgeschichte*, II (1962), opposite p. 96.

14. Franz, "Aus Briefen Konrad Haenischs," pp. 476–77.

15. A possible clue to when the Radeks began to live together may be found in Radek's best known anthology, *In den Reihen der deutschen Revolution*. The dedication page reads: "To my wife Rosa I dedicate the selection of the fruit of our labor derived from ten years of common struggle and common thought." Since Radek's preface to the book is dated 1919, this suggests that they either met or were "married" in 1909.

16. Reprinted as Appendix 2 to Otto Ernst Schüddekopf, "Karl Radek in Berlin: Eine Kapital deutsch-russischer Beziehungen in Jahre 1919," *Archiv für Sozialgeschichte*, II (1962), p. 11.

17. For evidence that Radek remained married to Rosa to the end of his life, see Dewey *et al.*, *The Case of Leon Trotsky*, p. 133.

18. *Huitième Congrès Socialiste International tenu à Copenhagen du 28 août au 3 septembre 1910. Compte rendu analytique* (Ghent: Secrétariat du Bureau Socialiste International, 1911), pp. 181–83.

19. *Ibid.*, pp. 116–17. For a fuller view of Lenin's views on cooperatives, see Lenin, XIX, pp. 345–54.

20. Karol [Karl] Radek, "Ruch współdzielczy na usługach kontrrewolucji i kapitału," *Przegląd Socjaldemokratyczny*, IV, No. 3 (May 1908), p. 206. Radek expressed similar sentiments in other articles: "Z

historji ruchu współdzielczego," *Trybuna*, I, No. 5 (April 30, 1910),
pp. 5–6 and "Granice ruchu współdzielczego," *Trybuna*, I, No. 2 (April
9, 1910), pp. 5–7.

21. Radek, "Kooperativy i Internatsional," *Sotsial-Demokrat*, No.
15/16 (December 12/30, 1910), pp. 2–3.

22. Lenin, XLVII, pp. 266–67.

23. *Ibid.*, pp. 274–75.

24. The Lenin-Luxemburg disputes have been examined in a number
of studies. See, for example, Frölich, pp. 101–8; Dziewanowski, pp. 34–
36; and Nettl, I, pp. 224–28, 285–94.

25. See, for example, his article, "Vor dem Parteitag."

26. This was of course Lenin's rationale for the vanguard theory of a
party, developed in his famous work *What Is To Be Done?* For a good
discussion of the impact of this work, see Ulam, pp. 176–93.

27. See below, pp. 94–103.

28. [Karl Radek], "Kritisches über Kopenhagen," *Leipziger Volkszeitung*, No. 214 (September 15, 1910), pp. 1–2 and No. 215 (September 16, 1910), pp. 1–2; "Sozialdemokraties und Rüstungsbeschrän-
kung," *Bremer Bürgerzeitung*, No. 88 (April 3, 1911), p. 1, No. 89
(April 15, 1911), p. 2, No. 90 (April 18, 1911), p. 1, No. 91 (April 19,
1911), p. 1.

29. The role of the SDKPiL in the Russian party and Lenin's annoy-
ance over Luxemburg's maneuvers are best seen in the correspondence
of Lenin with the International Socialist Bureau. See Haupt, *passim*.

30. Dziewanowski, pp. 51–52.

31. Radek, "Avtobiografiia," p. 153.

32. Radek, "Zur Abwehr," *Bremer Bürgerzeitung*, No. 88 (April 13,
1911), p. 1.

33. Franz, "Aus Briefen Konrad Haenischs," p. 473. Marchlewski
was showing some signs of impatience with Radek even before the challenge on disarmament. Shortly after the Copenhagen Congress, on October 4, 1910, Marchlewski, reporting on the Congress in a letter to
Dzierżyński, wrote: "Radek has been scribbling exaggerated things and
has become overly pessimistic." Tych and Schumacher, pp. 209–10.

34. Radek, *Meine Abrechnung.*

35. Nettl, I, pp. 391–92.

36. For a typical example of how the SPD leadership evaluated the
Bremen organization, note the remarks of Herman Müller in *Protokoll
... 1913*, pp. 539–40.

37. [Karl Radek], "Ein Gewaltstreich," *Leipziger Volkszeitung*, XIX,
No. 126 (June 4, 1912), pp. 1–3. This article was originally published
anonymously, but its authorship was established during a discussion of
the article at the SPD Congress of 1912.

38. These views were presented by Kautsky in a series of articles in *Die Neue Zeit* in 1911 and 1912. See Schorske, pp. 245–46.

39. Radek, "Zu unserem Kampfe gegen den Imperialismus," *Die Neue Zeit*, XXX, Book 2, No. 32 (May 10, 1912), pp. 194–99; No. 33 (May 17, 1912), pp. 233–41.

40. *Ibid.*, pp. 233–34.

41. Karl Radek, "An die Redaktion N. Z.," manuscripts dated July 17 and July 24, 1912, "In Sachen Radek."

42. Radek, "Wege und Mittel im Kampfe gegen den Imperialismus," *Bremer Bürgerzeitung*, No. 216 (September 14, 1912), Beilage 4, p. 4.

43. Galley proofs of the article as set for *Die Neue Zeit* are in the file "In Sachen Radek."

44. Radek, "An die Redaktion N. Z., manuscript dated August 16, 1912, "In Sachen Radek."

45. Radek, "An die Redaktion N. Z., manuscripts dated August 25 and August 29, 1912, "In Sachen Radek."

46. Franz, "Aus Briefen Konrad Haenischs," p. 472.

47. Luxemburg, "Blinder Eifer," p. 3.

48. Cited in Note 43 above.

49. *Protokoll . . . 1912*, p. 213.

50. Franz, "Aus Briefen Konrad Haenischs," p. 472.

51. *Ibid.*, pp. 473–77.

52. *Ibid.*, pp. 475–77.

53. *Ibid.*, p. 475. With perhaps a bit of malice, Haenisch observes that Lensch's desertion of Radek was to be expected.

54. *Protokoll . . . 1913*, pp. 540–41.

55. *Ibid.*, p. 536.

56. An accurate summary of the events leading to the exclusion of Radek from the SPD may be found in Schorske, pp. 254–56; another summary, highly biased in favor of Radek, is Franz, "Der Fall Radek," pp. 389–93.

57. "Die Lex Radeks," *Bremer Bürgerzeitung*, No. 211 (September 9, 1913), pp. 1–2.

58. Franz, "Aus Briefen Konrad Haenischs," p. 483.

59. Schorske (p. 256) maintains that the case was closed. Strictly speaking, he is correct, since the SPD did not rescind the expulsion. However, World War I broke out before the 1914 SPD Congress could meet. There are substantial indications that if the war had not intervened, there would have been mounting pressure to void the 1913 decision. See Franz, "Der Fall Radek," p. 392.

60. See, for example, Heilmann, pp. 1267–76. Heilmann, a member of the SPD's Right, found little cause for satisfaction in the manner in which Radek was excluded from the SPD in 1913.

NOTES TO CHAPTER 3

1. The full text of the Basel statement may be found in Gankin and Fisher, pp. 81–85.

2. Joll, pp. 167–68.

3. Schorske (p. 286) maintains that the manifesto owed its strident tone to the fact that most of the conservatives on the Executive Committee were on vacation when it was issued. The full text of the statement appears in Carl Grünberg, p. 51.

4. Landauer, pp. 495–96.

5. See Berlau, pp. 73–77.

6. Support for the government's request was by no means unanimous, but in the interests of party unity the fourteen dissidents agreed to cast their votes in favor of the war credits. For diverse interpretations of this crucial decision, see Schorske, pp. 286–91; Berlau, pp. 67–91; Fainsod, pp. 18–30.

7. In his last article before the war credits vote, Radek spoke in terms of socialist opposition to the war, rather than Left opposition alone, presumably hoping that even the revisionists would oppose the war. On this occasion he did not differentiate between revisionist and radical socialists. See Radek, "Wofür sollen wir bluten?" *Bremer Bürgerzeitung*, No. 176 (July 31, 1914), p. 2.

8. Radek, "Avtobiografiia," p. 155.

9. *Ibid.*, pp. 155–56.

10. Quoted in Wohlgemuth, pp. 56–57. Wohlgemuth claims to have a copy of the full letter in his possession.

11. Schorske, p. 290.

12. Parabellum [Radek], "Zwei Parteien," *Berner Tagwacht*, No. 53 (March 5, 1915), p. 1; Parabellum, "Bettler!" *Berner Tagwacht*, No. 54 (March 6, 1915), p. 2.

13. Angelica Balabanoff, who represented the Italian socialists, does not report any contact with Radek in Switzerland prior to 1915. See Balabanoff, *My Life as a Rebel*, p. 143.

14. Litwak, p. 34.

15. See Radek, "Erklärung," *Die Neue Zeit*, XXIX, Book 1, No. 1 (October 7, 1910), p. 27.

16. Interview with the Menshevik in question, who has asked me not to reveal his sister's identity. Rosa Radek did not arrive in Switzerland until the late summer of 1915 (see Radek, "Avtobiografiia," p. 155). Whether she knew of Karl's mistress in Berne is uncertain.

17. The full text may be found in Gankin and Fisher, pp. 140–43.

18. There is some reason to believe that the International Socialist

Bureau had intended to read Lenin out of the Second International at the 1914 Congress in Vienna. Cf. Ulam, p. 300.

19. Parabellum, "Vor dem Zusammentritt des Reichstages," *Berner Tagwacht*, No. 277 (November 26, 1914), p. 1; Parabellum, "Von Stufe zu Stufe," *Berner Tagwacht*, No. 287 (December 8, 1914), p. 1; Parabellum, "Die Hetze gegen Deutschland," *Berner Tagwacht*, No. 18 (January 23, 1915), p. 1.

20. Radek, "Avtobiografiia," p. 158.

21. Schorske, pp. 296–302.

22. Parabellum, "Das Budget angenommen," *Berner Tagwacht*, No. 67 (March 22, 1915), p. 1.

23. Parabellum, "Ein Schritt vorwärts in Deutschland," *Berner Tagwacht*, No. 91 (April 21, 1915), p. 1.

24. G. Shklovskii, "Bernskaia Konferentsiia 1915 g.," *Proletarskaia Revoliutsiia*, No. 5 (40) (1925), p. 187. The concept of a "United States of Europe" was one of the matters debated at the Bolshevik Conference held at Berne from February 27 to March 4, 1915. Lenin was in the odd position of having his idea accepted by the Conference after he himself was ready to drop the matter, partially as a consequence of his talks with Radek.

25. There is a good deal of confusion on exactly which party or parties Radek may have joined during his stay in Switzerland. He had earlier been publicly excluded from both the SDKPiL and the SPD, so he could not claim membership in either of these two important parties. However, in retorting to a statement in the German socialist press that he had no party affiliation, Radek claimed that he was a member of both the Swiss and the Russian Social Democratic Parties (Karl Radek, "Notiz," *Die Neue Zeit*, XXXIII, Book 2, No. 9, May 28, 1915, p. 288). Possibly he joined the Swiss Social Democratic Party after his emigration; it is worth noting, however, that he never identified himself with the Swiss party at any other time, even when such identification would have been of advantage to him (see pp. 38–39). The claim that he was a member of the Russian party is supported by Lenin in a letter dated March 31, 1914, "An den Landesvorstand der Sozialdemokratie Russ. Polens u. Litauens [SDKPiL]," to be found in the file "In Sachen Radek." In this letter, Lenin avers that Radek is a "fully qualified member" of the Russian Social Democratic Labor Party. Offsetting this evidence, however, is the authoritative article by Shklovskii, "Bernskaia Konferentsiia 1915 g.," in which it is specifically stated that Radek was not a Bolshevik in 1915. Moreover, in many of his later writings, Radek dated his membership in the Russian party from 1917. It is possible that Lenin offered him membership in the Bolshevik Party, but that Radek, still German-oriented, did not avail himself of it. The most plausible ex-

planation of his letter to *Die Neue Zeit* ("Notiz") is that Radek was lying, confident that no one would bother to check his story.

26. The text of the manifesto may be found in Gankin and Fisher, pp. 295–97.

27. Cf. *ibid.*, pp. 307–8, for the text of this resolution.

28. The very first issue carried an article by Radek, "Jugend vor die Front!" *Jugend-Internationale*, No. 1 (September 1, 1915), pp. 7–8.

29. For Lenin's acknowledgment of the letter, see Lenin, XLIX, p. 80.

30. For Zinoviev's view of the conference, see Gankin and Fisher, pp. 312–15.

31. Grimm did make inquiries to see if he could get Radek credentials from a member of the International Socialist Bureau. See the letter of H. Kamienski to Grimm, August 3, 1915, in Lademacher, II, pp. 88–89.

32. Lenin, XLIX, pp. 94–95, 128–29.

33. Lademacher, II, p. 71.

34. Lenin, XXII, pp. 288–92.

35. See *ibid.*, XLIX, p. 96.

36. It is noteworthy that most of the letters Lenin sent to Radek in 1915 carry the formal salutation "Dear Comrade Radek," and none refer to him by his first name. In contrast, letters from Lenin to Safarov during this period were addressed "Dear Georgi"; to Gorky, "Dear Alexei Maximich"; to Shliapnikov, "Dear Alexander"; and so on. The closest Lenin ever came to an informal salutation to Radek was a rare "Dear Radek."

37. See Lenin, XLIX, pp. 125–26.

38. Radek, "Der Entwicklung der Internationale," Part Two, *Lichtstrahlen*, II, 15 (September 5, 1915), p. 15.

39. See Schorske, pp. 301–4.

40. Luxemburg had been imprisoned for treason since February 8, 1915.

41. Cf. Gankin and Fisher, p. 335.

42. Liebknecht did, however, send a letter of solidarity to the conference, urging socialist activism. See Gankin and Fisher, pp. 326–28.

43. See Lenin's letter of August 19, 1915; Lenin, XLIX, pp. 125–26.

44. Trotsky, *My Life*, p. 249.

45. For an analysis of the groups that gathered at Zimmerwald and of their diverse viewpoints, see Gankin and Fisher, pp. 338–42; see also Fainsod, pp. 61–68. Two Lenin-oriented monographs are Ia. G. Temkin, *Tsimmerval'd-Kintal* (Moscow: Izadtel'stvo "Vysshaia Shkola," 1967), and Arnold Reisberg, *Lenin und die Zimmerwalder Bewegung* (Berlin: Dietz Verlag, 1966).

46. The complete text of the manifesto and the names of the signatories may be found in Gankin and Fisher, pp. 329–33.

47. See *ibid.*, p. 333, n.44. Gankin and Fisher state that a "reliable source" places Hanecki at the conference, but they do not cite the source. Hanecki's official biographical notices in Polish and Soviet works skim over his wartime activities without telling exactly where he was at any given time. According to one recent work, Hanecki left Switzerland and moved to Scandinavia in the summer of 1915. See Zeman and Scharlau, p. 163. Lademacher's account indicates that Hanecki was not there.

48. Lademacher, I, p. 164.

49. Gankin and Fisher, p. 353.

50. *Ibid.*, p. 348.

51. [Radek] "Die Zimmerwalder Linke über die Aufgaben der Arbeiterklasse. Zur Einführung," *Internationales Flugblatt*, No. 1 (November 1915), pp. 1–5.

52. Although the article was first published anonymously, Radek reprinted it a decade later in a Russian translation and admitted authorship. See Radek, *Germanskaia Revoliutsiia*, Vol. I (Moscow: Gosizdat, 1925), pp. 466–78.

53. In recent years, a number of studies have strongly suggested that Lenin was on the payroll of the German government all through World War I, and that he received huge sums of money from this source. One such charge is made in Possony, pp. 176–99; another is to be found in Moorhead, pp. 122–30. Both of these works are based on extensive research (actually, in the case of Moorhead, the research was done at second hand), and cannot be dismissed lightly. Yet it is hard to imagine why Lenin would have allowed others to control the journal if he had millions of marks at his disposal. As Radek's letters to Roland-Holst indicated, the original intention was to include Lenin as an editor, and the only anticipated difficulty was Lenin's reaction to contributions by Trotsky (Lademacher, II, pp. 165–66). Yet the issue of control was to prove important, and Lenin's lack of finances at this time definitely weakened his position. One scholar who has thoroughly plumbed the archives of the German Foreign Ministry states that there is no evidence of any direct contact between Lenin and the German Foreign Office. See Zeman, p. x. I do not doubt that the German government invested large sums in attempts to subvert the Russian war effort, or that Lenin would have accepted these funds if offered; I am less convinced, however, that Lenin himself directly benefited from these funds, since there are many indications that Lenin was constantly plagued with financial difficulties.

54. See Carr, *The Bolshevik Revolution*, pp. 418–28; Wolfe, pp. 578–90; Low, pp. 36–78; Leder, pp. 186–208.

55. Parabellum, "Annexionen und Sozialdemokratie," *Berner Tagwacht*, No. 252 (October 28, 1915), Beilage, p. 1, and No. 253 (October 29, 1915), Beilage, p. 1.

56. *Ibid.*, Part 2, p. 1.

57. *Ibid.*

58. "Revoliutsionnyi proletariat i pravo natsii na samoopredelenie," in Lenin, XXVII, p. 61. This was not published at the time, but circulated in manuscript form.

59. *Ibid.*, pp. 62–68.

60. Parabellum, "Das Selbstbestimmungsrecht der Völker," *Lichtstrahlen*, No. 3 (December 5, 1915), p. 50.

61. *Ibid.*, p. 52.

62. This portion of Radek's article, together with Lenin's underlining and remark, is reproduced in *Leninskii Sbornik*, XVII.

63. [Radek] "Thesen über Imperialismus und nationale Unterdrückung," *Vorbote*, No. 2 (April 1916), pp. 44–51. The theses are translated in full in Gankin and Fisher, pp. 507–18.

64. *Ibid.*, p. 512.

65. Lenin, XLIX, pp. 177–78.

66. *Ibid.*, pp. 234–35.

67. Radek was rumored by some to have been the go-between for the German government and the Bolsheviks and to have dispensed German funds liberally to Bolsheviks in Switzerland. In most of these allegations, the supposed source of funds is the German socialist Alexander Helphand (Parvus), a former radical who during the war was entrusted with large sums of money. See Possony, p. 182. There is no evidence, however, that Radek had access to any German money in Switzerland, or that he ever met Helphand in Switzerland. Considering Radek's relations with Lenin in 1916, there is little reason to believe that he would have procured funds for Lenin. Note the account of A. Litwak, one of the socialist émigrés in Switzerland, who knew Radek fairly well and saw him often in 1915 and 1916. Although Litwak's account of Radek's activities in Switzerland is almost completely hostile, he specifically states that Radek did not receive funds from Helphand. Zeman and Scharlau, p. 156, tend to back Litwak, although their account is more suggestive. For Radek's later contacts with Helphand, see pp. 56–57.

68. Lenin, XLIX, pp. 181–82.

69. *Ibid.*, pp. 183, 193–95, 199, 223.

70. Lademacher, I, pp. 251–52, 308, 323.

71. He was eventually denied the Dutch mandate by the Conference. See *ibid.*, I, p. 361.

72. Gankin and Fisher, p. 458.

73. Lademacher, I, p. 372.

74. *Ibid.*, p. 379.

75. See the text of the manifesto in Gankin and Fisher, pp. 418–21.

76. *Ibid.*, pp. 424–26.

77. Radek, "Thesen über Imperialismus und nationale Unterdrückung."

78. Lenin, XLIX, pp. 233–34, 344.

79. *Ibid.*, p. 370.

80. In later years Radek regretted his bad relations with Lenin in 1916. In his autobiographical article of 1929 he attempted to conceal the facts with a vague statement that he kept in "close touch" with Lenin during that year (Radek, "Avtobiografiia," p. 162). The published record of Lenin's correspondence in 1916, however, shows only one letter to Radek—the curt dismissal quoted in the text, p. 47.

81. Nettl, II, *passim*. At this time Luxemburg was still in prison.

82. See Parabellum, "Die Weihnachtsbotschaft aus Deutschland," *Berner Tagwacht*, No. 300 (December 23, 1914), p. 1.

83. Radek was always proud of these articles, and he reprinted them in later years as his own. Several appear in *In den Reihen der deutschen Revolution*.

84. [Radek] "Einheit oder Spaltung der Partei," *Die Arbeiterpolitik*, I, No. 4 (July 15, 1916), pp. 27–28; No. 5 (July 22, 1916), pp. 35–37; No. 6 (July 29, 1916), pp. 43–45; No. 7 (August 5, 1916), pp. 50–53; No. 8 (August 16, 1916), pp. 58–60; No. 10 (August 26, 1916), pp. 74–76. Most of the views discussed here are from the August 5 installment.

85. Nettl, II, pp. 630–31.

86. [Radek] "Im Fangnetz der Widersprüche," *Die Arbeiterpolitik*, I, No. 6 (July 29, 1916), p. 45.

87. *Ibid.*, No. 8 (August 16, 1916), p. 60.

88. Radek's last signed article in the *Berner Tagwacht* appeared on May 9, 1916.

89. Gankin and Fisher, pp. 532–38.

90. Arnold Struthahn [Radek], "Vor dem Parteitag der Schweizer Sozialdemokratie," *Die Arbeiterpolitik*, I, No. 18 (October 21, 1916), pp. 138–41.

91. The first article signed Struthahn is the one cited above. At least a dozen major articles and pamphlets were issued under this pseudonym in the next two years.

92. Lenin, XLIX, p. 370.

93. *Ibid.*, p. 373. A mildly amusing account of the casual manner in

which Radek dashed off the brochure appears in V. Miuntsenberg [W. Münzenberg], S. *Libknechtom i Leninym* (Moscow: Molodaia Gvardiia, 1930), p. 139.

94. Lenin, XLIX, p. 378.
95. *Ibid.*, p. 392.
96. Miuntsenberg, p. 139.
97. Radek, "Avtobiografiia," p. 162.

NOTES TO CHAPTER 4

1. Lenin, XLIX, pp. 404–5.
2. Futrell, p. 154.
3. Platten, p. 34.
4. The Bolshevik version of these negotiations is presented in Platten, *passim.* Alan Moorhead's *The Russian Revolution* also deals with this episode (pp. 173–83) but tries to suggest a more sinister atmosphere than the evidence warrants. Pertinent documents from the files of the German Foreign Office have been reprinted in Zeman, pp. 25–44. Another account based on the German documents is found in Hahlweg, *passim.*
5. Platten, pp. 37–38.
6. Radek, "Avtobiografiia," p. 168.
7. *Ibid.*, p. 169. Voikov did not accompany Lenin's party through Germany, but made a similar trip at a later date—presumably without his passport.
8. A photostat of the agreement may be found in Platten, between pp. 72 and 73. It might be noted that although there were thirty-two people in the sealed train, only thirty are accounted for by the signatures on the agreement. The thirty-first person was Platten, who acted as the intermediary with German officials; the thirty-second was obviously Radek. Why the German officials did not question the presence of an extra person on the train is still a mystery.
9. *Ibid.*, pp. 46, 128.
10. Futrell, Chapter VII, *passim.*
11. Litwak, p. 34.
12. Zeman and Scharlau, pp. 217, 227–28.
13. Zeman, p. 50.
14. Zeman and Scharlau, p. 217.
15. Futrell, pp. 179–92.
16. Mayer, pp. 262–63.
17. In keeping with long-established practice, Bolshevik historians speak only of Hanecki and Vorovsky as the leading members of the Stockholm group. Vorovsky had the historical "good fortune" to be as-

sassinated in 1923 while on a diplomatic mission and thus is remembered as a hero. Hanecki, like Radek, was purged in 1937; however, unlike Radek, Hanecki was posthumously rehabilitated in the late 1950's. For a typical example of the omission of Radek, see "Vozzvaniia zagranichego predstavitel'stva TsK RSDRP(b)," *Voprosy Istorii KPSS*, No. 3 (1957), p. 159.

18. Futrell offers some information in an incomplete biographical sketch of Hanecki, pp. 168ff. For Lenin's requests for money, see Lenin, XLIX, pp. 438–39.

19. Karl Radek, Jakob Hanecki, V. V. Worowski [sic], "Das Komplott gegen das russischen revolutionären Sozialdemokraten/Bolschewiki," *Russische Korrespondenz "Prawda,"* No. 11 (July 22, 1917), p. 506. This article was intended as a refutation to the rumors that the Bolsheviks were paid agents of the German Foreign Office. In Petrograd the rumors had manifested themselves as open charges.

20. [Radek] "Unterm eigenen Banner, *Arbeiterpolitik*, II (February 17, 1917), pp. 50–52; 8 (February 24, 1917), pp. 59–60; 9 (March 3, 1917), pp. 67–68.

21. See Schorske, pp. 314–21.

22. [Radek] "Das Zentrum der Partei und die Kriegsfragen," *Arbeiterpolitik*, II, 9 (March 3, 1917), pp. 68–70; 10 (March 10, 1917), pp. 77–79; 13 (March 31, 1917), pp. 100–2.

23. "Aufruf!," *Arbeiterpolitik*, II, 18 (May 5, 1917), p. 1. Knief's trip to Stockholm is mentioned in Radek, "Avtobiografiia," p. 166.

24. [Radek] "Die Treibkräfte der russischen Revolution" [Part 5], *Arbeiterpolitik*, II, No. 18 (May 5, 1917), p. 140; also see his "Burgschaften," *Arbeiterpolitik*, II, No. 14 (April 7, 1917), p. 106.

25. Futrell, p. 157.

26. A photograph opposite p. 161 in Futrell shows Radek in this unaccustomed garb.

27. *Leninskii Sbornik*, XIII, pp. 257–59.

28. Balabanoff was a Russian émigré who had spent several years in the Italian socialist movement. She appears to have been highly sympathetic to the Bolsheviks, but her first loyalty was to international socialism as expressed through the Zimmerwald Movement.

29. Balabanoff, *Erinnerungen und Erlebnisse*, pp. 143–51.

30. Balabanoff, *My Life*, p. 167. This book is not an English translation of *Erinnerungen und Erlebnisse*, despite the implication in the title.

31. Gankin and Fisher, pp. 617–28.

32. See Lenin's letter to Radek dated June 17, 1917, in Lenin, XLIX, pp. 443–44.

33. *Ibid.*, p. 440.

34. See Radek, "Zimmerwald auf der Scheidewege," *Jugend-Internationale*, No. 9 (September 1, 1917), pp. 2–4.
35. Lenin, XLIX, p. 440.
36. Mayer, p. 278.
37. See Mayer's letter to his wife, dated July 9, 1917, and quoted in *ibid.*, p. 276; also see Lademacher, I, 519.
38. Mayer records that he did just that. *Ibid.*, p. 278.
39. *Ibid.*, pp. 276–77.
40. Zeman, p. 69.
41. Futrell, p. 186.
42. Gankin and Fisher, pp. 680–83.
43. Balabanoff, "Die Zimmerwalder Bewegung," pp. 232–33.
44. Balabanoff, *My Life*, pp. 169–70.
45. Radek, "Die Revolution und der Bruch mit der Bourgeoisie in Russland," *Bote der Russischen Revolution*, No. 4 (October 6, 1917), pp. 1–5; also see Radek, "Die Weltlage und die russische Revolution," *Bote der Russischen Revolution*, No. 7 (October 27, 1917), pp. 4–7.
46. Balabanoff, *My Life*, pp. 169–70.
47. *Ibid.*, pp. 171–72.
48. Gankin and Fisher, p. 683.
49. Radek, "Der Bürgerkrieg in Russland," *Bote der Russischen Revolution*, No. 9/10 (November 17, 1917), p. 15.
50. Radek, "Parvus," *Pravda*, No. 285 (December 14, 1924), p. 2. This personal recollection was written on the occasion of Helphand's death.
51. V.V. Vorovskii, *Stat'i i materialy po voprosam vneshnei politiki* (Moscow: Izdatel'stvo sotsial'no-ekonomicheskoi literatury, 1959), pp. 181–82.
52. Radek's description of Helphand in "Parvus" suggests that he believed that Helphand regretted his dubious connection with the German Foreign Office and was interested in helping the revolutionary cause.
53. Lenin, XXXIV, pp. 30–31.
54. Radek, "Parvus," p. 2.
55. Zeman and Scharlau, p. 248.
56. Radek, "Avtobiografiia," p. 170.
57. Lockhart, p. 255.
58. Leon Trotsky, *My Life*, p. 239.
59. Radek, "Avtobiografiia," p. 159.
60. Gankin and Fisher, p. 348.
61. Quoted in Deutscher, *The Prophet Armed*, p. 361.
62. For the text of the appeal, see Ioffe, pp. 171–75.

63. The texts of this appeal and similar documents are reprinted in Drahn and Leonhard, *passim*.
64. Wheeler-Bennett, pp. 218–19.
65. Trotsky, *My Life*, p. 387.
66. For further details on the episode of Left-Communism, see Schapiro, pp. 130–46; see also Daniels, pp. 70–91.
67. *Sedmoi s"ezd Rossiiskoi Kommunisticheskoi Partii (Bol'shevikov)* (Moscow: Partiinoe Izdatel'stvo, 1923), pp. 123–24.
68. Radek, "Pobeda imperializmu nad russkoi revoliutsii," *Kommunist* [Petrograd], No. 1 (March 5, 1918), p. 1.
69. *Ibid.*, p. 2.
70. Radek, "Oborona revoliutsii," *Kommunist* [Petrograd], No. 2 (March 6, 1918), p. 2.
71. Radek, "Pobeda imperializmu . . . ," p. 2.
72. Schapiro, p. 142.
73. Radek, "Krasnaia armiia," *Kommunist* [Moscow], No. 2 (April 27, 1918), pp. 14–15.
74. *Trudy pervogo vserossiiskogo s"ezda sovetov narodnogo khoziaistvo, 25 maia–4 iiunia 1918 g. Stenograficheskii otchët* (Moscow: Gosudarstvennoe Izdatel'stvo, 1918), pp. 16–19.
75. At the Seventh Congress of the Bolshevik Party in March 1918, the Bolsheviks renounced the designation "Social Democrats" and began to call themselves "Communists." After 1918, Radek used the term "Social Democrat" interchangeably with "revisionist" or "reformist."
76. Radek, "Razvitie sotsializma ot nauki k deistvo [September 1918]," in *Piat' let Kominterna*, Vol. I (Moscow: Krasnaia Nov', 1924), pp. 29–30.
77. *Ibid.*, pp. 21–22, 27.
78. *Ibid.*, pp. 23, 25–26.
79. Radek, "Brest-Litovsk [October 1918]," in *Vneshniaia politika Sovetskoi Rossii* (Moscow: Gosudarstvennoe Izdatel'stvo, 1923), p. 22.
80. Radek, "Mezhdunarodnoe polozhenie i vneshniaia politika sovetskoi vlasti," Part 2, *Izvestiia*, No. 194 (September 8, 1918), p. 2.

NOTES TO CHAPTER 5

1. Radek, *Vneshniaia politika*, p. 27.
2. "Akten betreffend: den russischen Bolschewik, Karl Radek, 1917–1919," St. Antony's Collection of the Records of the German Foreign Office, Microfilm Roll No. 38, National Archives, Washington, D.C. (Hereafter this material will be cited as "Akten betreffend: Radek.") This description of Radek is taken from MS No. 4848 (January 31, 1918).

3. *Ibid.*, MS No. 17890 (April 27, 1918).

4. *Ibid.*, MS No. 32560 (August 2, 1918).

5. Struthahn [Radek], *Die deutsche Revolution* (Moscow: publisher unknown, 1918), pp. 5, 13.

6. See *ibid.*, pp. 25–26.

7. Until his departure from Switzerland, Radek had been the major contributor to *Arbeiterpolitik*. Since most of his articles were unsigned, he quite possibly continued to write the lead articles even after this time. Articles openly signed by Radek began to appear in *Arbeiterpolitik* in 1918, but they were translations of the Russian press rather than items written specifically for *Arbeiterpolitik*.

8. See Lowenthal, p. 26.

9. On November 22, 1918, the German ambassador to Sweden warned his superiors that he had received information that Radek was preparing to go to Berlin. See "Akten betreffend: Radek," MS No. 2761 BII (November 22, 1918).

10. Radek, "Noiabr'," p. 145.

11. *Ibid.*, p. 146.

12. For a brief treatment of the work of the Reich Congress, see Ryder, pp. 177–84.

13. This cool reception is noted in many accounts. See, for example, Nettl, II, p. 747. Radek wrote a long memoir ("Noiabr'") on his activities in Germany but understandably preferred not to dwell on his continued rebuff from Luxemburg. Yet even in Radek's memoir Luxemburg appears to have had only the briefest of conversations with him and not overly friendly ones at that. Although these memoirs were not published until 1926, Radek appears to have written his account much earlier. For translated excerpts of "Noiabr'," see Carr, "Radek's Political Salon," pp. 411–30. "Noiabr'," and several other documents—including some not readily available elsewhere—have been reproduced in Schüddekopf, "Karl Radek in Berlin," pp. 87–166.

14. See for example her famous critique of the Bolshevik regime in Luxemburg, *Leninism or Marxism*, pp. 25–80.

15. Radek, "Noiabr'," p. 150.

16. See, for example, Johannes Knief, "Internationale Kommunisten und Unabhängige," *Arbeiterpolitik*, III, 48 (November 30, 1918), pp. 289–92, and the unsigned article (probably also by Knief) "Kritisches zu der Berliner revolutionären Bewegung," *Arbeiterpolitik*, III, 49 (December 7, 1918), pp. 296–97.

17. Radek, "Noiabr'," p. 151.

18. *Illustrierte Geschichte*, p. 264.

19. [Rosa Luxemburg] "Was will der Spartakusbund?" (Berlin: Komissionsdruck der K.P.D., n.d.)

20. *Bericht über den Gründungsparteitag der Kommunistischen Partei Deutschlands (Spartakusbund) vom. 30, Dezember 1918 bis. 1. Januar 1919* (n.p.: Kommunistischen Partei Deutschlands [Spartakusbund], n.d.), p. 42.

21. Radek, *Die russische und die deutsche Revolution*, p. 15. Radek's speech was not included in the stenographic report but was separately printed.

22. *Ibid.*, p. 31. Had Radek been calling for an immediate revolution, he would undoubtedly have compared the position of the German Communist Party to the Bolshevik position in November 1917, since it was on November 7, 1917, that the Bolsheviks seized power in Russia. In April 1917, however, the Bolsheviks—with the notable exception of Lenin—were not even considering a take-over. Although Radek's words are ambiguous, it seems likely that they were intended as a warning that the KPD was not yet in position to try to take over Germany.

23. "Akten betreffend: Radek," MS No. A54719 (December 31, 1918). Others have also interpreted Radek's speech as a call to revolution. Fainsod (p. 180) did so, but apparently he did not have access to the stenographic report of Radek's speech cited above. Freund, pp. 35–36, interprets Radek's speech as an attempt to get the German Communists to rise. Freund did have access to the stenographic report, but he appears to have based his interpretation on the report of the police spy and on Radek's revolutionary phraseology.

24. A. A. Rubinshtein [Tomas], "Interview with Boris Nicolaevsky [1955]," MS, p. 5. In the Nicolaevsky Collection of the Hoover Institution on War, Revolution and Peace, Stanford University, Stanford, California. Rubinshtein was an important figure in the early years of the Communist International. Under the name "Thomas" he became an important though little-known troubleshooter for the Comintern. See Radek, "Noiabr'," p. 168.

25. See Frölich, pp. 290–315.

26. Rubinshtein, p. 5.

27. See Nettl, II, pp. 765–72. It might be noted that most of the Spartacists were unhappy about becoming involved in what Luxemburg and others regarded as the wrong battle, with the wrong allies (the Revolutionary Shop Stewards and USPD dissidents, who, ironically enough, were later referred to as Spartacists), at the wrong time.

28. Radek, *Germanskaia Revoliutsiia*, II, 94.

29. *Ibid.*, p. 95.

30. For some interesting speculation on why Wilhelm Pieck (later a

leader of Communist East Germany), who was apprehended with Lieb-knecht and Luxemburg, did not suffer a similar fate, see Waldman, p. 195n, and Nollau, pp. 332–33. Waldman implies and Nollau categorically states that Pieck made a deal with his captors and betrayed his comrades. In his own account, Pieck (p. 28) claims that he survived by playing dead after his captors shot at him.

31. "Akten betreffend: Radek," MS No. B45567 BII (January 23, 1919).

32. *Ibid.*, MS No. A14116 (April 30, 1919).

33. For Radek's claims, see his "Noiabr'," p. 156. Schüddekopf's "Karl Radek in Berlin," p. 95, cites evidence from the Brockdorff-Rantzau papers to deflate Radek's heroic claims.

34. Schüddekopf, "Karl Radek in Berlin," p. 95.

35. There is a photographic reproduction of one of these posters in the picture section following p. 82, and in *Illustrierte Geschichte*, p. 265.

36. Radek, "Noiabr'," p. 162.

37. Schüddekopf, "Karl Radek in Berlin," pp. 114–18.

38. Radek, "Noiabr'," p. 163.

39. *Ibid.*, pp. 164–65.

40. *Ibid.*, p. 169.

41. For example, see F. L. Carsten, *The Reichswehr and German Politics*, p. 70. Carsten, who did exhaustive research on the subject, does not list any new noteworthy contacts; neither does Meier-Welcker in *Seeckt*. Of course, there is always the possibility that the two Turkish émigrés, who did have contacts with some German military figures, sounded Radek out for the German generals.

42. Mayer, pp. 319–22.

43. Radek, "Noiabr'," pp. 166–67.

44. Possony (p. 182) suggests that Moor was a wartime contact between Lenin and the German Foreign Office.

45. Radek, "Noiabr'," p. 163. Possony (p. 300) does raise some reasonable doubts.

46. See for example her "character sketch" of Radek; Ruth Fischer, pp. 201–2.

47. Radek, "Noiabr'," pp. 167–68.

48. Radek records that Friedrich Stampfer, the editor of *Vorwärts*, visited him, but apparently Stampfer chose to omit the visit from his own memoirs (Stampfer, *Erfahrungen*). Mr. Philips-Price's account has been incorporated into Carr, "Radek's Political Salon," pp. 428–30.

49. Radek, "Noiabr'," pp. 169–72.

50. Paquet, pp. vii–xi.

51. Radek, *An die Reich Konferenz der Kommunistischen Partei Deutschlands* (no publication data cited, but known to have been published in 1919, probably in Berlin), p. 5.

52. Radek, "Avtobiografiia," p. 156.

53. Radek, "Noiabr'," p. 168.

54. Karl Radek [letter to Paul Levi, dated October 16, 1919], MS (photostatic copy), Hoover Institution, Stanford University, Stanford, California.

55. Ruth Fischer, p. 207; Radek, "Noiabr'," p. 168.

56. Levi's speech is reproduced in *Bericht über den 2. Parteitag der Kommunistischen Partei Deutschlands (Spartakusbund) vom 20. bis 24. Oktober 1919* (Berlin: KPD, n.d.), pp. 6–26.

57. The Hamburg group were not entirely without grounds in making such inferences. See Schüddekopf, *Linke Leute von Rechts*, pp. 114–18.

58. Struthahn [Radek], "Die auswärtige Politik des deutschen Kommunismus," pp. 332–46.

59. Ruth Fischer, p. 92. Radek certainly does not mention the visit either in "Avtobiografiia" or in "Noiabr'."

60. Radek, "Noiabr'," p. 169.

61. See Radek, *Die Entwicklung der Weltrevolution*, pp. 28–29.

NOTES TO CHAPTER 6

1. Nettl, II, p. 629.

2. Borkenau, p. 89.

3. *Der I. Kongress der Kommunistichen Internationale*, p. 183.

4. *Ibid.*, p. 6.

5. *Ibid.*, pp. 115–29, 168–72, 202–6, 218–20, 222.

6. *Ibid.*, p. 225.

7. Cf. the chapter entitled "The Roads to Moscow" in Draper, pp. 114–30.

8. These travelers included the American anarchist Emma Goldman and the writers Romain Rolland and Lincoln Steffens. Among those who thought they might be Communists but discovered once they came to Russia that they were not, Bertrand Russell is the most prominent. Radek satirized Russell's disillusionment in his article: "Mr. Bertrand Russell's Sentimental Journey to Russia," in *Portraits and Pamphlets*, pp. 210–16.

9. Hulse, p. 21.

10. Balabanoff, *My Life as a Rebel*, p. 247.

11. Although many members had grave misgivings about Radek, only Ruth Fischer, who thoroughly disliked him, was decidedly more sympathetic to Zinoviev in her memoirs.

12. Balabanoff, *My Life as a Rebel*, p. 244.

13. Carr, *Socialism*, p. 156.

14. Radek is alleged to have been deliberately careless on one occasion with secret Comintern documents, merely in order to embarrass Zinoviev. See Rubinshtein, p. 13.

15. Louis Fischer, *The Life of Lenin*, p. 315.

16. Herzog, pp. 809–10.

17. *Ibid.*, pp. 806–7.

18. Radek's appetite for material comfort is noted with distaste by Balabanoff in *My Life as a Rebel*, pp. 247–48.

19. Radek, *Die Entwicklung der deutschen Revolution*, p. 37.

20. *U.S. Department of State Papers . . . The Paris Peace Conference*, XIII, p. 793.

21. The correspondence is collected in *Krasnaia Kniga*.

22. The fact that this denial of collusion was included is in itself interesting. The Germans had received unofficial inquiries from the Bolshevik regime as to what the German reaction would be to a Russian march into Poland. See Korbel, pp. 28–29. The full text of the note from the Soviet government to Poland can be found in *Krasnaia Kniga*, pp. 84–85.

23. *Ibid.*, pp. 86–89.

24. This preparation is discussed in some detail in Komarnicki, pp. 454–56. Komarnicki adduces a convincing amount of evidence but he evidently has anti-Russian axes to grind and vitiates his case in doing so. Korbel (pp. 26ff) gives further evidence.

25. Radek, "Mezhdunarodnoe Znachenie Pol'skogo Voprosa," *Izvestiia*, February 15, 1920.

26. Radek, *Voina*, p. 17.

27. Tukhachevskii, p. 232.

28. Radek, *Voina*, p. 17.

29. Zetkin, p. 20. Later editions of this book omit the conversations between Lenin and Zetkin concerning Lenin's admission of having berated Radek for defeatism.

30. *Der zweite Kongress der Kommunist. Internationale*, p. 661.

31. See for example his intervention in the quarrels of the American delegation; *ibid.*, pp. 607–10.

32. *Ibid.*, pp. 482–501.

33. Reed's case is well presented in Draper, pp. 256–58.

34. *Der zweite Kongress der Kommunist. Internationale*, pp. 614–25.

35. See Lenin, XLI, pp. 281–85.

36. Radek, *Piat' let Kominterna*, I, p. 228.

37. Reed's last days and thoughts are a matter for considerable dispute, in part because of the confused accounts offered at various times

by his widow. Draper (pp. 284–93) makes a valiant effort to sift through these accounts and arrive at a plausible explanation of Reed's physical and mental condition during the last month of his life.

38. *Ibid.*

39. Radek, "Noiabr'," p. 149. In a letter to his wife, Radek implied that he had patched up his differences with the SDKPiL (Schüddekopf, "Karl Radek in Berlin," p. 113), but this appears to have been wishful thinking. According to Ruth Fischer (p. 76), Levi interceded with Luxemburg and told her that she simply could not ignore Radek. Whatever the truth of the matter, it seems generally agreed that Levi did not share Luxemburg's hostility to Radek.

40. Ruth Fischer, pp. 118–19.

41. Radek, *Die Entwicklung der Weltrevolution*, pp. 15–17.

42. Cf. Carr, *The Bolshevik Revolution*, III, p. 188.

43. Willy Brandt and Richard Lowenthal, p. 138.

44. Degras, *The Communist International*, I, pp. 250–51.

45. Willy Brandt and Richard Lowenthal, pp. 138–39. The authors suggest that Radek even joined forces with Zinoviev in trying to form an anti-Levi faction in the German delegation. If so, it was not a collaboration that Radek pursued for long.

46. Radek, *Die Masken sind gefallen, passim.*

47. Radek, "Avtobiografiia," p. 168. Also see the note by M. Philips-Price to Carr, "Radek's Political Salon," pp. 428–29. Price confirms Radek's presence in Berlin at this time.

48. Carr, *The Bolshevik Revolution*, III, p. 223.

49. Willy Brandt and Richard Lowenthal, p. 141.

50. "Offener Brief," *Die Rote Fahne*, No. 6 (January 8, 1921), p. 1. The term Zentrale simply means an executive body. The name Central Committee, chosen in emulation of the Bolshevik Party structure, was not adopted until years later.

51. *Piatyi Vsemirnyi Kongress Kommunisticheskogo Internatsionala*, p. 89.

52. Drachkovitch and Lazitch, pp. 275–82.

53. *Ibid.*, pp. 285–92.

54. *Ibid.*, p. 298.

55. Excerpts from the letters are reprinted in Gruber, pp. 347–50.

56. Paul Levi, *Unser Weg: Wider den Putschismus* (Berlin: A. Seehof Verlag, 1921).

57. Radek, "Die Lehren eines Putschversuche," in *ibid.*, pp. 58–64.

58. Radek, "Der Fall Levi," *Kommunistische Internationale*, No. 17 (1921), pp. 55–71.

59. *Protokoll des III. Kongresses*, pp. 465–72, 481.

60. *Ibid.*, pp. 597–602. Klara Zetkin at first joined Levi in his resignation from the Zentrale, but was later reconciled with the ECCI.

61. Ruth Fischer, p. 179n.

62. Willy Brandt and Richard Lowenthal, pp. 112–13.

63. *Ibid.*, pp. 187–88.

64. This was by no means the end of Friesland's career in German politics. Under the name Ernst Reuter, he eventually joined the SPD again, and subsequently enjoyed a long and distinguished career in German socialism, becoming Lord Mayor of West Berlin after World War II and serving in this capacity until his death in 1953. The story of his expulsion is well told in Angress, pp. 197–222. In general, Angress tends to accept the Friesland-Reuter view given in Willy Brandt and Richard Lowenthal, *passim*.

65. *Protokoll des III. Kongresses*, pp. 434–35.

66. Degras, I, pp. 250–51.

67. Radek, "Obmanshchiki iz II Internatsionala," *Pravda*, No. 268 (November 26, 1922), p. 1.

68. Radek's meetings with Seeckt are explored in Carsten, "The Reichswehr and the Red Army, 1920–33," *Survey*, No. 44/45 (October 1962), pp. 119–20. Also see Hallgarten, pp. 28–34. Hans Meier-Welcker's *Seeckt* offers a little more detail but no new revelations on any Radek-Seeckt contacts. Radek's mission to Seeckt was of course separate from his Comintern activities; this was one of the few times Lenin used Radek as a diplomatic emissary, and apparently he did so only because of Radek's knowledge of German politics. For the entire situation, much of it out of Radek's hands, see Carr, *The Bolshevik Revolution*, III, p. 305–38, and Freund, pp. 108–15.

69. The latter group was a new organization of Leftist socialists led by the Austrian Social Democrat Otto Bauer and including the Menshevik émigrés, the British Independent Labour Party (ILP), and several others. It briefly served to attract radicals who could accept neither the Comintern nor the Second International. In May 1923 it merged with the Second International into a new organization, the Socialist Workers' International. For Radek's caustic summary of the short life of the Second-and-a-Half International, see his article "The Balance of the Hamburg Socialist Conference: Without Sail or Rudder," *International Press Correspondence*, III, 46 (May 31, 1923), pp. 369–71.

70. See *The Second and Third Internationals, passim*.

71. Lenin, XLV, pp. 140–44.

72. A copy of this speech was smuggled to the U.S. Embassy in Brussels and is now in the National Archives. See Decimal Files, Department of State Archives, File No. 7600.61/692.

73. Gustav Hilger, a German diplomat stationed in Moscow, wrote: "I once devised an easy way of finding out whether Radek had recently been in Germany or not. All that was necessary was to invite him for lunch. If he came wearing his characteristic beard, we could be sure that he had not gone on an illegal trip abroad; but if he came clean-shaved or with stubbles there could be only one reason why he had taken off his beard." See Hilger and Meyer, p. 155.

74. *Protokoll des Vierten Kongresses der Kommunistischen Internationale*, p. 318.

75. Radek, "Obmanshchiki."

76. Degras, "United Front Tactics," p. 9.

77. *Piatyi Vsemirnyi Kongress*, I, p. 450.

78. The Treaty of Rapallo (1922) was the first major international treaty between the Soviet regime and a Great Power. By this treaty Germany and Russia, in recognition of their status as pariahs in European affairs, exchanged diplomatic representatives and made diplomatic and economic concessions to each other; important military agreements were ancillary to the treaty, although not part of it. The fullest discussion of the background of the treaty may be found in Freund, *passim*. Radek had no part in the actual negotiations, but could be said to be a major contributor in that he had facilitated Soviet-German contacts since 1919. In *Deutschlands Weg nach Rapallo*, Wipert von Blücher mentions Radek's activities but does not credit him with the consummation of the rapprochement. Carr, on the other hand (*The Bolshevik Revolution*, III, p. 381), calls Radek "one of the chief artificers of the Rapallo policy."

79. *Protokoll des Vierten Kongresses*, pp. 219–31.

80. This was essentially the point Radek had made in his policy statement to the Fourth Comintern Congress. See *ibid.*, pp. 306–9.

81. According to Hilger (p. 122), Radek told him that neither he nor the Soviet regime hoped for a Communist take-over in Germany at this time.

82. See Angress, pp. 254–56.

83. *Protokoll des Vierten Kongress*, pp. 83–84.

84. *Ibid.*, pp. 95–98.

85. *Ibid.*, pp. 100–103.

86. *Ibid.*, pp. 141–43.

87. See Carr, *The Interregnum*, pp. 154–56.

88. A hostile account of Radek's actions in Leipzig may be found in Ruth Fischer, pp. 225–29. The official record of the meeting does not mention Radek's presence.

89. Ruth Fischer, p. 229.

90. See Angress, pp. 281ff.

91. *Ibid.*, p. 315, n.6.

92. See Carr, *The Interregnum*, p. 176.
93. Ruth Fischer, pp. 92–93.
94. Freund, p. 157.
95. Radek *et al.*, *Schlageter: Eine Auseinandersetzung*, pp. 3–6.
96. *Ibid.*, p. 12.
97. *Ibid.*, p. 8.
98. *Piatyi Vsemirnyi Kongress*, p. 304.
99. One of the most celebrated remarks was Ruth Fischer's alleged exhortation against "Jewish capitalists." Miss Fischer repeatedly denied that she had made any such remark, but failed to convince many. See Angress, p. 340.
100. Carr, *The Interregnum*, pp. 186–87.
101. Radek, "Priblizhaiushcheesia bankrotstvo germanskoi burzhuazii i zadachi germanskoi kompartii," *Pravda*, No. 171 (August 1, 1923), p. 2.
102. Bajanov, *Avec Staline dans le Kremlin*, p. 191. Bajanov had been made a secretary to the Politburo just prior to this meeting; later he emigrated from the Soviet Union and published this memoir. It must be remembered that Bajanov wrote largely from personal recollection and may well have been mistaken in his summary of Radek's views. He does not specifically quote Radek.
103. *Ibid.*, pp. 192–94.
104. Radek, "Kapituliatsiia germanskoi burzhuazii," *Pravda*, No. 220 (September 29, 1923), p. 1.
105. Radek, "Imperialisticheskaia Frantsiia i perspektivy razvitiia Germanii," *Pravda*, No. 232 (October 2, 1923), p. 2.
106. *Die Lehren der deutschen Ereignisse*, p. 60.
107. Ruth Fischer (p. 323), who was also in Moscow, has recorded a highly emotional farewell between Brandler and Trotsky.
108. *Die Lehren der deutschen Ereignisse*, p. 60.
109. Carr, *The Interregnum*, pp. 212–13.
110. *Ibid.*, pp. 218–19.
111. Von Dirksen, p. 52. Von Dirksen's source is Radek himself.
112. The story of the Hamburg putsch is best told in Angress, pp. 444–51.
113. *Die Lehren der deutschen Ereignisse*, pp. 6, 8.

NOTES TO CHAPTER 7

1. The injustice of this allegation is amply proved in Carr, *The Interregnum*, pp. 201–52, and in Angress, pp. 426–60.
2. Cf. Deutscher, *The Prophet Unarmed*, pp. 203–5.
3. Radek, "Lev Trotskii-organizator probedy," *Pravda*, No. 58 (March 14, 1923), p. 4.

4. This reaction is recorded in the memoirs of a Menshevik observer, N.N. Volskii (Valentinov), p. 85.

5. Trotsky was extremely sensitive to such charges; he even explained his relinquishment of his post as Commissar of War in 1925 as one means of putting to rest the accusations that he sought a military coup. See Trotsky, *My Life*, p. 518.

6. Deutscher, *The Prophet Unarmed*, pp. 94–95.

7. Volskii, pp. 91–92.

8. Carr, *The Interregnum*, p. 229.

9. Lenin's last days are sensitively detailed in Louis Fischer, *The Life of Lenin*, pp. 625–76.

10. Quoted by Ruth Fischer, pp. 374–75.

11. *Die Lehren der deutschen Ereignisse*, pp. 92–93.

12. The resolution is quoted in full in Carr, *The Interregnum*, p. 236.

13. *Die Lehren der deutschen Ereignisse*, pp. 5–23.

14. *Ibid.*, p. 13.

15. *Trinadtsataia Konferentsiia*, pp. 179–80.

16. *Die Lehren der deutschen Ereignisse*, pp. 92–94.

17. *Trinadtsatyi S"ezd RKP (b), Mai 1924 goda*, p. 334.

18. *Ibid.*, pp. 349–53, 355–62.

19. *Ibid.*, p. 362.

20. *Ibid.*, pp. 681–82.

21. See *Protokoll des III. Kongresses*, p. 24.

22. *Piatyi Vsemirnyi Kongress Kommunisticheskogo Internatsionala*, I, pp. 51–52, 64.

23. *Ibid.*, pp. 173–92.

24. *Ibid.*, pp. 143–72.

25. *Ibid.*, pp. 449–51.

26. *Ibid.*, II, p. 237.

27. *Rasshirennyi plenum Ispolkoma Kommunisticheskogo Internatsionala*, p. 587.

28. In a letter from prison (Schüddekopf, "Karl Radek in Berlin," p. 113) to his wife, Radek suggested that the child be named Sophie, presumably after his mother. Hilger notes (in Hilger and Meyer) that Radek was always extraordinarily fond of the child.

29. Radek, *Portraits and Pamphlets*, p. 268.

30. For example, see Hilger and Meyer, p. 73.

31. She wrote, among other things, a book on Afghanistan, numerous articles, and a melodramatic account of the Hamburg putsch of 1923 (Larissa Reissner, *Hamburg auf den Barrikaden*, Berlin, Neuer Deutscher Verlag, 1925; reprinted Berlin, Dietz Verlag, 1960). Although her journalistic, emotional style may be passé, her works are constantly reprinted—without the prefaces by Radek that adorned earlier printings

—see, for example, Larisa Reisner, *Izbrannoe* (Moscow: Khudozh, Lit., 1965) and Larisa Reisner, *Izbrannye Proizvedenie* (Moscow: Gosizdat, 1958).

32. Cf. U.S. Department of State, Decimal Files, MS No. 760/7718 B2, dateline Riga, January 18, 1925.

33. Radek, "Era demokraticheskogo patsifizma," *Krasnaia Nov'*, No. 6 (October/November 1924), p. 235.

34. *Ibid.*, p. 267.

35. See Deutscher, *The Prophet Unarmed*, p. 267.

36. Alexandrov, p. 27. Alexandrov also relates a tasteless remark of Stalin's about Larissa Reissner, but does not document it.

37. In later years Trotsky claimed to have always been opposed to the entrance of the Chinese Communists into the Kuomintang (Trotsky, *Problems of the Chinese Revolution*, pp. 12–20). The available evidence, however, including the Trotsky Archive at Harvard University, not only fails to support his claim but tends to refute it. Also see Conrad Brandt, pp. 31–36.

38. Chiang's views towards the various Russian leaders are contained in his own memoir: *Soviet Russia in China: A Summing Up at Seventy* (London: Harrap, 1957).

39. Roots, p. 472.

40. Radek, "Vozhd' kitaiskogo naroda," *Pravda*, No. 60 (March 14, 1925), pp. 2–3; "Sotsial'nopoliticheskoi idei Sun-Iat-Sena," *Pravda*, No. 59 (March 12, 1926), pp. 3–4.

41. Radek, "Voprosy kitaiskoi revoliutsii," *Krasnyi Internatsional Profsoiuzov*, No. 10 (October 1925), p. 37.

42. *Protokoll des Vierten Kongresses der Kommunistischen Internatsionale*, p. 632.

43. Radek, "Voprosy kitaiskoi revoliutsii," p. 30.

44. *Ibid.*, p. 28.

45. Radek, "Mezhdunarodnoe obozrenie," *Izvestiia*, No. 233 (October 11, 1925), p. 2.

46. *Protokoll des Vierten Kongresses*, p. 141.

47. Radek, "Voprosy kitaiskoi revoliutsii," p. 37.

48. The Trotsky Archive shows virtually no correspondence between Trotsky and Radek during this period, which suggests that Radek was not cooperating very closely with Trotsky at this time.

49. Latourette, p. 144, refers to the role of Chinese students from Sun Yat-sen University in helping the Kuomintang. He also sets the number of students at six hundred. Schwartz, p. 148, describes the *esprit* and importance of the alumni of the university, although in reference to events long after Radek's involvement there.

50. Conrad Brandt, pp. 77–79.

51. Radek, "Porazhenie narodnykh armii v Kitae," *Pravda*, No. 69 (March 26, 1926), p. 2.

52. Radek, "Izmena kitaiskoi krupnoi burzhuazii natsional'nomu dvizheniiu" [hereafter cited as Radek "Izmena"], ms., p. 2. In the Nicolaevsky collection.

53. Louis Fischer, "China," p. 613.

54. For an authoritative treatment of the emergence of the Zinoviev Opposition, see Daniels, pp. 253–72.

55. Deutscher, *Stalin*, p. 305.

56. Trotsky, *Problems of the Chinese Revolution*, p. 98.

57. The letter is quoted in *ibid.*, pp. 384–85.

58. "Preniia po dokladu V. Miliutina," *Vestnik Kommunisticheskoi Akademii*, No. 17 (1926), pp. 248–49.

59. Stalin, VIII, pp. 278–79.

60. Radek ["A Letter to Klara Zetkin"], ms., Trotsky Archive. The letter is undated but appears to have been sent early in 1927. The book Radek mentions was probably his work (listed in Knizhnaia Letopis', *Istoriia revoliutsionnogo dvizheniia v Kitae*, Moscow, Trud Kitaia, 1927). Whether the book was actually ever released is uncertain; in any case, I have not been able to locate a copy either in the United States or in the major European libraries.

61. Radek, "Izmena," p. 31.

62. *Ibid.*, p. 32n.

63. *Ibid.*

64. Radek, "Novyi etap kitaiskoi revoliutsii," *Novyi Mir*, No. 3, (March 1927), pp. 157–59.

65. Radek, "Izmena," p. 32n.

66. Radek ["Letter of March 3, 1927"], ms., Trotsky Archive.

67. Trotsky, "Pis'mo Radeku [March 4, 1927]," ms., Trotsky Archive.

68. Radek, "Izmena," p. 32n.

69. Quoted by Vuyo Vuyovich in the Appendix to Trotsky, *Problems of the Chinese Revolution*, p. 386.

70. This prediction is mentioned in at least two different sources: Trotsky, *"The Real Situation in Russia,"* p. 336, and Louis Fischer, *Men and Politics*, pp. 85–86. Fischer's source of information was the Soviet Commissar of Foreign Affairs, Georgi Chicherin, who requested that the information be withheld during his lifetime.

71. Quoted by Vuyovich in Trotsky, *Problems of the Chinese Revolution*, pp. 389–90.

72. Radek, "Izmena." Stalin's speech of May 13, 1927 (*Sochineniia*, IX, pp. 239–68), seems to indicate that he had read or at least was familiar with the ideas put forth by Radek in this document.

73. Radek, "Izmena," pp. 42–43.

74. *Ibid.*, pp. 43–46, 52.

75. Dan, "Tuchi s vostoka," p. 4.

76. Radek, "Izmena," pp. 42, 46–47.

77. *Ibid.*, pp. 14–26; p. 5n.

78. Trotsky, *Problems of the Chinese Revolution*, p. 386.

79. Radek, "Izmena," pp. 53, 55.

80. *Ibid.*, p. 54.

81. Trotsky, "Pis'mo Radeku."

82. Radek, "Izmena," pp. 52–57.

83. Stalin, IX, pp. 240–45, 260–64.

84. For the text of this telegram see Eudin and North, pp. 379–80. Actually the Left Kuomintang learned of the telegram through a deliberate leak by the Comintern emissary M. N. Roy. See Conrad Brandt, p. 138.

85. Deutscher, *The Prophet Armed*, pp. 328–29.

86. Evdokimov, Zinoviev, Radek, Safarov, and Trotsky, "Novyi etap kitaiskoi revoliutsii: ot Chan-Kai-Shi do Van-Tsin-Veiu," ms., dated July 2, 1927. Trotsky Archive. A penciled notation on the first page in Trotsky's hand identifies Zinoviev as the author.

87. Deutscher, *The Prophet Unarmed*, p. 312.

88. *KPSS v Rezoliutsiiakh i Resheniiakh: S"ezdov, Konferentsii i Plenumov TsK*, 7th ed., Vol. II (Moscow: Gosudarstvennoe Izdatel'stvo Politicheskoi Literatury, 1954), pp. 387–94.

89. Radek, "Termidorianskaia opasnost' i oppozitsiia," ms., pp. 7, 8. Trotsky Archive.

90. Radek, "Itogi avgustovskogo plenuma," ms., p. 5, Trotsky Archive.

91. Deutscher, *The Prophet Unarmed*, Chapter 5, *passim*.

92. Serge, p. 227.

93. *Piatnadtsatyi S"ezd VKP/b/, dekabr' 1927 goda: Stenograficheskii otchët*, II (Moscow: Gosudarstvennoe Izdatel'stvo Politicheskoi Literatury, 1962), pp. 1392, 1400.

94. Trotsky, *My Life*, pp. 539–43, offers a melodramatic account of these events.

95. Deutscher, *The Prophet Unarmed*, p. 390.

96. Radek ["Letter of February 1928"], ms., Trotsky Archive.

97. For some reason Alexandrov makes repeated references in *The Tukhachevsky Affair* to Radek's being sent to Orangenburg in the Ural Mountains, relatively close to Moscow, supposedly as a personal favor on the part of Stalin. Alexandrov offers no documentation, however, and the assertion seems to be incorrect, since Radek's presence in Tobolsk and Tomsk can be reasonably well established.

98. Radek ["Letter to Preobrazhensky"] dated May 5, 1928, ms., Trotsky Archive.

99. *Ibid.*

100. Radek ["Letter to Sosnovsky"], dated July 14, 1928, ms., Trotsky Archive.

101. Radek, "Nado dodumat' do kontsa," ms., p. 2, Trotsky Archive.

102. *Ibid.*, p. 5.

103. Radek, "Razvitie i znachenie lozunga proletarskoi diktatury," ms., pp. 4–29, Trotsky Archive. The extent to which this document meant a break with Trotsky can best be seen in Trotsky, *Permanent Revolution*, where Trotsky makes it clear that he rejects Radek's views on permanent revolution.

104. Radek, "Neskolko zamechanii," ms., Trotsky Archive.

105. E. M. Yaroslavskii, "Etot son knochen," *Izvestiia*, No. 121 (May 30, 1929), p. 2.

106. Deutscher, *The Prophet Unarmed*, p. 452.

NOTES TO CHAPTER 8

1. For a description of the formation and collapse of the Right Opposition, see Daniels, pp. 322–69.

2. "Psikhologicheskaia podopleka kapituliantstva," *Biulleten Oppozitsii*, No. 6 (October 1929), p. 25.

3. "Zaiavlenie v TsKK byvshikh rukoviditelei trotskistskoi oppozitsii tt. Y. Preobrazhenskogo, K. Radeka, i I. Smilgi o razryvye s. oppozitsiei," *Pravda*, No. 158 (July 13, 1929), p. 3. The capitulation of Smilga and Preobrazhensky, both of whom were less volatile than Radek and of somewhat tougher political and moral fiber, must have seriously dampened any hopes Trotsky had for keeping an Opposition organization alive in the Soviet Union.

4. Dewey *et al.*, *The Case of Leon Trotsky*, p. 101.

5. Even Isaac Deutscher, who tends to give Trotsky the benefit of the doubt, does not believe that Bliumkin's meeting with Trotsky's son was fortuitous. See Deutscher, *The Prophet Outcast*, p. 86.

6. Dewey *et al.*, *The Case of Leon Trotsky*, p. 105.

7. Several Menshevik émigrés have told me personally that they always received sympathetic treatment from Radek. According to one informant, during a Menshevik hunger strike in 1922, Radek secretly encouraged the Mensheviks to hold their ground so as to win release from prison.

8. Serge, p. 257; also see Drachkovitch, p. 178.

9. "Kak i za shto Stalin rasstrelial Bliumkina?" *Biulleten Oppozitsii*, No. 9 (February/March 1930), pp. 9–11.

10. Cf. Orlov, p. 194.

11. Testimony at Radek's trial in 1937 revealed that some of the luxuries enjoyed by the major Bolsheviks, such as a house in the country, had been restored to him after 1933. See *Report of the Court Proceedings in the Case of the Anti-Soviet Trotskyite Center . . . Verbatim Report* (Moscow: People's Commissariat of Justice of the USSR, 1937), p. 443.

12. Most of these articles were reprinted in Radek, *Podgotovka bor'by za novyi peredel mira.*

13. Radek, "Reviziia Versal'skogo dogovora," *Pravda*, No. 127 (May 10, 1933), p. 2.

14. Scott, pp. 109–15.

15. One of the non-Soviet participants in the Geneva Conference has told me that Radek was constantly in the company of two security guards at Geneva. On one occasion, Radek did manage to get into a car that had no room for the guards, but they followed in a second car, greatly distressed lest Radek make some indiscreet comment in their absence.

16. Komet, p. 133. The American Embassy also took note of Radek's visit to his mother in Tarnov and his favorable reception in Poland. (U. S. Department of State, Decimal Files, MS #760C.61/657, dated July 24, 1933).

17. Budorowycz, pp. 32–33.

18. There is a visa file on Karl Radek for 1933 in the decimal files of the U. S. State Department. Since all visa files are automatically closed for seventy-five years, however, there is no way of knowing whether Radek's trip was canceled because of action by the U. S. State Department or on Stalin's orders.

19. Radek, *Portrety i pamflety.*

20. *Ibid.*, I, p. 321.

21. See Radek, "V kloake Kontrrevoliutsii," *Izvestiia*, No. 297 (December 12, 1934), p. 2.

22. "Trotskistsko-Zinov'evskaia fashistskaia banda i eë getman Trotskii," *Izvestiia*, No. 194 (August 24, 1936), p. 3.

23. Radek, "The Bases of Soviet Foreign Policy," *Foreign Affairs*, XII, No. 2 (January 1934), p. 199.

24. Louis Fischer, *Men and Politics*, p. 88.

25. Radek, "Zodchii sotisialisticheskogo obshchestva," *Pravda*, No. 1 (January 1, 1934), pp. 3, 4.

26. Orlov, pp. 195–96.

27. *Problems of Soviet Literature*, pp. 79–82.

28. *Ibid.*, p. 153.

29. Auswärtiges Amt, *Documents on German Foreign Policy, 1918–*

1945, Series C, II (Washington: Government Printing Office, 1959), p. 297; also see pp. 333–34.

30. Cummings, in Radek, *Portraits and Pamphlets,* p. xix.

31. For an educated guess, see Nicolaevsky, p. 92n.

32. This last explanation is implied in "The Letter of an Old Bolshevik" reprinted in *ibid.,* pp. 26–27. Nicolaevsky drew the information for the "letter" from Bukharin, who visited him in Paris in 1936.

33. Dewey, *The Case of Leon Trotsky,* p. 101.

34. Memo from Bullitt to Hull, Decimal Files, U. S. Department of State Archives, File No. 7600.61/692.

35. *Ibid.*

36. This thesis has been developed in many works and has been reconstructed, step by step, in Orlov, pp. 3–24. A more recent study develops this line further. See Conquest, pp. 43–61.

37. *Ibid.,* p. 114.

38. Radek, "Trotskistsko-Zinov'evskaia fashistskaia banda," p. 3. Ironically, it was the last article ever published by Radek.

39. Alexandrov (pp. 21–39, 51–56) has woven a highly fictionalized account in which an unwilling Radek is employed by Stalin to prepare the frameup of Mikhail Tukhachevsky. Unfortunately, because of Alexandrov's obvious fabrication of supposedly verbatim conversations, his thin documentation, and his careless and erroneous citation of known dates and facts, his account is not acceptable.

40. *Ibid.,* p. 56.

41. Conquest, p. 156, hints that Radek was purged merely because Stalin needed a big name to keep in the spotlight until he could construct a case against Bukharin; this is, however, an unlikely theory.

42. Alexandrov, pp. 91–92.

43. Hutton, p. 137. Hutton, who lived in Moscow from 1934 to 1938, knew Radek and may well have heard the story from him. Budënny was a military man whose political fortunes had always been tied to those of Stalin.

44. Orlov, p. 197. In many ways, the story sounds as if it is a story and nothing more. Ordinarily the accounts of secret police defectors must be used with great care, but Orlov's seems more reliable than most. As Conquest (p. 570) points out, Orlov's information through 1937 (the last time he was in the Soviet Union) has checked out very well. Radek did testify to the effect that during the long interrogation he "tortured" the police by his behavior (*Report of Court Proceedings,* p. 549).

45. Radek either let slip or intentionally inserted into his trial testimony an oblique hint that he knew he was going to be exiled again. In discussing his activities in 1928, he referred to that year as the period of his first exile. There would be no reason for him to think of it as a first

exile unless he had reason to believe that a second exile was in the offing. See *Report of Court Proceedings*, p. 542. Orlov (p. 207) maintains that Radek had made a deal with Stalin prior to the trial.

46. *Report of Proceedings*, p. 85.

47. *Ibid.*, pp. 113–15.

48. *Ibid.*, pp. 124–25.

49. Cf. Conquest, p. 503.

50. See Dewey *et al.*, *Not Guilty*. Dewey's volume leaves much to be desired, but is valuable for the testimony by Trotsky that it contains.

51. Dewey *et al.*, *The Case of Leon Trotsky*, pp. 204–7, 115–16.

52. *Ibid.*, p. 212.

53. The most famous instance was the alleged meeting of Trotsky's son with E. S. Holtzman—a defendant in the Zinoviev trial—at the Hotel Bristol in Copenhagen. Much to the embarrassment of the Soviet Union, it was revealed that the Hotel Bristol had burned to the ground in 1917. See *ibid.*, pp. 167–72.

54. *Report of Court Proceedings*, p. 543.

55. Conquest, pp. 163, 183.

56. Hilger, p. 72.

57. *Report of Court Proceedings*, p. 135.

58. *Ibid.*, p. 543.

59. Orlov, p. 212.

60. After this date, Radek's wife and daughter were never seen again. Hilger (p. 72) gloomily suggests that they were sent to a labor camp; also see Conquest, p. 183.

61. Orlov, pp. 280–81.

62. Petrov and Petrov, p. 69.

63. Duranty, p. 10.

64. This story was repeated to me in Warsaw and Cracow during the winter of 1957–58.

65. In the fall of 1964 I received a visitor from the Soviet Union, an academician of moderately important rank. When the conversation passed to Radek, my visitor interjected, "Radek is alive—living in Moscow and collecting a pension!" The prospect was indeed interesting, but was dissipated when I showed him a recent volume of the fifth edition of Lenin's *Sochineniia*. He looked at the imprint—Moscow, 1964— and then in the Appendix at the biographical notation that Radek had died in 1939. Sadly he shook his head and remarked, "No, Radek does not live." His disappointment was as great as my own.

66. Soviet historians have not been able to do much more than supply a death date for Radek. For a discussion of this problem, see Warren Lerner, "The Unperson in Communist Historiography," *South Atlantic Quarterly*, LXV, 4 (Autumn 1966), pp. 438–47. The editors of the

Soviet historical encyclopedia continued the practice of omitting Radek's name (*Sovetskaia Istoricheskaia Entsiklopediia*, XI, Pegram-Renuven, Moscow: Isdatel'stvo Sovetskaia Entsiklopediia, 1968).

NOTES TO CHAPTER 9

1. Ruth Fischer, p. 208.

2. It is noteworthy how little correspondence Lenin had with Radek from 1918–1923; see Lenin, XLIX, L, LI, *passim.*

3. Letter counts may be an inadequate means of determining the nature of relationships, but we may note that the Trotsky Archive indicates very little correspondence between Radek and Trotsky in the same period.

4. U. S. Department of State, Decimal Files, MS No. SSOE1/189, Letter No. 1465, dated March 27, 1922, p. 2.

5. Brupbacher, p. 262.

6. Hilger's evaluation (p. 73) is worth noting: "This revolutionary by profession, this convinced internationalist, had one great weakness: Germany. The Polish Jew from Austrian Galicia felt himself tied to Germany by the closest bonds, and he spoke German better than any other language."

7. A few Jews—Lazar Kaganovich is the best-known example—survived in high places throughout Stalin's rule. It was long rumored that Kaganovich's sister had been secretly married to Stalin; if true, this might well explain Kaganovich's survival.

8. Freund, p. 65n.

9. Borkenau, p. 164.

10. Information given me by Menshevik émigrés.

11. Drachkovitch, p. 178.

12. Leon Trotsky, "Radek i oppozitsiia," *Biulleten Oppozitsii*, No. 1/2 (July 1929), pp. 10–11.

13. Conquest, p. 156.

14. Souvarine, amongst others, doubts any such intent on Radek's part; see Drachkovitch, p. 179.

15. *Report of Court Proceedings*, p. 543.

16. Balabanoff, p. 210.

Radek's Publications

Few Bolsheviks have written more than Karl Radek: he was the author of hundreds of articles as well as numerous books and pamphlets. I give here an annotated list of his major publications, that is, those separately published, and of the various newspapers and journals to which he contributed the majority of his articles. His most significant articles have been cited in the notes to the text. (In the case of a periodical or newspaper difficult to obtain, I list at least one library where the pertinent issues may be found, with no intent to imply that the material is unavailable elsewhere.)

MAJOR PUBLICATIONS

Die auswärtige Politik Sowjet-Russlands. Hamburg: Carl Hoym, 1921.—A collection of articles on Soviet foreign policy.

"Avtobiografiia," *Entsiklopedicheskii slovar'.* 7th ed. Vol. XLI, Part 2. Moscow: Russkii Bibliograficheskii Institut Granat, 1929, pp. 138–69.—Radek's own account of his early career.

Der deutsche Imperialismus und die Arbeiterklasse. Bremen: Buchhandlung der Bremer Bürgerzeitung, 1912.—A contribution by Radek to the body of socialist theory concerning the relationship of imperialism to the collapse of capitalism.

Deutschland und Russland. N.p.: Redaktion Russische Korrespondenz, 1920.—The title hints at future cooperation between the two countries.

Die deutsche Revolution: oder trau, schau—wem? Moscow: no publisher cited, 1918.—Published under the pseudonym of Arnold Struthahn. This is a polemic against the Social Democratic leaders who came to power in Germany in November 1918.

Die Entwicklung der deutschen Revolution und die Aufgaben der Kommunistischen Partei. 2d ed. Hamburg: Carl Hoym, 1920.—One of Radek's many pieces of cautious advice to the KPD.

Die Entwicklung der Weltrevolution und die Taktik der Kommunistischen Parteien im Kampfe um die Diktatur des Proletariats. Berlin: Berliner Buch und Kunstdruckerei, 1919.—Both this and the preceding book were written while Radek was in jail in Berlin in 1919; they reflect his depression over the failure of the Spartacist revolt and urge caution in the drive for world revolution.

Germanskaia Revoliutsiia (The German Revolution), 2 vols. Moscow: Gosizdat, 1925.—Volume I consists largely of Russian translations of the articles contained in *In den Reihen der deutschen Revolution*; for the most part, Volume II duplicates *Na sluzhbe germanskoi revoliutsii.* A projected third volume was never published, probably because it would have included articles dealing with Radek's discredited German policy of the 1920's.

In den Reihen der deutschen Revolution, 1909–1919. Munich: K. Wolff, 1921.—A valuable collection of Radek's major articles from the German socialist press, by means of which one can identify those articles in *Arbeiterpolitik* that were actually written by Radek. The book is dedicated to Radek's wife.

Istoriia revoliutsionnogo dvizheniia v Kitae (The History of the Revolutionary Movement in China).—I have been unable to ascertain whether this book was actually published; in view of Radek's problems in 1927, it may well have been recalled from the press without publication. I have been advised that students from Sun Yat-Sen University did produce in Chinese translation a volume whose contents may be identical with the one listed here: La-te-k'o [Radek], *Chung-kuo ko-ming yün-tung shih* (A History of the Chinese Revolutionary Movement), n.p., 1929. The original edition may be found in the library of Keio University in Tokyo; a later edition is at Harvard University. (I am grateful to Professor Richard Kagan of Boston State College for this information.)

Der Kampf der K. I. gegen Versailles u. gegen d. Offensive des Kapitals. Hamburg: Carl Hoym, 1923.—Reprint of a speech to the Comintern.

Kitai v ogne voiny (China in the Fire of War). Moscow: Rabochaia Moskva, 1924.—A propaganda brochure concerning the need for supporting the revolutionary nationalist armies in China, written when Comintern-Kuomintang cooperation was just beginning.

Krushenie germanskogo imperializma i zadachi mezhdunarodnogo rabochego klassa (The Collapse of German Imperialism and the Tasks of the International Working Class). Moscow: Central Executive Committee of the Soviets, 1918.—Written when Radek believed that a German revolution was imminent.

Die Masken sind gefallen: eine Antwort an Crispien, Dittman, und Hilferding. Hamburg: Kommunistischen Internationale, 1920.—Radek's contribution to the wooing of the USPD.

Meine Abrechnung. Bremen: J. H. Schmalfedlt, 1913.—Radek's justification of his actions in the SDKPiL and his defense against accusations that he had embezzled party funds.

Mezhdunarodnaia Politika (International Politics). Vol. I. Moscow: Gosizdat, 1925.—Although there were to have been two volumes of this work, the second never appeared, presumably because of the intra-party struggle. Volume I is a collection of articles on "capitalist stabilization" that contains little of a controversial nature.

Na sluzhbe germanskoi revoliutsii (In the Service of the German Revolution). Moscow: Gosizdat, 1921.—Russian translations of some of Radek's articles in the German press.

Piat' let Kominterna (Five Years of the Comintern), 2 vols. Moscow: Krasnaia Nov', 1924.—These two volumes contain almost every important speech Radek gave to the Comintern.

Podgotovka bor'by za novyi peredel mira (Preparation of the Struggle for a New Partition of the World). Moscow: Partizdat, 1934.—Reprints of Radek's articles of 1933 denouncing German foreign policy and suggesting the possibility of Soviet cooperation with the West to protect the Versailles system.

Portraits and Pamphlets. Translation and Introduction by A. J. Cummings; Notes by Alec Brown. London: McBride, 1935.—The articles in this book span the years 1918–34, but most were written between 1930 and 1933. Many of the articles are incorrectly dated.

Portrety i pamflety (Portraits and Pamphlets), 2 vols. Moscow: Gosizdat, 1927.

Portrety i pamflety (Portraits and Pamphlets), 2 vols. Moscow: Sovetskaia Literatura, 1933–34.—Volume I is very similar to the 1927 edition cited above but there are significant differences. Cummings's English version is not a translation of either Russian edition, although it contains many articles from both.

Das Programm der Kommunistischen Partei Russlands. Zurich: Internationaler Verlag, 1920.

Programma kommunisticheskogo stroitel'stva na pervoi faze ego razvitiia (The Program of Communist Construction in the First Phase of Its Development). Moscow: Knigo-Izdatel'stvo RFKPA, 1921.— This work and the preceding one are routine explanations of the importance of saving the Soviet economy, not only for the sake of Russia, but also for the sake of the world revolution.

Proletarische Diktatur und Terrorismus. Hamburg: Carl Hoym, 1920.—
This book, similar to Trotsky's more famous book of the same title,
is a reply to Kautsky's criticism of the terror tactics used by the Soviet
regime against its political enemies.

Rosa Luxemburg, Karl Liebknecht, Leo Jogiches. Hamburg: Carl Hoym,
1921.—A sensitive tribute to the fallen leaders of the Spartacist revolt.

Die russische und die deutsche Revolution und die Weltlage. Berlin:
O. Godemann, 1919.—This is the text of the controversial speech
given by Radek before the founding congress of the KPD in December 1918.

Schlageter: Eine Auseinandersetzung. Berlin: Vereinigung Internationaler Verlagsanstalten, 1923.—This book contains Radek's speeches
and articles on the "Schlageter line" of 1923. It also includes some
articles by German Rightists.

*Soll die Vereinigte Kommunistischen Partei Deutschlands eine Massen-
partei der revolutionäre Aktion oder eine zentristische Partei des War-
tens sein?* Hamburg: Carl Hoym, 1921.—Radek's thoughts on the
union of the Left USPD and the KPD.

Vneshniaia politika Sovetskoi Rossii (The Foreign Policy of Soviet Russia). Moscow: Gosizdat, 1923.—This collection of Radek's articles on
foreign policy is not a duplicate of *Die auswärtige Politik Sowjet-
Russlands.*

Voina Pol'skikh belogvardeitsev protiv Rossii (The War of the Polish
White Guards against Russia). Moscow: Gosizdat, 1920.—This work
of propaganda, written during the Russo-Polish War of 1920, contains
many implied warnings against a Bolshevik incursion into Poland.

*Zur Taktik des Kommunismus: ein Schreiben an den Oktober-Parteitag
der K.P.D.* Berlin: Kommissions-Druckerei, 1919.—Writing from
prison, Radek warns the KPD not to repeat the mistakes that led
to the Spartacist *putsch.*

NEWSPAPERS AND PERIODICALS TO WHICH RADEK CONTRIBUTED

Die Arbeiterpolitik: Wochenschrift für wissenschaftlichen Sozialismus.
—A weekly journal published by the Bremen Left-Radicals from
1916 to 1918. A number of articles published anonymously here by
Radek appeared later in his *In den Reihen der deutschen Revolution.*
A complete file may be found in the Staatsbibliothek in Bremen;
fairly complete sets are kept in the New York Public Library and in
the Hoover Institution at Stanford University.

*Berner Tagwacht: Offizielle Publikationsorgan der sozialdemokratischen
Partei der Schweiz.*—The official newspaper of the Swiss Social Dem-

ocratic Party. During the first two years of World War I, Radek published a column almost every day, using the pseudonym "Parabellum." A complete file is kept in the Landsbibliothek, Berne.

Bol'shevik: politiko-ekonomicheskii dvukhnedelnik TsK VKP (b): (Bol'shevik): political-economic biweekly of the Central Committee of the All-Russian Communist Party.—The major theoretical journal of the Bolshevik Party, published since 1921. It is now published under the title *Kommunist.*

Bote der Russischen Revolution.—Published by Radek and Hanecki in Stockholm in 1917 as an official Bolshevik journal abroad. A nearly complete run is kept in the Duke University Library. A copy of the rare number 11 may be found in the Archives of the Jewish Bund in New York.

Bremer Bürgerzeitung.—The daily newspaper of the Bremen organization of the SPD. Radek was one of its most important contributors from 1908 to 1914. A complete file is kept in the Staatsbibliothek in Bremen.

Czerwony Sztandar (The Red Flag).—Published intermittently by the SDKPiL. Radek was editor during 1907 and 1908. A file is available in the Biblioteka Narodowa, Warsaw.

Die Fackel.—A newspaper printed and distributed by Radek at the Brest-Litovsk negotiations. I have been unable to locate a file of this newspaper.

Freie Volkszeitung.—Radek's brief tenure in 1912 as editor of this socialist newspaper in Göppingen led to his exclusion from the SPD. I have been unable to locate any file of this newspaper.

Gazeta Robotnicza (Worker's Newspaper).—This was the organ of the "Warsaw Committee" of the SDKPiL. Some issues are in the Hoover Institution, Stanford University.

International Press Correspondence (also known as *Inprecorr* and *World News and Views*).—A translation service that carried dozens of Radek's articles in the 1920's.

Die Internationale: Eine Zeitschrift für Praxis und Theorie des Marxismus.—A journal of the KPD. It carried several of Radek's articles prior to his disgrace in 1924. A complete run can be found in the combined holdings of the New York Public Library and Columbia University.

Internationale Presse Korrespondenz (Inprekorr).—The German counterpart of *International Press Correspondence.* In general, the translations here are fuller and more accurate than those in the English version. A complete set is kept in the New York Public Library.

Internationales Flugblatt.—Published by the Zimmerwald Left in Zurich in 1915. Radek edited the first and only issue. A copy is kept in the Duke University Library.

Izvestiia (News).—The official newspaper of the Soviet government. Radek contributed many articles over the years and served as an editor in the 1930's.

Jugend-Internationale: Kampforgan der Kommunistischen Jugend-Internationale.—During World War I, Radek wrote a few articles for this journal, explaining why socialist youth had no responsibility to defend their fatherland. An almost complete file is kept in the New York Public Library.

Kommunist.—The Left Communists published both a newspaper and a periodical with this title during 1918 in their fight against the Treaty of Brest-Litovsk. A complete file is kept in the Saltykov-Shchedrin Library, Leningrad.

Der Kommunist: Organ der KPD. Nordwest. Published by the Bremen Left-Radicals from 1918–1920. Radek occasionally contributed to it. An incomplete collection may be found in the New York Public Library.

Kommunisticheskii Internatsional: Organ Ispolnitel'nogo Komiteta Kommunisticheskogo Internatsionala (The Communist International: Organ of the ECCI).—The official publication of the Comintern, which appeared simultaneously in several languages.

Krasnaia Nov'.—A remarkable journal combining articles on cultural and political subjects. Radek's most notable contribution was his account of his activities in Germany during 1919, which was published in 1926. A complete file is in the Columbia University Library.

Krasnyi Internatsional Profsoiuzov (The Red International of Trade Unions).—The official journal of the trade union movement. During the 1920's Radek contributed occasional articles.

Leipziger Volkszeitung.—Prior to World War I, this paper, under the influence of Rosa Luxemburg, became the most important publication of the German Left. A complete file of the paper for these years is in the Columbia University Library.

Lichtstrahlen.—An outspoken Leftist journal published at the beginning of World War I. The New York Public Library has a complete file.

Mirovoe Khoziaistvo i Mirovaia Politika (The World Economy and World Politics).—A theoretical journal to which Radek contributed a few articles after his return in 1929.

Młot (The Hammer).—A semi-secret publication of the SDKPiL. Because of harassment by the censor, its name was changed successively to *Nasze Drogi* (Our Roads), *Nasza Sprawa* (Our Cause), *Wolna Trybuna* (The Free Tribune), *Wolny Głos* (The Free Voice), and

Praca (Labor). The New York Public Library has an almost complete file.

Naprzód (Forward).—An organ of the PPSD, edited in the first part of the century by Emil Haecker. A file is kept in the Jagellonian Library, Cracow.

Nasza Sprawa (Our Cause).—See Młot.

Nasze Drogi (Our Road).—See Młot.

Die Neue Zeit: Wochenschrift der deutschen Sozialdemokratie.—The official journal of the SPD. Prior to World War I, it was by far the most influential socialist journal. A complete set may be found in the Duke University Library.

Praca (Labor).—See Młot.

Pravda (Truth).—The official newspaper of the Bolshevik Party.

Przegląd Socjal-Demokratczny (The Review of Social Democracy.)— The official theoretical journal of the SDKPiL from 1902 to 1904 and again from 1908 to 1910. A fairly complete file may be found in the International Instituut voor Sociale Geschiedenis, Amsterdam.

Die Rote Fahne: Zentralorgan der Kommunistischen Partei Deutschlands (Sektion der Kommunistischen Internationale).—The official newspaper of the KPD, which featured many articles by Radek prior to 1924. A file is available at the New York Public Library.

Russische Korrespondenz "Prawda."—Published and edited by Radek from Stockholm in 1917. A nearly complete file is available at the Duke University Library.

Sotsial-Demokrat (The Social Democrat).—Published irregularly and at various places by the Bolshevik Party prior to 1917.

Vorbote: Internationale Marxistische Rundschau.—A journal of the Zimmerwald Left edited by Radek in 1916. Copies of the two numbers issued are available at the Hoover Institution.

Vorwärts.—The official newspaper of the SPD.

Wolna Trybuna (The Free Tribune).—See Młot.

Wolny Głos (The Free Voice).—See Młot.

Bibliography

ARCHIVAL MATERIALS

"Akten betreffend: den russischen Bolschewik, Karl Radek, 1917–1919."
St. Antony's Collection of the Records of the German Foreign Office,
Microfilm Roll No. 38, National Archives, Washington, D.C.—This is
a dossier on Radek's activities kept by the German Foreign Office
once it became aware that he was involved in Bolshevik designs on
Germany. It contains police reports, relevant correspondence (some
of it illegible), and other documents.

"In Sachen Radek [1912–1914]." International Instituut voor Sociale
Geschiedenis, Amsterdam.—This file is part of the larger archive on
German Social Democracy stored at the Institute. It contains published and unpublished materials pertaining to Radek's troubles with
the SPD in 1912–14.

The Nicolaevsky Collection. This collection, now at the Hoover Institution, contains numerous unique materials on the history of socialism
and communism.—For the purposes of this study, the most important
items in the collection are the memoranda by Rubinshtein ("Thomas")
and Balabanoff, as well as a long memorandum by Radek, "Izemena-
kitaiskoi krupnoi burzhuazii natsional'nomu dvizheniia" (The Infi-
delity of the Chinese Big Bourgeoisie to the National Movement).
Written after the Shanghai massacre of 1927, this paper is essential
to an understanding of Radek's position on and role in the Chinese
question. For some reason, there is no copy of this memorandum in
the Trotsky Archive, although Trotsky must have certainly received
a copy.

The Trotsky Archive.—This well-known collection of Trotsky's personal
papers is deposited at the Houghton Library, Harvard University. It
is my understanding that the documents have been recatalogued re-

cently, and therefore I give no references to document numbers in the footnotes.

U. S. Department of State. "Decimal Archives, 1919–1939." National Archives, Washington, D.C.

Volskii [Valentinov], N. N. "Moi vospominaniia" (My Memoirs). Archive of Russian and East European History and Culture, Butler Library, Columbia University.—unpublished memoirs of a Menshevik émigré. They provide a reliable commentary on the first decade of the Bolshevik regime.

PUBLISHED MATERIALS

Alexandrov, Victor. *The Tukhachevsky Affair,* translated by John Hewish. Englewood Cliffs, N.J.: Prentice-Hall, 1963.

Angress, Werner T. *Stillborn Revolution: The Communist Bid for Power in Germany, 1921–1923.* Princeton, N.J.: Princeton University Press, 1963.

Ascher, Abraham. "Russian Marxism and the German Revolution, 1917–1920," *Archiv für Sozialgeschichte* VI/VII (1966/67), pp. 391–439.

————, and Guenter Lewy. "National Bolshevism in Weimar Germany —Alliance of Political Extremes against Democracy," *Social Research,* XXIII, 4 (Winter 1956), pp. 450–80.

Baevskii, D. "Bol'sheviki v Tsimmerval'de" (The Bolsheviks in Zimmerwald), *Proletarskaia Revoliutsiia,* 5 (1935), pp. 27–48.

————. "Lenin i Tsimmerval'da Levaia" (Lenin and the Zimmerwald Left), *Bor'ba Klassov,* 3 (March 1934), pp. 34–47.

Bajanov, Boris. *Avec Staline dans le Kremlin.* Paris: Les Éditions de France, 1930.

Balabanoff, Angelica. *Erinnerungen und Erlebnisse.* Berlin: E. Laubsche Volksbuchhandlung, 1927.

————. *My Life as a Rebel.* New York: Harper & Bros., 1938.

————. "Die Zimmerwalder Bewegung," *Archiv für die Geschichte des Sozialismus und der Arbeiterbewegung,* XII (1926), pp. 310–413; XIII (1927), pp. 232–84.

Bantke, Samuil S., ed. *Bor'ba Bol'shevikov za sozdanie Kommunisticheskogo Internatsionala. Materialy i Dokumenty, 1914–1919 gg.* (The Struggle of the Bolsheviks for the Creation of the Communist International. Materials and Documents, 1914–1919). Moscow: Partinnoe Izdatel'stvo, 1934.

Beloff, Max. *The Foreign Policy of Soviet Russia, 1929–1941.* 2 vols. London: Oxford University Press, 1947–49.

Berlau, Joseph A. *The German Social Democratic Party, 1914–1921.* New York: Columbia University Press, 1949.

Bernstein, Eduard. *Evolutionary Socialism: A Criticism and Affirmation.* Translated by Edith C. Harvey. New York: Huebsch, 1909.

Bluecher, Wipert von. *Deutschlands Weg nach Rapallo.* Wiesbaden: Limes Verlag, 1951.

Borkenau, Franz. *World Communism.* New York: Norton, 1939.

Brandt, Conrad. *Stalin's Failure in China.* Cambridge, Mass.: Harvard University Press, 1958.

Brandt, Willy, and Richard Lowenthal. *Ernst Reuter: Ein Leben für die Freiheit.* Munich: Kindler Verlag, 1957.

Brupbacher, Fritz. *60 Jahre Ketzer.* Zurich: B. Ruppli, 1935.

Bukharin, Nikolai. "O tov. Radekom" (Concerning Comrade Radek), *Pravda,* No. 121 (May 30, 1924), p. 3.

Buszko, Jozef. *Ruch socjalistyczny w Krakowie, 1890–1914* (The Socialist Movement in Cracow, 1890–1914). Cracow: Wydawnicto Literackie, 1961.

Carr, Edward Hallett. *The Bolshevik Revolution, 1917–1923.* 3 vols. London: Macmillan, 1950–53.

――――. *The Interregnum, 1923–1924.* London: Macmillan, 1954.

――――. "Radek's Political Salon in Berlin, 1919," *Soviet Studies,* III (April 1952), pp. 411–30.

――――. *Socialism in One Country, 1924–1926,* 3 vols. London: Macmillan, 1958–64.

Carsten, F. L. *The Reichswehr and German Politics, 1918–1933.* London: Oxford University Press, 1966.

――――. "The Reichswehr and the Red Army, 1920–1933," *Survey,* No. 44/45 (October 1962), pp. 114–32.

Cole, G. D. H. *A History of Socialist Thought.* Vol. III: *The Second International 1889–1914;* Vol. IV: *Communism and Social Democracy, 1914–1931.* London: Macmillan, 1956–58.

Collard, Dudley. *Soviet Justice and the Trial of Radek and Others.* London: Gollancz, 1937.

Communist International. *Der I. Kongress der Kommunistischen Internationale: Protokoll der Verhandlungen in Moskau vom 2. bis zum 19. März 1919.* Petrograd: Verlag der Kommunistischen Internationale, 1920.

――――. *Piatyi Vsemirnyi Kongress Kommunisticheskogo Internatsionala 17 iiunia–8 iiulia 1924 g. Stenograficheskii otchët* (Fifth World Congress of the Communist International, June 17–July 8, 1924. Stenographic Report), 2 vols. Moscow: Gosizdat, 1925.

――――. *Protokoll des III. Kongresses der Kommunistischen Internationale (Moskau, 22. Juni bis 12. Juli, 1921).* Hamburg: Carl Hoym, 1921.

――――. *Protokoll des Vierten Kongresses der Kommunistischen Interna-*

tionale. Petrograd-Moskau vom 5. November bis 5. Dezember, 1922. Hamburg: Carl Hoym, 1923.

―――. *Der Zweite Kongress der Kommunist. Internationale: Protokoll der Verhandlungen vom 19. Juli in Petrograd und vom 23. Juli bis 7. August, 1920 in Moskau.* Hamburg: Carl Hoym, 1921.

―――. Executive Committee (ECCI). *Bericht über die Tätigkeit des Präsidiums und der Exekutive der Kommunistischen Internationale für die Zeit vom 6. März bis 11. Juni 1922.* Petrograd: Verlag der Kommunistischen Internationale, 1922.

―――. *Die Lehren der deutschen Ereignisse. Das Präsidium des Exekutivkomitees der Kommunistischen Internationale zur deutschen Frage. Januar 1924.* Hamburg: Carl Hoym, 1924.

―――. *Rasshirennyi plenum Ispolkoma Kommunisticheskogo Internatsionala 21 marta–6 aprelia 1925 g. Stenograficheskii otchët* (The Enlarged Plenum of the Executive Committee of the Communist International, March 21–April 6, 1925. Stenographic Report). Moscow: Gosizdat, 1925.

―――. *Rasshirennyi plenum Ispolnitel'nogo Komiteta Kommunisticheskogo Internatsionala 12–23 iiunia 1923 g. Otchët* (The Enlarged Plenum of the Executive Committee of the Communist International, June 12–23, 1923. Report). Moscow: Krasnaia Nov', 1923.

―――. *Die Tätigkeit der Exekutive und des Präsidiums des E. K. der Kommunischen Internationale vom 13. Juli 1921 bis 1. Februar 1922.* Petrograd: Verlag der Kommunistischen Internationale, 1922.

―――. *Die Täktik der Kommunistischen Internationale gegen die Offensive des Kapitals: Bericht über die Konferenz der erweiteren Exekutive der Kommunistischen Internationale. Moskau, vom 24. Februar bis 4. März, 1922.* Hamburg: Carl Hoym, 1922.

Conquest, Robert. *The Great Terror: Stalin's Purge of the Thirties.* New York: Macmillan, 1968.

Dan, Feodor. "Bol'sheviki i 'Edinyi Front' " (The Bolsheviks and the "United Front"), *Sotsialisticheskii Vestnik,* No. 9 (31) (May 22, 1922), pp. 5–7.

―――. "Tuchi s vostoka" (Clouds out of the East), *Sotsialisticheskii Vestnik,* No. 8 (150) (April 23, 1927), p. 4.

Daniels, Robert Vincent. *The Conscience of the Revolution: Communist Opposition in Soviet Russia.* Cambridge, Mass.: Harvard University Press, 1960.

Degras, Jane. "United Front Tactics in the Comintern, 1921–1928," *St. Antony's Papers,* No. 9.

―――, ed. *The Communist International, 1919–1943: Documents.* Vols. I and II. London: Oxford University Press, 1956–60.

Deutscher, Isaac. *The Prophet Armed: Trotsky, 1879–1921.* New York: Oxford University Press, 1954.

————. *The Prophet Unarmed: Trotsky, 1921–1929.* New York: Oxford University Press, 1959.

————. *The Prophet Outcast: Trotsky, 1929–1940.* New York: Oxford University Press, 1963.

————. *Stalin: A Political Biography.* 2d ed. New York: Oxford University Press, 1966.

————. *The Non-Jewish Jew and Other Essays.* New York: Oxford University Press, 1968.

Dewey, John, *et al. The Case of Leon Trotsky.* New York: Harper, 1937.

————. *Not Guilty.* New York: Harper, 1938.

Dirksen, Herbert von. *Moscow, Tokyo, London: Twenty Years of German Foreign Policy.* Norman, Okla.: University of Oklahoma Press, 1952.

Drachkovitch, Milorad M., and Branko Lazitch, eds. *The Comintern: Historical Highlights; Essays, Recollections, and Documents.* New York: Praeger, 1966.

Drahn, Ernst, and Suzanne Leonhard. *Unterirdische Literatur in revolutionären Deutschland während des Weltkrieges.* Berlin: Verlag Gesellschaft und Erziehung, 1920.

"Drakon." "Roman Karla Radeka s 'poslednoi kukharoi' " (The Romance of Karl Radek with the "Last Cook"), *Sotsialisticheskii Vestnik,* No. 8 (May 20, 1921), p. 29.

Draper, Theodore. *The Roots of American Communism.* New York: Viking, 1957.

Drobner, Bołeslaw. *Bezustanna Walka: Wspomnienia, 1883–1918* (The Incessant Struggle: Memoirs, 1883–1918). Warsaw: Państwowy Instytut Wydawn., 1962.

Duranty, Walter. *Stalin & Co.: The Politburo—The Men Who Run Russia.* New York: William Sloane Associates, Inc., 1949.

Dziewanowski, Marian Kamil. *The Communist Party of Poland: An Outline of History.* Cambridge, Mass.: Harvard University Press, 1959.

Eastman, Max. *Since Lenin Died.* New York: Boni and Liveright, 1925.

Eudin, Xenia Joukoff, and Harold H. Fisher. *Soviet Russia and the West, 1920–1927: A Documentary Survey.* Stanford: Stanford University Press, 1957.

————, and Robert C. North. *Soviet Russia and the East, 1920–1927: A Documentary Survey.* Stanford: Stanford University Press, 1957.

Fainsod, Merle. *International Socialism and the World War.* Cambridge, Mass.: Harvard University Press, 1935.

Fanger, Donald M. "Radek's Role in the Soviet Opposition," Unpublished master's thesis, Department of History, University of California, Berkeley, 1953.

Fischer, Louis. "China—Seen from Moscow," *Nation*, CXXV, No. 3256 (November 30, 1927), pp. 613–14.

————. *The Life of Lenin*. New York: Harper and Row, 1964.

————. *Men and Politics*. New York: Duell, Sloan & Pearce, 1941.

————. *The Soviets in World Affairs*. 2d ed. 2 vols. Princeton: Princeton University Press, 1951.

Fischer, Ruth. *Stalin and German Communism*. Cambridge: Harvard University Press, 1948.

Flechtheim, Ossip K. *Die Kommunistische Partei Deutschlands in der Weimarer Republik*. Offenbach: Karl Drott, 1948.

Florinsky, Michael T. *World Revolution and the USSR*. New York: Macmillan, 1933.

Foster, William Z. *Questions and Answers on the Piatakov-Radek Trial*. New York: Workers Library Publishers, 1937.

Franz, Rudolf. "Aus Briefen Konrad Haenischs," *Archiv für die Geschichte des Sozialismus und der Arbeiterbewegung*, XIV (1929), pp. 444–84.

————. "Der Fall Radek von 1913," *Das Forum*, IV, 5 (February 1920), pp. 389–93.

Freund, Gerald. *Unholy Alliance*. New York: Harcourt, Brace, 1957.

Frölich, Paul. *Rosa Luxemburg, Her Life and Work*. Translated by Edward Fitzgerald. London: Gollancz, 1940.

Futrell, Michael. *Northern Underground: Episodes of Russian Revolutionary Transport and Communications Through Scandinavia and Finland, 1863–1917*. New York: Praeger, 1963.

Gankin, Olga Hess, and H. H. Fisher. *The Bolsheviks and the World War: The Origins of the Third International*. Stanford: Stanford University Press, 1940.

Gay, Peter. *The Dilemma of Democratic Socialism: Eduard Bernstein's Challenge to Marx*. New York: Columbia University Press, 1952.

Gruber, Helmut, ed. *International Communism in the Era of Lenin*. New York: Fawcett, 1967.

Grünberg, Carl. *Die Internationale und der Weltkrieg*. Leipzig: C. L. Hirschfeld, 1916.

Grünberg, K., and Cz. Kozłowski. *Historia Polskiego Ruchu Robotniczego, 1864–1918* (History of the Polish Worker Movement, 1864–1918). Warsaw: Książka i Wiedza, 1962.

Hahlweg, Werner. *Lenin's Rückkehr nach Russland 1917: Die deutschen Akten*. Leiden: E. J. Brill, 1957.

Hallgarten, George W. F. "General Hans von Seeckt and Russia," *Journal of Modern History*, XXI (March 1949), pp. 28–34.

Haupt, Georges, ed. *La Correspondance entre Lenine et Camille Huysmans, 1905–1914.* The Hague: Mouton, 1963.

Heilmann, Ernst. "Parteijustiz," *Sozialistische Monatshefte,* III, 21 (October 16, 1913), pp. 1267–76.

Heine, Wolfgang. "Zum Auschlusse Radeks," *Bremer Bürgerzeitung,* No. 229 (September 30, 1913), p. 1.

Herzog, Wilhelm. "Russisches Notizbuch, Mai–August 1920," *Das Forum,* IV, 11 (August 1920), pp. 791–865.

Hilger, Gustav, and Alfred G. Meyer. *The Incompatible Allies.* New York: Macmillan, 1953.

Huitième Congrès Socialiste International tenu à Copenhagen du 28 août au 3 septembre 1910. Compte rendu analytique. Ghent: Secrétariat du Bureau Socialiste International, 1911.

Hulse, James W. *The Forming of the Communist International.* Stanford: Stanford University Press, 1964.

Iaroslavskii, E. M. [Yaroslavsky]. "Etot son konchen" (This Dream Is Over), *Izvestiia,* No. 121 (May 30, 1929), p. 2.

Illustrierte Geschichte der deutschen Revolution. Berlin: Internationaler Arbeiter-Verlag, 1929.

Isaacs, Harold R. *The Tragedy of the Chinese Revolution.* Revised ed. Stanford: Stanford University Press, 1951.

"Iz tezisov Radeka ob Avgustovskom Plenume 1927 g. TsKVP(B)" (From the Theses of Radek Concerning the August Plenum of 1927 of the TsKVP[B]), *Biulleten Oppozitsii,* No. 3/4 (September 1929), pp. 35–38.

James, Cyril L. R. *World Revolution, 1917–1936.* London: Secker and Warburg, 1937.

Joffe, A., ed. *Mirnye peregovory v Brest-Litovske* (The Peace Negotiations in Brest-Litovsk). Moscow: Narkomindel, 1920.

Joll, James. *The Second International, 1889–1914.* London: Weidenfeld and Nicolson, 1955.

Kochan, Lionel. *Russia and the Weimar Republic.* Cambridge, England: Bowes and Bowes, 1954.

Komarnicki, Titus. *Rebirth of the Polish Republic.* London: Heinemann, 1957.

Komet, Abraham. "Tsu der geschichte fur yidn in Torne" (Toward a History of the Jews in Tarnov), *Torne: Kiyum un Khurbn fun a yidisher shtot* (Tarnov: The Life and Death of a Jewish City). Tel Aviv: Landsmanshaftn fun torner yidn, 1954.

Kommunistische Partei Deutschlands (KPD). *Bericht über den Gründungsparteitag der Kommunistischen Partei Deutschlands (Spartakusbund) vom 30. Dezember 1918 bis 1. Januar 1919.* [Berlin:] Kommunistische Partei Deutschlands (Spartakusbund), [1919].

———. _Bericht über die Verhandlungen des III. [8] Parteitages der Kommunistischen Partei Deutschlands: Abgehalten in Leipzig vom 28. Januar bis 1. Februar 1923._ Berlin: Vereinigung Internationaler Verlag, 1923.

———. _Bericht über die Verhandlungen des Vereinigungsparteitages der U.S.P.D. (Linke) und der K.P.D. (Spartakusbund); Abgehalten in Berlin vom 4 bis 7. Dezember 1920._ Berlin: Frankes Verlag G. m. b. H., 1921.

———. _Bericht über die Verhandlungen des 2. [7] Parteitages der Kommunistischen Partei Deutschlands (Sektion der Kommunistischen Internationale); Abgehalten in Jena vom 22. bis 26. August 1921._ Berlin: Vereinigung Internationaler Verlag, 1922.

———. _Bericht über den 2. Parteitag der Kommunistischen Partei Deutschlands (Spartakusbund) vom 20. bis 24. Oktober, 1919._ Berlin: Kommunistische Partei Deutschlands [1919].

Korbel, Josef. _Poland Between East and West: Soviet and German Diplomacy toward Poland, 1919–1933._ Princeton: Princeton University Press, 1963.

Koszutska, Maria (Wera Kostrzewa). _Pisma i Przemowienia._ Vol. I. Warsaw: Książka i Wiedza, 1961.

Lademacher, Horst, ed. _Die Zimmerwalder Bewegung: Protokolle und Korrespondenz._ 2 vols. The Hague: Mouton, 1967.

Landauer, Carl. _European Socialism: A History of Ideas and Movements._ Vol. I. Berkeley: University of California Press, 1959.

Laqueur, Walter. _Russia and Germany: A Century of Conflict._ London: Weidenfeld and Nicolson, 1965.

Lazitch, Branko [Branslav Stranjakovitch]. _Lénine et la IIIe Internationale._ Neuchâtel: La Baconnière, 1951.

Leder, V. "Natsional'nyi vopros v polskoi i russkoi sotsial-demokratii" (The National Question in Polish and Russian Social Democracy), _Proletarskaia Revoliutsiia,_ No. 2/3 (61/62) (1927), pp. 142–208.

Legters, Lyman H. "Karl Radek als Sprachrohr des Bolschewismus," _Forschungen zur Osteuropäischer Geschichte,_ Vol. VII (1959), pp. 1–128.

Leites, Nathan C., and Elsa Bernaut. _Ritual of Liquidation: The Case of the Moscow Trials._ Glencoe, Illinois: Free Press, 1954.

Lenin, Vladimir I. _Sochineniia_ (Works). 3d ed. 31 vols. Moscow: Partiinoe Izdatel'stvo, 1928–35.

———. _Polnoe Sobranie Sochinenii_ (Complete Collected Works). 5th ed. 55 vols. Moscow: Izdatel'stvo Politicheskoi Literatury, 1958–65. Citations in Notes are to this entry unless otherwise specified.

Leninskii Sbornik (Leninist Miscellany). 35 vols. Moscow: Partiinoe Izdatel'stvo, 1924– .

Lenz, Joseph. *The Rise and Fall of the Second International.* New York: International Publishers, 1932.

Levi, Paul. *Unser Weg. Wider den Putschismus.* Berlin: Seehoft, 1921.

"Die Lex Radeks," *Bremer Bürgerzeitung*, No. 211 (September 9, 1913), pp. 1–2.

Litwak, A. "Bletlekh zikhroynes" (Pages of Memories), *Unzer Tsayt*, IV, 1 (January 1944), pp. 33–36.

Low, Alfred D. *Lenin on the Question of Nationality.* New York: Bookman Associates, 1958.

Lowenthal, Richard. "The Bolshevisation of the Spartacus League," St. Antony's Papers, No. 9, *International Communism* (London: Chatto & Windus, 1960), pp. 23–71.

Luxemburg, Rosa, "Blinder Eifer," *Vorwärts*, No. 215 (September 14, 1912), p. 3.

———. *The Crisis in German Social Democracy* (the *Junius Pamphlets*). New York: Socialist Publications, 1918.

———. *Reform or Revolution.* Bombay: Modern India Publications, 1951.

———. *The Russian Revolution and Leninism or Marxism.* Ann Arbor: University of Michigan Press, 1961.

Mayer, Gustav. *Erinnerungen: Vom Journalisten zum Historiker der deutschen Arbeiterbewegung.* Munich: Verlag der Zwölf, 1949.

Miuntsenberg, V. [W. Münzenberg]. *S Libknechtom i Leninym.* Moscow: Molodaia Gvardiia, 1930.

Nettl, J. P. *Rosa Luxemburg.* 2 vols. New York: Oxford University Press, 1966.

Nicolaevsky, Boris I. *Power and the Soviet Elite,* edited by Janet D. Zagoria. New York: Praeger, 1965.

Nollau, Gunther. *International Communism and World Revolution: History and Methods.* New York: Praeger, 1961.

Nomad, Max. *Dreamers, Dynamiters, and Demagogues.* New York: Walden Press, 1964.

North, Robert C. *Moscow and the Chinese Communists.* Stanford: Stanford University Press, 1953.

Orlov, Alexander. *The Secret History of Stalin's Crimes.* New York: Random House, 1953.

Paetel, Karl O. *Versuchung oder Chance.* Göttingen: Musterschmidt Verlag, 1965.

Paquet, Alfons. *Der Geist der russischen Revolution.* Munich: Kurt Wolff Verlag, 1920.

Petrov, Vladimir and Evdokia. *Empire of Fear.* London: Deutsch, 1956.

Pieck, Wilhelm. *Die Gründung der KPD. Erinnerungen und die No-*

vember-Revolution. Berlin: Kommunistische Partei Deutschlands, 1928.

Platten, Fritz. *Lenin iz emigratsii v Rossiiu, mart 1917* (Lenin's Emigration to Russia, March 1917). Moscow: Moskovskii Rabochii, 1925.

Possony, Stefan T. *Lenin: The Compulsive Revolutionary*. Chicago: Henry Regnery, 1964.

Report of Court Proceedings in the Case of the Anti-Soviet Trotskyite Center. . . . Verbatim Report. Moscow: People's Commissariat of Justice of the USSR, 1937.

Report of the International Peace Congress Held at The Hague under the Auspices of the International Federation of Trade Unions, December 10–15, 1922. Amsterdam: International Federation of Trade Unions, 1923.

Roots, John McCook. "The Moscow End of China-Soviet Affairs," *Asia*, XXVII (June 1927), pp. 468–73.

Rosenfeld, Günter. *Sowjetrussland und Deutschland, 1917–1922*. Berlin: Akademie Verlag, 1960.

Russian [later All-Union] Communist Party [Bolsheviks]. *Desiatyi s"ezd RKP/b/, mart 1921 goda. Stenograficheskii otchët* (Tenth Congress of the RKP/b/. March 1921. Stenographic Report). Moscow: Gosizdat, 1963.

————. *Deviatyi s"ezd RKP/b/, mart–aprel' 1920 goda. Protokoly* (Ninth Congress of the RKP/b/, March–April 1920. Protocols). Moscow, Gosizdat, 1960.

————. *Dvenadstatyi s"ezd Rossiiskoi Kommunisticheskoi Partii (Bol'shevikov). Stenograficheskii otchët* (Twelfth Congress of the Russian Communist [Bolshevik] Party. Stenographic Report). Moscow: Krasnaia Nov', 1924.

————. *KPSS v rezoliutsiiakh i resheniiakh: S"ezdov, konferentsii, i plenumov TsK* (CPSU in Resolutions and Decisions: Congresses, Conferences, and Plenums of the CC). 3 vols. Moscow: Gosizdat, 1954.

————. *Odinnadstatyi s"ezd RKP/b/, mart–aprel' 1922 goda. Stenograficheskii otchët* (Eleventh Congress of the RKP/b/, March–April 1922. Stenographic Report). Moscow: Gosizdat, 1961.

————. *Piatnadtsatyi s"ezd VKP/b/, dekabr' 1927 goda. Stenograficheskii otchët* (Fifteenth Congress of the VKP/b/, December 1927. Stenographic Report). Moscow: Gosizdat, 1962.

————. *Protokoly desiatoi vserossiiskoi konferentsii RKP (B), mai 1921 g.* (Minutes of the Tenth All-Russian Conference of the RKP [B], May 1921). Moscow: Partiinoe Izdatel'stvo, 1924.

————. *Sedmoi ekstrennyi s"ezd RKP/b/, mart 1918 goda. Stenografi-*

cheskii otchët (Seventh Special Congress of the RKP/b/. March 1918. Stenographic Report). Moscow: Gosizdat, 1962.

――――. *Trinadstatyi s''ezd RKP/b/, mai 1924 goda. Stenograficheskii otchët* (Thirteenth Congress of the RKP/b/, May 1924. Stenographic Report). Moscow: Gosizdat, 1963.

Ryder, A. J. *The German Revolution of 1918: A Study of German Socialism in War and Revolt.* Cambridge, Eng.: Cambridge University Press, 1967.

Schapiro, Leonard. *The Communist Party of the Soviet Union.* New York: Random House, 1959.

――――. *The Origin of the Communist Autocracy: Political Opposition in the Soviet State: First Phase, 1917–1922.* London: Bell, 1955.

Schorske, Carl E. *German Social Democracy, 1905–1917.* Cambridge, Mass.: Harvard University Press, 1953.

Schüddekopf, Otto-Ernst. *Linke Leute von Rechts: Die nationalrevolutionären Minderheiten und der Kommunismus in der Weimarer Republik.* Stuttgart: Kohlhammer, 1960.

――――. "Karl Radek in Berlin: Eine Kapitel deutsch-russischer Beziehungen in Jahre 1919," *Archiv für Sozialgeschichte,* II (1962), pp. 87–166.

Schurer, H. "Radek and the German Revolution," Part I, *Survey,* No. 53 (October 1964), pp. 59–69; Part II, *Survey,* No. 55 (April 1965), pp. 126–40.

Shaynfeld, S. "Der yunger Karol Radek" (The Young Karl Radek), *Torne: Kiyum un Khurbn fun a yidisher shtot* (Tarnov: The Life and Death of a Jewish City). Tel Aviv: Landsmanshaftn fun torner yidn, 1954.

Shklovskii, G. "Bernskaia Konferentsiia 1915 g.," *Proletarskaia Revoliutsiia,* No. 5 (40) (1925).

Sozialdemokratische Partei Deutschlands (SPD). *Protokoll über die Verhandlungen des Parteitages der sozialdemokratischen Partei Deutschlands abgehalten in Chemnitz vom 15. bis 21. September 1912.* Berlin: Buchhandlung Vorwärts, 1912.

――――. *Protokoll über die Verhandlungen des Parteitages der sozialdemokratischen Partei Deutschlands abgehalten in Jena vom 14. bis 20. September 1913.* Berlin: Buchhandlung Vorwärts, 1913.

――――. *Protokoll über die Verhandlungen des Parteitages der sozialdemokratischen Partei Deutschlands abgehalten zu Jena vom 17. bis 23 September 1905.* Berlin: Buchhandlung Vorwärts, 1905.

Stalin, Iosif V. *Sochineniia* (Works). 13 vols. Moscow: Gosudarstvennoe Izdatel'stvo Politicheskoi Literatury, 1946–53.

Stampfer, Friedrich. *Erfahrungen und Erkentnisse: Aufzeichnungen aus meinen Leben.* Cologne: Verlag für Politik und Wirtschaft, 1957.

Stern, Leo, ed. *Die Auswirkungen der grossen sozialistischen Oktober-revolution auf Deutschland.* Vol. IV. Berlin: Rütten and Loening, 1959.

Temkin, Ia. G. *Tsimmerval'd-Kintal* (Zimmerwald-Kienthal). Moscow: Izdatel'stvo "Vysshaia Shkola," 1967.

Troeltsch, Ernst. *Spektator-Briefe.* Tübingen, 1924.

Trotsky, Leon. *My Life.* Translated by Max Eastman. New York: Scribner, 1930.

————. *Permanent Revolution.* Calcutta: Gupta, Rahman & Gupta, 1947.

————. "Po povodu tezisov. t. Radeka" (In Connection with the Theses of Comrade Radek), *Biulleten Oppozitsii,* No. 1/2 (July 1929), pp. 11–14.

————. *Problems of the Chinese Revolution.* Translated by Max Shachtman. New York: Pioneer Publishers, 1932.

————. "Radek i oppozitsiia" (Radek and the Opposition), *Biulleten Oppozitsii,* No. 1/2 (July 1929), pp. 10–11.

————. *The Real Situation in Russia.* Translated by Max Eastman. New York: Harcourt, Brace, 1928.

————. *The Third International after Lenin.* Translated by John G. Wright. New York: Pioneer Publishers, 1957.

Trudy I vserossiiskogo s"ezda sovetov narodnogo khoziaistva 25 maia–4 iiunia 1918 g. Stenograficheskii otchët (Transactions of the First All-Russian Congress of the National Economy, May 25–June 4, 1918. Stenographic Report). Moscow: Gosizdat, 1918.

Tukhachevskii, Mikhail. "La marche au-delà de la Vistule," in Joseph Pilsudski, *L'Année 1920.* Paris: Renaissance du Livre, 1929.

Tych, Feliks, and Horst Shumacher. *Julian Marchlewski: Szkicz biograficzny* (Julian Marchlewski: A Biographical Sketch). Warsaw: Książka i Wiedza, 1966.

Ulam, Adam. *The Bolsheviks: The Intellectual and Political History of the Triumph of Communism in Russia.* New York: Macmillan, 1965.

Vavilin, I. "Bol'sheviki i Tsimmerval'd" (The Bolsheviks and Zimmerwald), *Krasnaia Letopis',* No. 2 (59) (1934), pp. 10–23.

Vorovskii, V. V. *Stat'i i Materialy po voprosam vneshnei politiki* (Articles and Materials on Problems of Foreign Politics). Moscow: Izdatel'stvo sotsial'noekonomicheskoi literatury, 1959.

Waldman, Eric. *The Spartacist Uprising of 1919 and the Crisis of the German Socialist Movement. A Study of the Relation of Political Theory and Party Practice.* Milwaukee: Marquette University Press, 1958.

Walecki, Henryk. *Wybór Pism* (Selected Writings). Vol. I. Warsaw: Książka i Wiedza, 1967.

Warski [Warszawski], Adolf. *Wybór Pism i Przemówień* (Selected Writings and Speeches). Vol. I. Warsaw: Książa i Wiedza, 1958.

Wheeler-Bennett, John W. *Brest-Litovsk: The Forgotten Peace.* New York: St. Martin's Press, 1956.

Wohlgemuth, Heinz. *Burgkrieg nicht Burgfriede!* Berlin: Dietz Verlag, 1963.

Wolfe, Bertram D. *Three Who Made a Revolution.* Boston: Beacon Press, 1955.

Zeman, Z. A. B., ed. *Germany and the Revolution in Russia, 1915–1918.* New York: Oxford University Press, 1958.

———, and W. B. Scharlau. *The Merchant of Revolution: The Life of Alexander Israel Helphand (Parvus), 1867–1924.* New York: Oxford University Press, 1965.

Zetkin, Klara. *Reminiscences of Lenin.* London: Modern Books, 1929.

Index